FAMOUS MEN & WOMEN
OF
PITTSBURGH

LEONORE R. ELKUS

EDITOR

FAMOUS MEN & WOMEN
OF
PITTSBURGH

Pittsburgh History & Landmarks Foundation

Manufactured in the United States of America
Library of Congress Catalogue Card No. 80-84822

Hardbound ISBN 0-916670-04-X
Softbound ISBN 0-916670-05-8

CONTENTS

FOREWORD

As we approached the Bicentennial year of our country, some of us felt an urgency to develop a project that would express the rich contributions of individuals in our state (and particularly those who had begun life or had spent important years of their lives), in Pittsburgh & Western Pennsylvania.

After checking the calendars of a number of educational institutions in this area and discovering they were not planning any similar project, I developed a list of outstanding men and women from this area—some, surprisingly little known—whose contributions were of outstanding value to our area and to our country. At a joint meeting of the City of Pittsburgh Bicentennial Commission, headed by Arthur Ziegler, and the Pittsburgh History & Landmarks Foundation (where Mr. Ziegler is President), it was unanimously decided to develop such a series with Arthur Ziegler and myself as the co-chairmen.

The die was cast and with considerable work and the excellent cooperation of those asked to develop the lectures, and from others who helped us with suggestions for speakers, a series of seventeen Bicentennial lectures, "Famous Pittsburghers," was developed. The series began September 29, 1976 with Lowell Innes, (Pittsburgh's beloved Mr. Chips), discussing Benjamin Bakewell and the Pittsburgh Glass Industry, introduced by Mr. Ziegler, and ended with Arthur W. Lindsley's lecture on June 7, 1977 on Charles Martin Hall, Inventor of Aluminum. Mr. Lindsley was introduced by Alfred M. Hunt, a Board Member of the Pittsburgh History & Landmarks Foundation.*

Our grateful thanks are due to many! William Oliver (a member of the Pittsburgh History & Landmarks Foundation Board) and Dr. Graham Netting were extremely helpful in their suggestions and advice. Our thanks to all the sponsors and donors who made the lecture series possible including a generous anonymous friend. Their names:

*We must note here that the lectures are not reproduced here in chronological order.

Donors and Sponsors of the Bicentennial Lectures—
September 1976-June 1977

DONORS

Mr. Reed Albig
Mr. James S. Balter
Mr. & Mrs. James H. Beal
Mr. & Mrs. James Bibro
Mr. & Mrs. William Block
Mr. & Mrs. J. Donald Cannon
Mr. & Mrs. John P. Davis, Jr.
Mr. & Mrs. Robert Dickey, III
Mr. & Mrs. David L. Genter
Mrs. O. H. Gruner
Mr. Alfred M. Hunt
The Freda T. and Oliver M. Kaufmann Fund
Mr. Aaron P. Levinson
Mr. David Owsley
Mr. & Mrs. Nathan W. Pearson
Mrs. Cleveland D. Rea

SPONSORS

Mr. & Mrs. Allen H. Berkman
Mrs. Guy Burrell
Mr. Henry Chalfant
Mr. & Mrs. M. A. Cancelliere
Mr. & Mrs. Richard D. Edwards
Mr. John Eichleay
Leonore Elkus
Mr. Leon Falk, Jr.
Mr. & Mrs. James A. Fisher
Mr. Leland Hazard
Mrs. B. F. Jones, III
The Junior League of Pittsburgh
Mr. John C. Oliver, Jr.
The Donald & Sylvia Robinson Foundation
Mr. Harold L. Tweedy
Mrs. James M. Walton

Our thanks to Patricia Wiley who assisted me patiently and diligently in a thousand ways and was never too busy with her many other duties to follow through with the tasks given to her. The project would never have been completed without her!

Thanks to my co-chairman Arthur Ziegler who in the midst of work on a large project, was always there to help when needed! Our thanks also to Eliza Smith who edited the Abel lecture.

Unbounded thanks to every lecturer for his and her willingness to cooperate and in a number of cases to create, original pieces of research in order to develop the lecture he or she had been requested to give.

Each lecturer has a scholarly and creative personality and it is a sad duty indeed to record our deepest thanks to the late Theodore L. Hazlett, Jr., who spoke so movingly about his own father Dr. T. Lyle Hazlett, and who died in July, 1979, two years after delivering his fine lecture. In this book Pittsburgh and Pennsylvania have a permanent record inspired by our Bicentennial, a book made possible by grants from:

A. W. Mellon Educational and Charitable Trust
Alcoa Foundation
Howard Heinz Endowment
Vesuvius Crucible Company Charitable Foundation
Anonymous donor
Mary McCune Edwards
The Historical Foundation of Pennsylvania
Harry M. Bitner Charitable Trust
Alexander Speyer and Tillie S. Speyer Foundation

As a continuance, we are now working on a series of booklets for children about most of these great men and women who lived here. We hope these will be distributed to the schools and museums to help the children of Western Pennsylvania learn more about the people who helped make their city, Western Pennsylvania, and their country a great place to live and to grow.

Leonore R. Elkus
Editor

Benjamin Bakewell, c. 1835, Carnegie Library of Pittsburgh

BENJAMIN BAKEWELL

by Lowell Innes

I was shocked to find that Benjamin Bakewell is not recorded in the Dictionary of National Biography and that he is not noted outside of Pittsburgh except among glass collectors. To understand the town to which Benjamin Bakewell came in 1808, we should look at it through the eyes of a Revolutionary soldier who visited there in 1784. His account of the future Birmingham of the Ohio Valley is written in *Family Magazine* of the early 1840's.

> Pittsburgh is inhabited almost entirely by Scotch and Irish, who live in paltry log houses, and are as dirty as in the north of Ireland, or even Scotland. There is much small trade carried on: goods are brought at the vast expense of forty-five per cent from Philadelphia and Baltimore. They take, in the shops, money, wheat, flour and skins. They have four attorneys, two physicians, one schoolhouse, two taverns, and no chapel; so they are likely to be damned without benefit of clergy. The rivers so encroach on the town, that I was told the Allegheny had, in thirty years, carried away one hundred yards. *The place, I believe, will never be very considerable.*

In 1796 the population of 1,395 was largely English, Scottish-Irish, German and French. There were only 102 houses. Three churches had been established: German Evangelical, Presbyterian, and Methodist Episcopal. A weekly newspaper, the *Pittsburgh Gazette*, had been serving to communicate as early as 1788, two years after the first post-office.

Artist George Catlin came to Pittsburgh thirty-five years after this and took note of the land which had been offered to Revolutionary soldiers as a reward for service.

> I saw on my route the 20 cents per acre land in Pennsylvania, so much talked about among our neighbors, but I cannot recommend it.

The two quotations picture for us frontier and social conditions far different from the stratified and cultured English society in which Benjamin Bakewell was born. In America men had to depend on character, on valor, or on instinct.

Benjamin was born August 1, 1767 in Derby, England, the son of Joseph Bakewell and Sarah Woodhouse. The youngest of three children, Benjamin was orphaned at an early age. With his sister Sarah he was brought up by an aunt, Elizabeth Woodhouse Gifford. The Reverend Richard Gifford, her husband, was a wealthy Church of England divine. Steeped in the tenets and ceremonies of the Anglican faith, Gifford drilled Ben rigidly in the

1

church catechism and services. Ben seems to have been a chore boy around the house, even being given menial tasks. One biographer believes these years brought out the strength of his character.

At fourteen he was taken out of school to be apprenticed to a haberdasher at Derby. Seven years later he went to London as a shopman in a mercer's. By August 1790 he had opened his own store in London opposite Cornhill.

Here he brought his bride, Anne White, daughter of the Presbyterian minister who had baptized him. Anne had been living in Birmingham with her sister, the wife of John Palmer, a retired Unitarian minister of independent means. At that time Palmer was assisting Dr. Joseph Priestley, noted scientist, naturalist, theologian and political writer. Bakewell listened to their radical ideas on politics and religion. Since his Cornhill shop imported French goods, his trips to Paris placed him in all the republican ferment of the French Revolution. When war between England and France checked his lucrative business, Ben sailed for America with ideas of freedom. Coincidentally, Dr. Priestley traveled the same year with probably the same hope, though the two men had not consulted about it.

Apparently the Bakewell family had income from a lead mine, for brother William, already established in America, furnished capital for Ben to run a brewery in New Haven, Connecticut. Ben was an able chemist, perhaps from having worked with Dr. Priestley. At any rate, with his energy and integrity, the brewery prospered, the ale being equal to the celebrated Burton-on-Trent.[1]

The brewery burned in 1803 or '04, which was fortunate for the American glass industry. Bakewell returned to New York and established an extensive importing business with England, France and the West Indies. At this time J.J. Audobon speaks of him as a rich merchant with a summer house five miles out on Bloomingdale Road. In 1806 Thomas Bakewell, his nephew, and Thomas Pears, lately from England, became his clerks. But President Jefferson's Embargo, 1807, which placed heavy bonds and special licenses on all foreign bound vessels and for United States ports, hampered trade severely.

Bakewell failed and assigned his assets to Thomas and Arthur Kinder. In September 1808 Thomas Kinder and Benjamin Page chose Benjamin Bakewell for qualities of leadership, character and industry to go to Pittsburgh for a new industry with a promising domestic market. They bought a small glass plant that had belonged to George Robinson and Edward Ensell. We like to say it was America's first industry and Pittsburgh's first smokestack!

There were difficulties: lack of skilled workmen and a need to bring in red lead and sand and clay for pots. Pearlash was more readily obtained where settlers were clearing the land. Bakewell was a real entrepreneur with energy and suavity. By 1810 he had a ten-pot furnace and was aiming for clear *flint* glass and a variety of forms.

Bakewell was a natural leader and with the establishment of his family in Pittsburgh—four children, Thomas, Nancy, John, Euphemia, there was an incentive for other men to join him, like the Campbells, Palmers, Pages, Pears and Atterburys. His nephew and clerk, Thomas, wrote of his uncle's attempts to make "good colorless glass that would not fly to pieces on the shelves."

In the eighteenth century Stiegel had sought skilled workmen from the Old Countries. When Bakewell followed his example it was much more dangerous because glass was sorely needed after the war in France and England and the Low Countries. Luring gaffers[2] from Europe was punishable by imprisonment and/or death. Yet Ben himself went before 1815, then Thomas Bakewell, and Tom Pears twice, 1816-1818. The workmen who wished to come to the new world used various disguises such as blackened faces, bakers' costumes, sailors' dress. After 1820 Bakewells spoke openly of hiring Belgians.

The fame of the factory was meteoric. Guide books like Cramer's *Navigator,* Darby's *Emigrant Guide,* Anne Royall's *Travels in Pennsylvania,* Fearon's *Sketches,* and Nuttall's *Journal* emphasized the importance of Bakewells.

This letter from Ben to his brother William at Fatland Ford evidences the general importance. October 1, 1817—

> We have had the President here and he expressed himself much pleased with our manufactury. He promised to order a set of glass for his own use when he arrived at home. Joseph Bonaparte passed through Pittsburgh last week incognito and it was not known until he had left.
>
> Our own business has suffered very much by the excessive importation of glass, and the . . . which have followed. We . . . blowing about five weeks . . . but whether we shall be able to prosecute it to advantage if Congress affords us no help remains to be ascertained.
>
> Adieu my dear Brother—accept of our united regards and present them to Mrs. B.
>
> Yrs. ever affec.

Thomas Nuttall in *A Journal of Travels into the Arkansas Territory During the Year 1819* wrote:

> I went through the flint glass works of Mr. Bakewell, and was surprised to see the beauty of this manufacture in the interior of the United States, in which the expensive decorations of cutting and engraving (amidst every discouragement incident to a want of taste and wealth) were carried to such perfection.

One of the pleasing accolades came from Deming Jarves in *Reminiscences of Glassmaking.* He honored Bakewell with a Magister Artium degree for quality in glass manufacture.

We should note that Bakewell's factory took first prize for a pair of cut decanters at the Franklin Institute show of 1825, surpassing the New England Glass Company; Jackson and Bagget, New York; and the Brooklyn Flint Glass Company. But we still think of the firm as the first flint glass company in America. Of particular interest are the two vases presented to Lafayette on his visit to Pittsburgh and the Bakewell factory in 1824-25. Another notable piece is the American System flask honoring

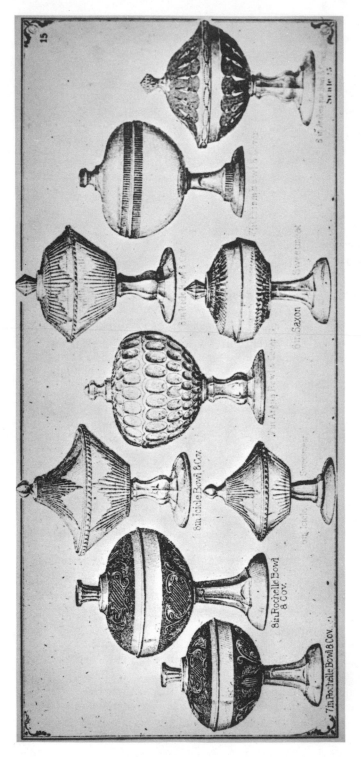

Page 15, Bakewell, Pears & Company Catalogue, c. 1875. Popular pressed patterns made over a period of time. Argus and Rochell were favorites. Carnegie Library

Henry Baldwin and Henry Clay for their efforts on the Protective tariff. The slogan, American System, carried other meanings—a strong National bank, and a national system of roads and canals. The Reynolds greyhound tumbler and various lacy panes marked *Bakewell* are treasured possessions at the Historical Society of Western Pennsylvania, Pittsburgh, landmarks in American glassmaking.

The factory submitted to the vicissitudes of a long life, 1808-1882. The fire of 1845 forced a move to the South Side and a new and enlarged factory emerged. Changing public taste, mechanical pressing and the soda-lime formula which set up a competition against flint glass, limited Bakewell styles somewhat. Throughout the glass world, however, the family ownership was respected. When the judges at the Centennial gave their commendation it was evident that the Bakewell standards had never been lowered:

> Moulded Glass Table Wares commended for the quality of the pieces and for the form of the wares. In a preceding general report the judges spoke of druggists' bottles, perfumers' wares etc. of ordinary qualities of form and metal. Yet they praised the Bakewell light tablewares as being well made.

Greyhound tumbler, c. 1828 presented to William Reynolds by Benjamin Bakewell, who said it was one of the first dozen made. Anne Royall described such a greyhound tumbler in her Pennsylvania or Travels Continued in the United States, 1829.

The Crockery and Glass Journal, December 30, 1875 notes:

> There is no house in the U. S. at the present day, whose reputation is more firmly established for turning out first class goods.

The best qualities of Bakewell were apparent in his business, civic and family life, not merely in his frequent meetings with leaders of his time. Before his retirement he had been head of the Pittsburgh City Council, and had been the prime mover in establishment of the City Water Works. After his retirement Bakewell became Director of Public Schools. Since he believed that improvement comes through reading and meditation, he was an understanding schoolman. Somehow I feel that his youthful experiences with Dr. Priestley and with the liberal thinkers in France won him away from Presbyterianism. Just as Dr. Priestley had guided his followers to Unitarianism, Bakewell founded the first Unitarian group in Pittsburgh.

The Daily Advocate and Advertiser, February 20, 1844 printed a long eulogy:

> His strict integrity and ingenuous dealing were universally acknowledged.
> In him were combined the affability and courtesy of a perfect gentleman, which were the spontaneous manifestation of a refined mind and a benevolent heart. In the very last moment of consciousness, he exhibited that kind consideration for others which distinguished his whole life.
> He steadily followed the path which his sense of duty marked out; and was not deterred by any obstacles, nor was his zeal cooled by sacrifice which any cause, dear to his heart, called upon him to make.

This man who had become a leader in his chosen industry had been an ideal host to men like President Monroe, Lafayette, DeWitt Clinton, skeptical travelers and critical journalists. They recognized Bakewell's sincerity and enjoyed his friendliness. It is one thing to establish and build a successful glass factory. It is quite another to grace it with a hospitality that lent dignity and honor to Pittsburgh.

---

[1] From a notebook—Bakewell Brewers, New Haven, Connecticut
Mr. Heyliger

Stock in Cellar Mar. 4,   5 barrels brown
    40 barrels ale

    4 Kegs
    2 Buts Wine   (126 gallons)
        Malaga   2 tuns   (252 gallons)
                          1 pip   (115 gallons)
                          6 barrels
        Madiera   1 keg
    B. Bakewell

---

[2] glassmakers

Lowell Innes
Lowell Innes, a native of Saco, Maine, is both an educator and an authority on 19th century American glass and on glass of the Midwest. As an educator, he taught English at Shady Side Academy in Pittsburgh, and became assistant head-master; he is now retired. He has been active in research, writing, and lecturing on American glass since the 1940's. He is an author of books on glass, including the definitive work **Pittsburgh Glass** *published by Houghton Mifflin in 1976, a contributor of articles, and a lecturer on glass at a number of museums and clubs concerned with the subject. Among other things, he arranged the first comprehensive show of American glass at the Carnegie Museum in Pittsburgh in 1949, and was the founder and first president of the Pittsburgh chapter of the National Early American Glass Club.*

Hugh Henry Brackenridge, by Gilbert Stuart, 1810. Original in University of Pittsburgh Chancellor's office.

HUGH HENRY BRACKENRIDGE

by Charles C. Arensberg

Early Life

"You will see in a spring evening the banks of the rivers lined with men fishing at intervals, from one another. This, with the streams gently gliding, the woods, at a distance green, and the shadows lengthening towards the town, forms a delightful scene . . .

This bank (of the Monongahela) is closely set with buildings for the distance of near half a mile, and behind this range the town chiefly lies, falling back on the plains between the two rivers . . .

The town consists at present of about an hundred dwelling houses, with buildings appurtenant. More are daily added, and for some time past it has improved with equal but continual pace. The inhabitants, children, men and women are about fifteen hundred; doubling almost every year from the accession of people from abroad, and from those born in the town . . .

There is not a more delightful spot under heaven to spend any of the summer months than at this place . . . Here we have the breezes of the river, coming from the Mississippi and the ocean; the gales that fan the woods, and are sent from the refreshing lakes to the northward; in the meantime the prospect of extensive hills and dales, whence the fragrant air brings odours of a thousand flowers and plants, or of the corn and grain of husbandmen, upon its balmy wings. Here we have the town and the country together. How pleasant it is in a summer evening, to walk out upon these grounds; the smooth green surface of the earth, and the woodland shade softening the late fervid beams of the sun; how pleasant by a crystal fountain in a tea party under one of those hills, with the rivers and the plains beneath . . .

In the fall of the year and during the winter season, there is usually a great concourse of strangers at this place, from the different states about to descent the river to the westward, or to make excursions into the uninhabited and adjoining country. These with the inhabitants of the town spend the evening in parties at the different houses, or at public balls, where they are surprised to find an elegant assembly of ladies, not to be surpassed in beauty and accomplishments perhaps by any of the continent.

It must appear like enchantment to a stranger, who after travelling an hundred miles from the settlements, across a dreary mountain, and through the adjoining country where in many places the spurs of the mountains still continue, and cultivation does not always shew itself, to see, all at once, and almost on the verge of the inhabited globe, a town with smoking chimneys, halls lighted up with splendor, ladies and gentlemen assembled, various music, and the mazes of the dance. He may suppose it to be the effect of magic, or that he is come into a new world where there is all the refinement of the former, and more benevolence of heart".

Hugh Henry Brackenridge wrote this praise of the town he had arrived in from Philadelphia five years before. He wrote it in the first number of the *Pittsburgh Gazette* which he had founded and published in 1786. He wrote it he said, as "intended to give some reputation to the town with a view to induce emigration to this particular spot".[1]

The writing shows his love of the frontier and of his adopted spot in it. It shows the romantic side of his writing which was to flower in *Modern Chivalry,* that lengthy, at times fascinating, but now dated novel which was a sort of primitive waystation between *Don Quixote* and the *Sot-Weed Factor.*

A man of contradictions, a man of wit, urbanity and integrity, a life-time politician who failed in his ambition to serve more than one term in the Pennsylvania legislature, a moderate in the great controversies of his time such as the Whiskey Insurrection and the battle to accept a federal constitution, he fell between two stools and lost on many an occasion the support of either side. His failures came from seeing too clearly the merits of both protagonist and antagonist.

Hugh Henry Brackenridge was born in Kintyre near Campbellstown, Scotland in 1748. His great grandfather a M'Donald, a "dead-doing" man, had given valiant service with his claymore at the Battle of Killicrankey, under Viscount Dundee (1689). His grandfather ("out with the '45") had been killed by the English at Culloden Moor. His father, worn out by the civil wars and the poverty of Scotland, emigrated to Pennsylvania in 1753 in the great celtic immigration to the New World of the 18th century.

Arriving in Philadelphia after the expensive voyage, the father had to sell the family's surplus clothing to get enough money to travel west. He leased a tract of cheap land in "The Barrens" of York County and began to eke out his living in the New World.

The official limit of settlement at that time was the Susquehanna River. Life was a battle against hardwood trees. General Braddock's defeat in 1755 and its aftermath of terror from the Indians formed a life-long aversion to Indians in the mind of the 7 year old boy.

The boy's mother and father dreamed he would become a clergyman and encouraged him to apply himself in the County School to the classics, a love which never left him and appears throughout his writings as well as his legal opinions. We feel his despair when, as he tells, his precious volume of Horace was eaten by the cow as he worked in the fields one day.

At 15 he applied for a teaching job in a free school in Gunpowder Falls, Maryland just over the state line and to every one's surprise was accepted. There the rustic bullies first made fun of him, but on the first attempt to defy his authority, Brackenridge "seized a brand from the fire, knocked the rebel down and spread terror around him". The bullies appealed to authority, but Brackenridge was "confirmed in his office with honor".

Gunpowder Falls became too small for him. He next applied to Princeton College which was becoming one of the intellectual centers of the country. Dr. Witherspoon, the President, accepted him and there he spent the next three years until graduation. There he began to write with Philip Freneau and the pair produced *Father Bamboo's Pilgrimage to Mecca*, a ludicrous and fantastic travel melange as well as *The Rising Glory of America,* a patriotic verse full of enthusiasm and hope for the American colonies.

Following the days at Princeton where he formed lifelong friendships with Freneau, James Madison and William Bradford, he went to teach school at Back Creek, Princess Anne on the Eastern Shore of Maryland. He was happy there. As his famous son Henry Marie wrote in the "Biographical Notice"[2] Brackenridge received a "handsome salary" and "in the midst of a wealthy polished society" he was "greatly respected as a man of genius and scholarship while his wit and superior social and conversational powers, always rendered him a welcome guest".

He was a successful teacher: "Into the minds of his pupils he infused a love of learning; and used to speak with pride of a Porson, of the Winders, the Murrays, the Purnells, and others who were afterwards distinguished".

Being a man of thought rather than action he opposed the Tories in the Revolution, became chaplain to the army and wrote tracts inveighing against George III and the British Parliament. He served as chaplain with Washington at Morristown and in the Pennsylvania campaign at Brandywine.

Following the Revolution he moved to Philadelphia in 1780 at the age of 32. Feeling as he wrote later that he could not get ahead in Philadelphia competing with the lawyers "Chew, Dickinson, Wilson etc.", he decided to move to the frontier in Pittsburgh and arrived there in 1781.

Brackenridge gradually became a lawyer of respect and local fame. He successfully defended twelve rioters accused of attacking the excise collector for whiskey, and lost his attempt to save the life of Mamachtoga the Indian, although he saved him from would-be lynchers.

He married "Miss Montgomery" of whom nothing is known except that she died two years later after giving birth to his son Henry Marie.

In 1786 he was elected for the first and last time to the Pennsylvania legislature and in a burst of activity procured the passage of the following bills:

1. To establish the Pittsburgh Academy (father of the University of Pittsburgh) and secure it an endowment of 5,000 acres of land to the north of Pittsburgh.
2. To erect a new county called Allegheny.
3. To establish a church in Pittsburgh.

Gilbert Stuart painted Brackenridge's picture in 1810 when Brackenridge was 62 and the portrait is now a proud possession of the University of Pittsburgh hanging in the Chancellor's office.

Brackenridge was now 42, a widower and lonely. His only child was being well taken care of by Madame Marie of Grants Hill. So he married the lovely Sabrina Wolfe. Here is a contemporaneous account of their whirlwind courtship from the journal of John Pope, a Virginian who visited Pittsburgh in October of 1790:

"Apprehending a Return of the Rheumatism, I resolved to await the Event in Pittsburgh . . . Here I saw the celebrated Hugh Henry Brackenridge . . . He had been lately married to a Miss Sabina Wolfe, Daughter of an old Dutch Farmer in Washington County. The circumstances of his Courtship, Marriage, and subsequent Conduct I shall relate, with some slight Reference to the Person, Temper and Disposition of the Man.

Mr. Brackenridge on his Way from Washington Court, called in to have his horse fed and escape a Rain which was then descending. The Horse was fed, the rain had subsided, and Mr. Breckenridge to avoid wet feet, ordered his Horse brought to the Door; Miss Wolfe was directed to perform that office.

> Nut brown were her Locks, her shape was full strait,
> Her Eyes were as block as a Sloe;
> Milk white were her Teeth, full smart was her Gait,
> And Sleek was Her Skin as a Doe.

These allurements made a deep Impression upon the susceptible Heart of Brackenridge—He prevented her in the servile Office, mounted his Nag and off he went. He had not gone more than a Sabbath Day's Journey, (for such his really was) before his Horse, at the Instigation of the Rider, turned short about and revisited Mr. Wolfe's. A familiar Application was made to the old Gentleman for his Daughter, which he considered nothing more than Pleasantry in Mr. Brackenridge, for which he is so remarkable. Mr. Brackenridge declared that he was serious, that his Intentions were honorable, and that his future Happiness rested on the Event of his then Application. Miss Sabina had been employed in shrubbing the old Man's Meadow, which saved him the annual Expence of about ten Dollars. This with him was an insuperable Objection to parting with his Girl—Mr. Brackenridge obviated the Difficulty by paying down a Sum of Money, obtained the Young Lady's Consent, married her, and sent her to Philadelphia, where she now is under the Governance of a reputable female Character, whose business will be to polish the Manners, and wipe off the Rusticities which Mrs. Brackenridge had acquired whilst a Wolfe . . ."

Last fall the writer and his wife visited the site of Jacob Wolfe's Fort—the home of Sabina—and there in still comparatively wild surroundings the old farmer showed us on "yonder pile of stones" where the foundation of the old fort lies buried in the field.

The Whiskey Insurrection

Perhaps the greatest event of Brackenridge's life, the one in which he accomplished the most and the one for which he got the least repute was the Whiskey Rebellion in 1794. His first-hand history of the insurrection is still the best account of that affair which was the first great test of the federal government to prevent insurrection and seccession.[3]

Brackenridge pointed out that the Mississippi River was closed, the western farmers could thus dispose of their grain only by converting it into whiskey; the country was new and recovering from Indian raids and spoliation and the excise tax imposed was a lethal blow to the settlers who had little agricultural machinery, poor transportation and scant labor help.

Throughout the meetings of the angry farmers in Mingo Creek, in Parkinson's Ferry (now Monongahela City), in Fort Couch back of Mt. Lebanon, in the burning of Bower Hill, the Neville mansion, and finally in the great gathering at Braddock's Field to march on Pittsburgh, capture it, and set it to the torch, Brackenridge played a double role if you will, but nevertheless the role of a skillful mediator.

David Bradford and Benjamin Parkinson were the firebrands; Albert Gallatin, of "Friendship Hill", later Secretary of the Treasury, and Brackenridge were the moderates.

Without recounting the long involved plots, meetings, and counterplots of this involved insurrection following the robbery of the U.S. Mail, the slaying of one of their group and the wounding of six others at Bower Hill, a few incidents may show the role that Brackenridge played in defusing the explosive situation.

Two or three thousand warlike citizens gathered at Braddock's Field on August 1, 1794 with murder in their hearts. The Washington County militiamen, Brackenridge notices, were dressed as if for war against the Indians. They amused themselves all day and night by shooting their guns and drinking usquebaugh. "There appeared a great wantonness of mind and disposition to do anything extravagant". Brackenridge noticed them using language of the French Revolution—not the "tarring and feathering" violence of the revolution of 1776, but the guillotining language of France.

During the night Brackenridge exerted himself particularly to prevent an attack on Pittsburgh. Passing from group to group, he appeared to support the proposal to attack the garrison. The general type of conversation was as follows:

> "Insurgent. 'Are we to take the garrison?'
> Brackenridge. 'We are.'
> Insurgent. 'Can we take it?'
> Brackenridge. 'No doubt of it.'
> Insurgent. 'At a great loss?'
> Brackenridge. 'Not at all; not above a thousand killed and five hundred mortally wounded.' (This last remark, so lightly uttered, always appeared serious to the more thinking part of those to whom he spoke)."

Nevertheless the crowd demanded to march on Pittsburgh. Brackenridge did not stop them but urged them to go: "Yes, by all means; and if with no other view, at least to give a proof that the strictest order can be kept and no damage done. We will just march through, and taking a turn, come out upon the plain of the Monongahela's banks; and taking a little whiskey with the inhabitants of the town, the troops will embark and cross the river".

The army marched to Pittsburgh and Brackenridge himself served out four barrels of his best old brew that day. He would rather spare that he said than a single quart of blood. He thought it better to be employed in extinguishing thirst than fire.

After a Washington County "Committee"—70 armed men—were about to burn one Quaker Jackson's house and mill because he had called the Committee a "scrub congress". First however they would try Jackson. At the trial which was held immediately, Brackenridge spoke to defuse the meeting with a tale:

13

"I recollect to have read, that, in the time of Oliver Cromwell, lord protector of England, when he was in the height of his glory, a person came to him, and gave him information of words, used by another, greatly contemptuous of his dignity; viz. he was said, that your excellency may kiss his - - -. You may tell him, said Oliver, that he may kiss mine. This Quaker has called us a Scrub Congress; let our sentence be, that he shall be called a Scrub himself".

The anecdote produced loud guffaws from the audience who took the Quaker off to bestow the epithet on him. He retaliated with whiskey and water and the incident was closed.

The federal troops arrived in Pittsburgh, Alexander Hamilton as special emissary from Washington, Generals Lighthorse Harry Lee and Morgan commanding. Lee took over Brackenridge's house on Market Street, not because he knew Brackenridge from Princeton, but because it was a large house. Hundreds were immediately arrested. Morgan parading near Brackenridge's house was heard to say "Hang the rascal, hang him".

Brackenridge lay on his bed fully dressed on the night of November 13, fully expecting to be arrested. He read Plutarch as he waited and meditated on Solon's law requiring that a citizen who did not take part in a "civil tumult" should be put to death, because moderate citizens, by mingling with the violent, could assist in bringing about an accommodation. This he thought he had done, but it all seemed to him to no avail.

The next morning Hamilton ordered Brackenridge to appear to give testimony. After two days of searching questions by Hamilton, Hamilton gave what should be history's final word on Brackenridge's part:

"Mr. Brackenridge, in the course of yesterday I had uneasy feelings. I was concerned for you as a man of talents; my impressions were unfavourable; you may have noticed it. I now think it my duty to inform you that not a single one remains. Had we listened to some people, I do not know what we might have done. There is a side to your account; your conduct has been horribly misrepresented, owing to misconception. I will announce you in this point of view to Governor Lee, who represents the executive. You are in no personal danger. You will not be troubled by a simple inquisition by the judge; what may be due to yourself with the public, is another question".

While Brackenridge was clear now of the threat of treason, his position with his peers was still not cleared. General Neville, hearing of the outcome, shouted:

"The most artful fellow that ever was on God Almighty's earth; he has put his finger in Bradford's eye, in Yates' eye, and now he has put his finger in Hamilton's eye too: I would not wonder if he is made attorney for the states, on the west of the Allegheny Mountain".

And even the next year when Brackenridge was summoned as a witness at the treason trials in Philadelphia, he was shunned there by his old friends and

Opposite: *The Whiskey Rebellion at Bower Hill. General Brackenridge described the event as, "A stand of the democratic poverty ridden west against the encroachments of the aristocratic Money Bags of the East." Reproduced with permission from Stefan Lorant. Painted by Idabelle Kleinhans especially for* **Pittsburgh,** The Story of an American City. *Carnegie Library of Pittsburgh.*

acquaintenances on the street when they walked by him. "I was driven to contemplate the buildings a good deal as I walked," Brackenridge narrated later. "A stranger would have thought me a disciple of Palladio, examining the architecture."

Brackenridge as a Supreme Court Justice
December 18, 1799 to June 26, 1816

As a reward for his services to the "Republicans" or Federalists Governor McKean of Pennsylvania appointed Brackenridge to the Supreme Court of Pennsylvania on December 18, 1799. When he was appointed (Supreme Court Judges are now elected by the people) Edward Shippen was Chief Justice, William Tilghman, Jasper Yeates and Thomas Smith were Associate Justices. Shippen resigned in 1807 as Chief Justice and William Tilghman took his place.

So Brackenridge the believer in federalism, the intellectually-minded, became Associate Justice with four others. At that time the Supreme Court Justices unlike nowadays were "nisi prius" or lower court judges riding on circuit and trying cases in the lower court. They travelled on horseback from Carlisle to Pittsburgh to Philadelphia. When they were not doing that they sat as appellate judges in Philadelphia.

One of the ways to tell what a judge is doing vis a vis the scene of the time is, of course, to study his cases. This is what I propose to do in the next few paragraphs to show that the judge was fashioning new legal tools since the Revolution out of old handles, shaping the precedents to come in the new republic or simply solving old problems between new litigants.

Horace Binney in his six volume reports of the Supreme Court of Pennsylvania (1809-1815) describes graphically, accurately and fully the work of the justices of that Court.

We must remember, for example, that the English "common law", that is the customs as well as the old statutes of the Kings of England, were adopted in Pennsylvania after the Revolution whenever and if the courts believed such adoption was practical and just, but adjustments had to be made nevertheless.

For example in a case in 1807 when Brackenridge was justice[4] one Boyer was indicted for stealing "2 $10 notes of the President and Directors of the Bank of the United States". The statute in Pennsylvania defined robbery or larceny in the terms of "promissory notes for the payment of money". The defense argued that the indictment misdescribed the crime since the crime was stealing *promissory notes* and the indictment mentioned only notes. The judgment was therefore arrested and the defendant was freed.

This case may be explained as a survival of the ancient British skill in pleading which was the only escape from the 200 or more crimes in the 18th Century which were punishable by death. After all, a 10 year old boy had been hung in the 18th Century in England for stealing a loaf of bread, and the people were beginning to wonder about the charm and wisdom of their criminal laws.

So the judges as well as the lawyers in human decency found linguistic ways to avoid the harshness of the British laws.

Thus it was in Pennsylvania after the Revolution that, although the common law of England was in large measure continued in the warp and woof of the American and Pennsylvania legal systems, the stringent punishments and capital executions were not considered fit for a happy and optimistic new world.

Thus with the failure to perpetuate the vast number of capital crimes for simple larceny or robbery, for example, lawyers no longer found it necessary to devise elaborate semantic escapes for their clients.

Another fruitful source of litigation in the early 1800's in Pennsylvania was whether insurance companies were liable for loss of cargo upon seizure by either the British or French privateers who were roaming the Atlantic Ocean and particularly the Caribbean ports. For example in *Calhoun v. The Insurance Company of Pennsylvania,* 1 Binney 293 (1808) an American brig was seized by a British privateer blockading Cadiz in Spain. The question involved as whether the American captain knew that there was a blockade and was trying to breach it. Was the American captain attempting to deliver goods to a peaceful port when the seizure occurred and was he unaware of any embargo?

Was the American captain on the other hand testing a known danger for a great reward and no insurance if he failed or was he an innocent transporter of goods haplessly seized by a hostile foe or pirate on the high or not so high seas?

The cases of which there are many during Brackenridge's incumbency on the court went both ways and the court gave them full and careful thought.

In 1808 in *Emerick v. Harris,* 1 Binney 425, Brackenridge ducked the issue which did not deter Justice Marshall in *McCullough v. Maryland.* This is whether a Supreme Court could decide whether an Act of Assembly was constitutional or not. Brackenridge said according to Binney the matter was a "vexata quaestio, very delicate and embarrassing in its nature; that he had made out his observations at a considerable length, in which the difficulties of the question were stated; but that at present he did not think it necessary to read them". He proceeded thereafter to duck the fundamental question of the supremacy of the court over the legislature.

In *Webb and Wife v. Isaac Evans,* 1 Binney 565, Isaac Evans died and left a will in which he gave his wife one bed and furniture at her choice, six chairs, 1 case of drawers, 1 looking glass, the whole of the tea furniture, 1/2 of the pewter, 1 horse creature, saddle and bridle and 1 cow. During her widowhood he also gave her use of the small cellar under the kitchen and with common use of the kitchen, oven, drawwell and springhouse. He also ordered his son William to provide sufficient firewood for her cut at a proper length and laid handy at her door during her widowhood. Brackenridge came to the aid of the poor lady even though she was remarried to Webb and held that was not enough for her and that she was entitled to her dower, that is, her rights in all the real estate during her life.

Brackenridge had short patience for the extreme technicalities of the law in many cases and inveighed against the formalities of the law on many an occasion. In Kelly v. Foster, 2 Binney 12 he said:

> "The forms of law do not make it a game of tric trac, a system of catches, nor is subtilty and discrimination useful, but to enable to reach the truth, and get at the justice of the case with certainty, and with despatch. A rule of law pushed to an extreme does not correspond with the intention of it; and a dissatisfaction with the administration of justice, under the technical form of systematic science. I am inclined in this case to affirm the judgment."

In *Campbell v. Spencer*, 2 Binney 129, we see the first great stirrings of equity in Pennsylvania that the system of strict law must yield in some instances to mercy and that the chancellor's "conscience" may avoid the rigid legal imperative. In that case the plaintiff and two of his friends sent for the defendant to meet them in a tavern in Somerset County. Defendant came early in the morning and the party drank bitters. How many we are not told. Finally a bargain was proposed between the plaintiff and the defendant to trade the defendant's farm of 450 acres to be paid for by some store goods belonging to the plaintiff. The defendant was a farmer unacquainted with merchandise. He had a wife and a large family of children who lived with him on the farm. The plaintiff was a store keeper. Immediately after the bargain the defendant wished to annul it but the plaintiff told him he did not make "child's bargains" but would stick to the agreement. The defendant was much distressed and said he had ruined his family and on the next morning applied to the plaintiff to let him off. The plaintiff refused. The matter went to the jury and Judge Yeates told the jury there was nothing in the evidence which would authorize the court to say that the contract was void however indiscreet it had been on the part of the defendant. The jury however found a verdict for the defendant and upon appeal Brackenridge found that the plaintiff had been overreaching. The bargain he said was "accompanied with such circumstances as will justify a court in refusing to lend their aid to the carrying it into effect."

Brackenridge on the Manumission of Slaves

The treatment of slaves in Pennsylvania was interesting since the Act of March 1, 1780 provided for the gradual freeing of all slaves under twenty-one years old upon their attaining the age of 28 years. In the meantime the right of possession was scrupulously maintained by the courts.

Commonwealth v. Clements, 6 Binney 206 (1814) was a slave case, decided in a novel manner by Brackenridge. You will remember that under the Act in Pennsylvania of 1780 for the gradual abolition of slavery a negro slave under the age of twenty-one years, might in consideration of manumission (freedom) bind himself for further service until the age of 28 or for 7 more years of slavery if the slave was already over the age of 21.

Under this generous and enlightened law Susan Stephens a black slave from Kent County, Maryland, ran off to Philadelphia and there married a free black. The master pursued her, seized her and was about to carry her back to Maryland, when one Clements agreed to pay the master $195 if the master would manumit (free) the slave, both Susan and her free husband agreeing to bind themselves as servants to Clements for three years. To make matters more complicated Susan was "in a state of pregnancy".

William Masters one of the society of abolitioners now got in the act and hired a lawyer to bring Susan before the court on habeas corpus. "In consequence of its novelty" the reporter Binney says, the case was heard before the whole court.

Susan's lawyer argued that the law was that she, a married person, couldn't bind herself to an indenture of service, that therefore the agreement of manumission was void and she should be free to go back to her husband.

Maxwell's lawyer, who had paid the $195, said not at all, she was not really married, she and her man were only living together and besides a slave couldn't contract marriage under the law because that would take control away from her master.

The court cut through the technicalities and held that since Pennsylvania was committed gradually to abolishing slavery, the contract of indenture for three years was the best thing possible for Susan, her husband and the child "en ventre sa mere" as the law says, and Susan would be remanded to the custody of him who paid the slaveholder $195.

Brackenridge agreed with his fellow judges. His opinion is amusing since he cites by way of analogy an old Irish case which is still good law in 1976, by the way.

He says he remembers an old case:

> "A person passing by a pool, missed a foot and slipt in. He was over his depth, and the bank was steep. A shepherd observing him from a height, hastened to his assistance, and entangling his crook in the garments of the drowning man, drew him out. But in attempting to fix his crook in the first instance, he had hurt the eye of the stranger in the pool, and which afterwards occasioned the loss of it. The stranger so rescued, brought his suit and claimed damages; for it is a principle of our law, derived from the civil, Southcote's case, Coke, Coggs V. Barnard, Ld. Raymond, and Jones on Bailments, that even voluntary service and without reward, if unskillfully performed, may partake of the nature of injury and require damages.
>
> The court decided, that the plaintiff should have his election to go back to the same pool, and put himself in the same place, and after having struggled a while and being half drowned, if he could get out of himself and without help he might come back and prosecute his action; this he declined, and was nonsuited. I would propose to give the applicant in this case the like election, which is to annul the evidence of her manumission, and procure her indenture to be taken up, and to put herself in her master's hands, as at the time when she was taken out of his possession, if this can be done. If she cannot do this, or procure it to be done, her complaint under this habeas corpus must be dismissed.

Justice Brackenridge was a man of integrity with a fine sense of "l'honnette homme" and decorum. In one case involving a stay of execution by a creditor against B, Brackenridge refused to take part in deciding the case because the defendant B was his landlord in the hotel where he lodged at the time. He went on to say that he always avoided accepting invitations from persons when he was on the circuit. He described it with his fine sensibility in this manner:

"But I take the liberty of remarking, what greater ground of exception there might be in the minds of counsel, where a judge has at any time suffered himself to be entertained by a party, and partaken of his viands, and where there has not been, and could not easily be an opportunity of making a return, and certainly not a propriety of offering compensation. Hence it is, that it may be adviseable to decline invitations of hospitality, even for the sake of the opinion of others . . .

In this age of Watergate and general bribery in all quarters the attitude of Brackenridge is refreshing as an example of old time rectitude. He was a judge and he took his office seriously.

Brackenridge on the Indians

It seems odd to us today that such a generally enlightened cultured man as Brackenridge had the view of Indians he had. Perhaps it may be derived originally from his undoubted experience with the savage retaliation of Indians against white incursions in Pennsylvania in the 18th Century. Perhaps his defense of the miserable Mamachtaga might have added fuel to his thoughts. After all his French contemporary Chateaubriand, who wrote about "le noble sauvage", roaming free in the beautiful wilderness became disillusioned, as did even more so the great Austrian poet Nicholas Lenau, who visited America and Pittsburgh in the year 1833, but despite his early enthusiasms,[5] ended his life in Austria with the same despair and disillusion.

At any rate Brackenridge felt the Indian was barbarous, uncouth and cruel and moreover was not entitled, as no person in the world was, to live off the land and its wild animals, never cultivating an inch of it for the greater support and stability of mankind. Such a person was no better than a beast, for a beast does the same thing on the land as the Indian. Listen to Brackenridge in Thompson v. Johnston[6] expatiating on this subject:

"It cannot be said that the proprietor (William Penn)[7] admitted an absolute dominion in the native to the ownership of the soil. In fact he considered the Indian title as but in the nature of a claim. Nor was it altogether without reason that he so considered it; not for the reason already hinted at, the not being a christian, but for the not being a man; in other words, the not living more human, and after the manner of men. For what distinguishes an Indian from a wild beast, an animal ferae naturae, who lives upon his prey and cultivates little or no soil? And hence it is that if he claims a right to what soil shall be necessary, living in this manner, it will be more than will fall to his share as one of the family of mankind; for the cultivation of the soil will support a greater population, than a life by hunting, and therefore this mode of life is less according to the law of nature. It is on this principle that the philosopher fastens in reducing the claim of the savage from that extensive range of a life by hunting, to a more confined extent of subsistence by tilling the ground. With regard to the whole of mankind, a savage cannot be said to have an absolute right to the soil he occupies, since he does not occupy it in a way that contributes to the civilization of man; for a close population and the scarcity of soil to a certain extent, are necessary to the improvement of the species. Arts and manufactures are the offspring of a close cohabitation, science also and all those endowments which elevate human nature. Hence cities, towns and dense settlements produce refinement in manners, and lead to the cultivation of literature and to all mental enjoyments. Can those therefore be said to have a perfect right to the soil, who do not use it themselves in a proper manner? Can they be said to have a right to hinder others to use it?"

He goes on to apply the Indian concept to the whole world and in the light of our modern problems of overpopulation seems to have a point.

"It will terminate in this, that with respect to the community of nations, there can be no absolute right of soil in any nation, unless where it can be ascertained that taking quantity and quality into view, and relative contiguity to marine productions, no more of the earth is occupied by one than another, or at least no more than in proportion to their size and the production of what is necessary for their subsistence. For to reduce it to strict principle, as the length and breadth of the place of interment is to the body of a man at death, so is his proportion of the soil during life."

Commonwealth v. Cornish
6 Binney 249 (1914)

Then there was the sad case of *Commonwealth v. Cornish* which was an indictment of one Cornish whose first name is never given, for perjury when he swore before a magistrate that one Jacob Miley shot him on November 8, 1813. It appeared that there was a great riot on the 8th of November at which several guns were fired. Cornish was shot in the face and as one witness swore, immediately said, "Jacob Miley has shot me". It was a great crowd of about 1,000 or 2,000 persons. The witness knew Miley and took the person who fired the gun, from his size and dress, to be Miley. On the 10th of November Cornish charged Miley on oath before the magistrate. A warrant was issued for Miley's arrest and Miley was brought up before the court on the 12th. Cornish was sworn again and said that Miley had shot him, that he knew him well and pointed at him and said that Miley was a mutton butcher from whom he had often bought mutton. Miley produced unquestionable evidence that he was about 20 miles from where the riot occured and swore that he did not even know Cornish nor that he had even seen him before. Miley was let off and Cornish was indicted for perjury. He was found guilty before the Chief Justice Tilghman and Judge Brackenridge sitting as a lower court and then the case was appealed to the Supreme Court where they were sitting again. Brackenridge had a tough time but finally decided that Cornish had been rash and quick-triggered and wrong and was guilty of perjury as having made an untrue statement without probable cause. The Judge said:

"We are between Scylla and Charybdis in this case. On the one hand, there is the risk of discouraging testimony given for the Commonwealth; on the other hand, there is the risk of individuals from rash and unadvised swearing . . . It ought to be at a man's risk to undertake to swear positively, under circumstances where he ought to have mistrusted his vision, and could not have been certain, as to what he undertook to say positively that he saw. This was the case here."

So the man who was shot ended up being convicted of a very serious crime in those days—perjury. We don't know what happened to him.

Chief Justice Tilghman, Justice Yeats and Brackenridge got along well together at least from the reports.

I can find only one instance in the six volumes of reports of the Supreme Court where Justice Brackenridge dissented from the opinions of his fellow judges. This was in *French v. Reed* in 6 Binney 308 (1814) involving the capture of a vessel in Hispaniola by a French privateer and whether or not insurance was owing. Oddly enough the report says: "Brackenridge J. delivered his opinion *contra;* but a part of it having been mislaid, the reporter is unable to publish it."

Brackenridge never retired from the bench. He died after a short illness in Carlisle on June 25, 1816, at the age of 68. His daughter Cornelia, by his second wife Sabina Wolfe, died at the age of 21 in 1823 and lies beside him. In the next lot rests perhaps the greatest of Pennsylvania jurists, John Bannister Gibson, who succeeded Brackenridge on the bench the day after Brackenridge's death.

When we view Brackenridge the young patriot, the romantic taleteller, the misunderstood mediator of the Whiskey Rebellion, the disappointed politician, the mature judge of a great state in its infant days, we believe he lived a full life and a useful one and that he met Justice Oliver Wendell Homes' test:

> "I think that as life is action and passion, it is required of a man that he should share the passion and action of his time at peril of being judged not to have lived."

---

[1] This quote and others here we have gleaned from the excellent biography of Brackenridge: "The Life and Writings of Hugh Henry Brackenridge" by Milton Newlin, Princeton University Press 1932.

[2] "Biographical Notice of Hugh Henry Brackenridge, Late of the Supreme Court of Pennsylvania" Southern Literary Messenger Vol. VIII pp. 1-119 (Jan. 1842). Reprinted in *Modern Chivalry*, (Eds of 1845, 1846).

[3] Incidents of the Insurrection in the Western Parts of Pennsylvania in the year 1794. Phila. 1795.

[4] 1 Binney 201 (1807).

[5] Der Indianerzug, Das Blockhaus, Niagara.

[6] 6 Binney 68 (1913).

[7] Brackenridge points out here too that the King claimed absolute right by discovery and no mention was made in his grant to Penn of any reservation of rights in the "Aborigines".

Charles Covert Arensberg

Charles Covert Arensberg is a life-time resident of Pittsburgh, and a partner in the law firm of Tucker, Arensberg, Very, and Ferguson. With Mrs. Henry P. Hoffstot, Jr., Mr. Arensberg was instrumental in founding the Pittsburgh History & Landmarks Foundation and has served as its president or chairman of the board since its inception. He is a graduate of Harvard University and Harvard Law School, an accomplished linguist and the author of many articles.

Jane Grey Swisshelm and Daughter Henrietta, c. 1860. Carnegie Library of Pittsburgh.

24

JANE GREY SWISSHELM

by Mary Ellen Leigh McBride

Twenty-five years ago I started newspaper work on the Pittsburgh Sun-Telegraph, which is now defunct. Each reporter had a brass spittoon beside his desk; that was an order of Mr. William Randolph Hearst, who owned the paper. But it was also a reminder that women didn't count . . . that all reporters, even those who worked on the women's pages, as I did, were presumed to be men. And truly, it was a man's world on the newspapers then.

Refinements had not yet come to the world of journalism. . . if you saw the movie "Front Page" you had a pretty good idea of the way the city room used to look. We even had the same kind of typewriters they used in the play. . . enormous monsters, that Mr. Hearst had bought back in the twenties. Whatever you hear about how lavish Mr. Hearst was with his money, he certainly did not waste it on his employees. Bad as it was, as Cleopatra says "in my salad days, when I was young and green" the newspaper world must have been infinitely worse when Jane Grey Swisshelm started as the first newspaperwoman.

I think Jane Swisshelm has had, over the years, an unwarranted sainthood thrust upon her. She was definitely unsaintly. . . she was outspoken, used to having her own way and doing as she pleased, quite an iconoclast, and not afraid of public opinion. These are hardly the attributes of sainthood.

But Jane Swisshelm was a good writer, an innovator, and a very shrewd and intelligent woman. She had a natural flair for writing which is rare; she taught herself to write and had the best equipment a reporter can have. . . a real feeling for and interest in people. And Jane Swisshelm didn't miss anything; like most women, she pounced upon every detail and fully used her powers of observation. Swisshelm's stories are full of life at a time when most stories, newspaper and otherwise, were sticky with the Victorian style. Simpering and languishing had no place in any of Jane's prose.

Jane Grey Cannon was born on December 6, 1815 in a log cabin on what is now Sixth Ave., across from Trinity Episcopal Church. In 1934 the Women's Historical Society of Pittsburgh placed a plaque on the side of Gimbels Department Store to commemorate her birthplace and it is still there.

At the time of Jane's birth, Trinity Church was not built but the property was a large graveyard, built up high off the street and surrounded by a railing. Jane used to go over and sit among the graves; she was never afraid to be alone, even as a young child, and she was never afraid of death.

Although her father, Thomas Cannon, was a merchant who was not terribly prosperous, her family was very close-knit and very happy. Jane's grandmother lived with them and Jane adored the old lady, who told her tales of her childhood and of Lady Jane Grey, for whom she was named. Grandmother was extremely religious and Jane learned her first scripture at her knee.

The Cannons were strict Calvinists; Jane always believed that the minister was talking directly to her and from her earliest days she was an earnest student of the Bible. Like so many who have few material possessions, the family's spiritual possessions meant a great deal to them.

Jane had brothers and sisters, but one by one they died of tuberculosis. To get the remaining family into the fresh country air and away from the city, in April of 1816, the Cannons moved to Wilkinsburg, where they opened up a store. It was here that Jane's beloved sister, Elizabeth, was born and Jane spent some of the happiest days of her life. Financial matters took a turn for the worse and in 1821 they moved back to the log cabin in Pittsburgh to see if they could attract more customers with a store there. But it was to no avail, they did not prosper and, what's worse, Jane's beloved father was found to have tuberculosis and died in 1823.

The bereaved widow, her daughters Elizabeth and Jane, and a son, William, survived. Mrs. Cannon was a brave woman and the little family struggled on. Mrs. Cannon made bonnets and Jane learned to make pillow lace, which was in vogue at the time, and for awhile they still lived on Sixth Avenue.

At age 12 Jane went to the Edgeworth Seminary in Braddock's Field with her cousin, Mary Alexander. The school was very good and run by a Mrs. Olever and Jane says she thought it the best thing she had ever done. . . she loved studying and was a born scholar and here at last she was able to learn things. Her roommate was a Pittsburgh girl named Helen Semple and Jane thought her very kind. But Jane had not been at the school too long when she developed a cough and Mrs. Olever wrote her mother and suggested Jane should be taken home. Fearing the fatal consumption, Mrs. Cannon agreed.

On her way to the Edgeworth Seminary something had happened to Jane that had a lasting effect on her future, and perhaps if it hadn't happened Jane's whole life might have been different. Jane and her cousin and another girl were picked up in Pittsburgh in a wagon driven by Mr. Olever to be taken out to Braddock's Field. Mr. Olever was late and by the time they got out around Edgewood it was dark. Mr. Olever got the horses stuck in a stream and the water had rushed into the bed of the wagon. The girls cried out and were about to drown. They were saved by a dark haired boy of about 16 who carried them all to safety, then got Mr. Olever and the horses out of the water and back on the road. The boy took them up to his home to dry out by the fire; his father and mother were there and welcomed the poor, wet, frightened things into the house. The self-confidence of the boy, the gallant way he pulled her from the stream, his handsome face, all left an indelible mark upon Jane. She admitted that she fell in love with him then but it was many years before she married the boy, who was James Swisshelm.

When Jane returned home, her mother decided to move back to the fresh air of Wilkinsburg and try and restore Jane to health.

Mrs. Cannon was a wonderful mother, she loved her children deeply and they were a very devoted family. With very little money they lived a happy life and were encouraged by their mother to develop their talents. Jane taught school in Wilkinsburg when she was 15 and she was apparently a good teacher; she says she did not have to whip any pupils. . . she did not believe in it. . . and felt they got on when their curiosity to know was aroused. In this she was way ahead of her time, for at that time punishment was considered the only spur to learning.

Jane and her sister, Elizabeth, and their mother all doted on William, and he on them. William had not received much formal schooling because as the oldest child he had been busy helping his mother, but apparently he was a natural mechanical genius and could build anything. . . windmills and toys and little whirligigs. . . that worked. He loved to figure out how to make things move by air power and was always engaged in building something.

The church elders, who had taken it upon themselves to be his guardians since his father had died, said this was the work of Satan and that William could find better things to do with his hands. Against Mrs. Cannon's wishes and against William's vehement protests, the church bound him as an apprentice to a cabinet maker. To spare his mother, William tried to do cabinet making but he really hated it; finally things came to an impasse and William decided to run away. It must have been a sad scene at the Cannon home. . . William came one night to say goodbye to his family. . . Mrs. Cannon torn between her love for her son and her blind devotion to her church. . . Jane and Elizabeth crying. . . and finally, William slipping out and down to the wharf to sign on as a deckhand on a steamboat going by.

The family heard from William. . . he ended up in New Orleans. . . he was happy and prosperous. . . then the letters stopped. Some time later through a friend they learned that William had died of yellow fever. They didn't even know where he was buried.

This had a great effect on all the Cannons and Mrs. Cannon never forgave herself. Jane does not say what the church elders said when they learned of the tragedy.

On November 18, 1836 against the wishes of her mother and sister, Jane Grey Cannon became the bride of James Swisshelm. She had met him again while she was teaching in Wilkinsburg. Jane was 21 years old; she said she was old enough to know what she was doing, but the heart plays strange tricks on one, even someone as intelligent as Jane. Jane and James were very different even in their physical traits. Jane was five feet tall and weighed a hundred pounds. She had a piercing gaze, a quick mind and could recite passages from the Bible for hours. She read incessantly and was a very positive person.

James Swisshelm was well over six feet, a strong, handsome man with black hair and a cheerful laugh who never read books. He was slow and careful, a good farmer, a good neighbor and a good son. Beyond that he had nothing, nor would most people expect more. But Jane did. Jane wanted an intellect to match hers, a broad minded man who could look to the future and see the changes coming, a man who would allow his wife great freedom to do as she

27

chose. Why she expected James to be like this is beyond explanation.

James' family had always been farmers, they had already lived in that same place for almost a hundred years; his father had been with George Washington at Valley Forge. They were devoted Methodists and had given land for a Methodist church. They were honest, hard-working people whose interest did not go beyond the next hill or the next planting. James only wanted his farm and Jane wanted the world.

Within a year of their marriage, James and Jane had separated. Jane went home to her mother, who told Jane she was making a mistake. Mrs. Cannon had opposed the marriage, feeling that the couple was temperamentally unsuited, but once it had taken place she wanted Jane to try and make it work.

Jane blamed it all on her mother-in-law and religion. . . they were trying to convert her to Methodism, she said.

To save face James built her a small house, where she lived by herself all week, and then on the weekends he would come to see her. They remained legally married for 20 years but after the first year they really led separate lives.

In June of 1838 James and Jane went to Louisville, Kentucky. His brother, Samuel, had preceded them and the brothers were going to open a store.

It was supposed to be a new start for all of them and for James' and Jane's marriage. But it turned out very differently.

It was in Louisville that Jane became an abolitionist, for here she saw for the first time the white men who bought female negro slaves and got them pregnant and then sold their own children into slavery. This was not hidden or deplored; this was a business.

For Jane it was a glimpse into hell.

Everything in her revolted against this inhuman practice and she tried on several occasions through her church work to do something about it. But Kentucky was a slave state and most all of the church goers owned slaves. The abuses she saw would not be cured by the feeble protests of a lady from Pittsburgh.

Then and there Jane made a declaration, as she notes in her memoirs, "Half a Century," from which she never wavered for the rest of her life.

> I promised the Lord then and there, that for life, it should be my work to bring 'deliverence to the captive, and the opening of the prison to them that are bound.'

Jane was as good as her word and made herself very unpopular by her vociferous defense of slaves. She tried to open up a school to teach negro children and was threatened with bodily harm. For Jane to try and reform Louisville was the same as Jane trying to tear down Mt. Everest with an iced tea spoon; the task was beyond her.

Jane received word from Pittsburgh that her mother was dying of cancer and she decided to leave Louisville, much against James' will. He claimed he needed her; she claimed her duty was with her mother. Besides, Jane hated Louisville. . . in addition to the ugly slave problems and the dreadful things she saw there, James' and Samuel's business had failed and things were not pleasant.

Jane returned home to find her mother suffering terribly. Mrs. Cannon lingered on and on until even Jane's great faith in God was shaken. Mrs. Cannon finally died in January, 1840. During this ordeal Jane had made up her mind she would not go back to Louisville and she wrote and told James. He was furious and when she and her sister, Elizabeth, went to settle her mother's estate, James refused to sign any papers as he had to do and furthermore, he sued her mother's estate for Jane's services as a nurse! This was all within the law, for at that time a married woman could not hold property in her own name.

Jane says in her memoirs:

> Mother's will was sacred to me. The money he proposed to put in improvements on the Swissvale mills. These, in case of his death before his mother, would go to his brothers. I had not even a dower right in the estate, and already the proceeds of my labor and income from my separate estate were put upon it. I refused to give him the money, and on my way alone from the lawyer's office it occurred to me that all the advances made by humanity had been through the pressure of injustice, and that the screws had been turned on me that I might do something to right the great wrong which forbade a married woman to own property. So, instead of spending my strength quarreling with the hand, I would strike for the heart of that great tyranny.
>
> I borrowed books from Judge Wilkins, took legal advice from Colonel Black, studied the laws under which I lived, and began a series of letters in the Journal on the subject of a married woman's right to hold property. I said nothing of my own affairs and confined myself to general principles.
>
> Lucretia Mott and Mary A. Grew, of Philadelphia, labored assidously for the same object, and in the session of '47 and '48, the legislature of Pennsylvania secured to married women the right to hold property.

This was Jane's first great triumph for women's rights but as the Bible says, "There were many like unto it."

One of the few lawyers to compliment her on her victory was a young man named Edwin M. Stanton who was passing through Pittsburgh on his way to Washington, D.C. Jane and he became great friends and corresponded frequently.

A distant relative in Butler, PA. the Rev. Isaah Niblock, ran a girls' seminary there and he asked Jane to come and take charge. She was to get $25 a month and board; she felt this was munificent.

While she was in Butler Jane tells us how she got started on her newspaper career:

> Petitions were presented in the Pennsylvania Legislature for the abolition of capital punishment. Senator Sullivan, chairman of the committee to which they were referred, wrote to Mr. Niblock for the scripture view. He was ill and requested me to answer, which I did, and Mr. Sullivan drew liberally from my arguments in his report against granting the petitions. The report was attacked, and I defended it in several letters published in a Butler paper—anonymously—and this was my first appearance in print, except a short letter published by George D. Prentiss,

in the Louisville Journal, of which I remember nothing, save the strangeness of seeing my thoughts in print.

James had returned from Louisville and since her sister Elizabeth was planning on getting married and moving to Ohio, Jane decided to give their marriage another try.

At this time Jane gave up the idea of being a teacher and decided to write.

> In April, 1842, my husband took possession of the old home in the valley, and we went there to live. There were large possibilities in the old house, and we soon had a pleasant residence. I had the furniture mother left me, and a small income from her estate. The farm I named "Swissvale," and such is the name thereof. When the Pennsylvania railroad was built it ran through it, but not in sight of the house and the station was called for the homestead.
>
> In the summer of '42 I began to write stories and rhymes, under the nom de plume of "Jennie Deans", for The Dollar Newspaper and Neal's Saturday Gazette, both of Philadelphia. Reece C. Fleeson published an anti-slavery weekly in Pittsburgh, The Spirit of Liberty, and for this I wrote abolition articles and essays on woman's right to life, liberty, and the pursuit of happiness. My productions were praised.

But this connubial bliss did not last. Jane's mother-in-law and two brothers-in-law came to live with them and keeping house for a lot of people was never Jane's forte.

Jane had become very active in the Abolitionist party in Pittsburgh; she could tell them firsthand what went on in the South and she wrote stinging letters to the Pittsburgh papers about conditions in Louisville.

But, sitting out on a farm in Swissvale was not Jane's idea of setting the world on fire so she left James and moved into Pittsburgh.

Charles Shiras, a wealthy Pittsburgh attorney, had backed an abolitionist newspaper, "The Albatross," and it had failed. Jane now proposed to step in and edit a new abolitionist newspaper which she called "The Pittsburg Saturday Visiter."

Pittsburgh was spelt without an "h" then and the spelling "visiter" came from Samuel Johnson's dictionary. . . a work Jane much admired.

It says a lot for Jane that the men who ran the newspapers knew her and respected her and some were willing to put cold cash on the line to let her publish. She was a tremendous presence and when people met her they felt the waves of her personality; she was no shrinking violet. There was one drawback. . . if Jane was going to be the editor she would have to stay in the office and work, just like every other newspaper writer. Would she do it? Try and stop her!

And so Jane Gray Cannon Swisshelm became the first woman to sit in an office in downtown Pittsburgh, the first woman salaried newspaper writer and the first woman newspaper editor.

Jane describes the situation:

> I have been publicly asserting the right of woman to earn a living as book-keepers, clerks, sales-women, and now shall I shrink for fear of a danger any one must meet in doing as I advised? This is my Red Sea. It can be no more terrible than the one which confronted Israel. Duty lies on the

> other side, and I am going over! 'Speak unto the children of Israel that they go forward.' The crimson waves of scandal, the white foam of gossip, shall part before me and heap themselves up as walls on either hand.

Let it be said to James Swisshelm's credit that he wholeheartedly supported Jane in her new venture as he was much against slavery and felt she could do some good with her paper.

> The coming advent was announced, but I had no arrangements for securing either advertisements or subscribers. Josiah King, now proprietor of the Pittsburg Gazette and James H. McClelland called at the Journal office and subscribed, and with these two supporters, the Pittsburg Saturday Visiter, entered life. The mechanical difficulty of getting out the first number proved to be so great that the forms were not on the press at 3 P. M. By five the streets were so blocked by a waiting crowd, that vehicles went around by other ways, and it was six o'clock, January 20th, 1848, when the first copy was sold at the counter. I was in the editorial room all afternoon, correcting proof to the last moment, and when there was nothing more I could do, was detained by the crowd around the doors until it was after eleven.

And so Jane was launched into the world of journalism. There were no footsteps for her to follow but that suited Jane just fine. She would make a path for others.

Jane continued to be a journalist until the day she died; in fact, five days before she died in July of 1884, an article by her appeared in the "Gazette."

As an editor, Mrs. Swisshelm took her position seriously and began to attack with her pen; there was a ready made situation which she used to advantage. The Mitchell case had been heard in the Pittsburgh Courts and the presiding judge, Judge Grier had handed down a verdict of guilty with which Jane did not agree.

Dr. Robert Mitchell of Indiana, PA had been taken into court in Pittsburgh in 1847 on the charge of aiding fugitive slaves and was found guilty by Judge Grier and fined $5,000 plus costs, which amounted to another $5,000. His house and land and furniture were sold at sheriff's sale to pay his debts but he said he would do it again if he got the chance.

Jane took off after Judge Grier, who was an elder in the Presbyterian Church, and pursued him with Biblical quotations and made such a spectacle of him that when the next case for slave harboring came before him, he reversed his former decision and there were no more cases on that issue heard in Pittsburgh courts.

It is a mistake to think that Jane was a "Woman's Libber" and wanted to open the doors of opportunity for all womankind. Far from it. . . Jane regarded most women as idiots who used their heads to put a hat upon and most women's movements as foolish. Three selections from her "Memoirs" give the state of her mind:

> The suffragettes created and spread the idea that masculine supremacy lay in the form of their garments, and a woman dressed as a man would be as potent as he.
> Strange as it may now seem, they succeeded in giving such efficacy to the idea, that no less a person than Mrs. Elizabeth Cady Stanton was led

astray by it, so that she set her cool, wise head to work and invented a costume, which she believed would emancipate woman from thraldom. Her invention was adopted by her friend, Mrs. Bloomer, editor and proprietor of the LILY, a small paper then in its infancy in Syracuse, NY, and from her the dress took its name. . . "the bloomer." Both women believed in their dress, and staunchly advocated it as the sovereignest remedy for all the ills that woman's flesh is heir to.

I made a suit and wore it at home parts of two days, long enough to feel assured that it must be a failure; and so opposed it earnestly, but nothing I could say or do could make it apparent that pantaloons were not the real objective point at which the discontented women aimed. The women themselves promulgated and pressed their claim to bifurcated garments and the whole tide of popular discussion was turned into that ridiculous channel.

In 1852 Jane's printers quit in a union dispute and Jane advertised for women to take their place in the composing room.

Jane picked three women from a hundred applications and Mr. Riddle, who was a partner in the "Visiter"' upbraided Jane because she did not pick the neediest of the applicants. Jane says she replied:

I do not propose to turn this office into an eleemosynary establishment. I want the women whom the work wants, not those who want the work. How long could a weak woman maintain her respectability among all these men? Would it be any kindness to put her in a place she is incapable of filling, and where she must inflict incalculable injury on herself, and the general cause of woman's right to labor? Do not let your generosity run away with your judgment.

And the third example:

By the pecks of letters I have been receiving, I had learned that there were thousands of women with grievances, and no power to state them or to discriminate between those which could be reached by law and those purely personal; and that the love of privacy with which the whole sex was accredited was a mistake, since most of my correspondents literally agonized to get before the public. Publicity! publicity! was the persistent demand. To meet the demand, small papers, owned and edited by women, sprang up all over the land, and like Jonah's gourd, perished in the night. Ruskin says to be noble is to be known, and at that period there was a great demand on the part of women for their full allowance of Nobility; but not one in a hundred thought of merit as a means of reaching it. No use waiting to learn to put two consecutive sentences together in any connected form, or for an idea or the power of expressing it. One woman was printing her productions, and why should not all the rest do likewise? They had so long followed some leader like a flock of sheep, that now they would rush through the first gap into newspaperdom.

Jane was also asked to be the president of one of the first women's suffrage conventions and she says:

I declined the presidential honors tendered me, on the ground of inability to fill the place; and earnestly entreated the movers to reconsider and give up the convention, saying:

"It will open a door through which fools and fanatics will pour in, and make the cause ridiculous."

The answer was that it was too late to recede. The convention was held, and justified my worst fears. When I criticised it, the reply was:

"If you had come and presided, as we wished you to do, the result would have been different. You started the movement and now refuse to lead it, but cannot stop it."

The next summer a convention was held in Akron, Ohio, and I attended, hoping to modify the madness, but failed utterly, by all protests I could make, to prevent the introduction by the committee on resolutions of this:

"Resolved, that the difference in sex is one of education"

Jane was getting bored with Pittsburgh. . . the action was all in Washington, DC and she liked to be where the action was. So she immediately did something about it and in her Memoirs says:

I longed to be in Washington, so I wrote to Horace Greeley, who answered that he would pay me five dollars a column for letters. It was said that this was the first time a woman had been engaged in that capacity.

I went to Washington in the early part of '50, going by canal to the western foot of the Alleghenies, and then by rail to the foot of the inclined plane, where our cars were wound up and let down by huge wind-lasses. I was in a whirl of wonder and excitement by this, my first acquaintance with the iron-horse, but had to stay all night in Baltimore because the daily train for Washington had left before ours came.

Jane was a great success in Washington and soon was in the thick of things. Her letters to the *New York Tribune* were vituperative, so much as that Jane was obliged to leave her hotel lodgings and move in with a friend, Mrs. Emma Southworth, the eminent writer of Victorian novels.

But Jane got things done. As she points out:

Among the legislative absurdities which early attracted my attention was that of bringing every claim against the government before Congress. If a man thought government owed him ten dollars, the only way was to have the bill pass both houses. In my Tribune letters, I ventilated that thoroughly, and suggested a court, in which Brother Johathan could appear by attorney. Mr. Greeley seconded the suggestion warmly and this, I think, was the origin of the Court of Claims.

There was yet one innovation I wanted to make, although my stay in Washington would necessarily be short. No woman had ever had a place in the Congressional reporter's gallery. This door I wanted to open to them, called on Vice-President Fillmore and asked him to assign me a seat in the Senate gallery. He was much surprised and tried to dissuade me. The place would be very unpleasant for a lady, would attract attention, I would not like it; but he gave me the seat. I occupied it one day, greatly to the surprise of the Senators, the reporters, and others on the floor and in the galleries; but felt that the novelty would soon wear off, and that women would work there and win bread without annoyance.

Jane's stay in Washington was highlighted by the fact that it was she who prevented Daniel Webster from becoming president of the United States.

Jane, of course, was violently abolitionist and so had been Daniel Webster but he realized to get to be president he would have to appeal to the Southern voters so he began to modify his position and to back down from his abolitionist stand.

Jane saw this as giving in to the slave dealers and she acted accordingly. Every newsman and in fact just about everybody in Washington knew that

Daniel Webster had a Negro mistress by whom he had several children. It had been known for years. . . yet Jane was the only one who dared write the story.
As she tells it:

DANIEL WEBSTER

Darkest of the dark omens for the slave, in that dark day, was the defalcation of Daniel Webster. He whose eloquence had secured in name the great Northwest to freedom, and who had so long been dreaded by the slave-power, had laid his crown in the dust; had counseled the people of the North to conquer their prejudices against catching slaves, and by his vote would open every sanctuary to the bloodhound. The prestige of his great name and the power of his great intellect was turned over to slavery, and the friends of freedom deplored and trembled for the result.

There was some general knowledge through the country of the immorality of Southern men in our national capital. Serious charges had been made by abolitionists against Henry Clay, but Webster was supposed to be a moral as well as an intellectual giant.

In the nation's capital lived some of our most prominent statesmen in open concubinage with negresses, adding to their income by the sale of their own children, while one could neither go out nor stay in without meeting indisputable testimony of the truth of Thomas Jefferson's statement: "The best blood of Virginia runs in the veins of her slaves." But the case which interested me most was a family of eight mulattoes, bearing the image and superscription of the great New England statesman, who paid the rent and grocery bills of their mother as regularly as he did those of his wife. I wondered and began to look at and inquire about him, and soon discovered that his whole panoply of moral power was a shell—that his life was full of rottenness. Then I knew why I had come to Washington. I gathered the principal facts of his life at the Capitol, stated them to Dr. Snodgrass, a prominent Washington correspondent, whose anti-slavery paper had been suppressed in Baltimore by a mob, to Joshua R. Giddings and Gamaliel Bailey. They assured me of the truth of what had been told me, but advised me to keep quiet, as other people had done.

But when I went to post the letter, I hesitated, walked back and forth on the street, and almost concluded to leave out that paragraph. I shuddered lest Mr. Julian's prediction should prove true. I was gratified by my position on the Tribune—the social distinction it gave me and courtesy which had been shown me. Grave Senators went out of their way to be polite, and even pro-slavery men treated me with distinguished consideration. My Washington life had been eminently agreeable, and I dreaded changing popularity for public denunciation. But I remembered my Red Sea, and my motto—"Speak unto the children of Israel that they go forward." The duty of destroying that pro-slavery influence was plain.

The surprise with which the Webster statement was received was fully equalled by the storm of denunciation it drew down upon me. The New York Tribune regretted and condemned. Other secular papers made dignified protests. The religious press was shocked at my indelicacy, and fellows of the baser sort improved their opportunity to the utmost. I have never seen, in the history of the press, such wide-spread abuse of any one person as that which I was favored; but, by a strange fatality, the paragraph was copied and copied. It was so short and pointed that in no other way could its wickedness be so well depicted as by making it a witness against itself.

Mr. Webster was a prominent candidate for President. Would his friends permit this story to pass without a word of denial? Mr. Julian was right; no one would dare deny the charge. He was, however, wrong in saying it would ruin me. My motive was too apparent, and the revelations too important, for any lasting disgrace to attach to it. On all hands it was assured that the disclosure had had a telling effect in disposing of a formidable power which had been arrayed against the slave, as Mr. Webster failed to secure the nomination.

Mr. Greeley continued to be my friend, and I wrote for the Tribune often after that time.

There was nothing left for Jane to do but leave Washington and return to Pittsburgh, which she did.

Jane was at this time 36 years old and had been married 15 years without any children but she became pregnant when she returned to Pittsburgh and her only child, a daughter named Henrietta, was born in 1851.

The child's birth was a terrible shock and physically very trying for the delicate Jane; she had a nervous breakdown and for several months afterward was in a bad state of mind and physical being.

James was delighted with the baby and he and his mother had almost complete charge of her as Jane soon went back to "The Pittsburg Saturday Visiter" and editorship.

Jane never mentions her pregnancy or the baby's birth in her autobiography "Half a Century" which she wrote in 1880. In the book she alludes to her daughter three times and then never by name, only as "the baby" even when the child is ten years old. Jane's nickname for the child was Zoe. It is from other sources we learn of Henrietta's education and marriage. Granted that bustling maternalism was not part of liberated Jane's makeup, it does seem strange that she barely acknowledges Henrietta's existence. Especially so since Jane and her own mother were so close and Mrs. Cannon was so devoted to her children.

The Swisshelm marriage got worse instead of better after the birth of their child. Things came to a head in 1857 and Jane decided to leave James for good.

She notes in her memoirs:

> In March '57, I resigned my place on the Family Journal and Visiter, feeling that my public work was over, and that no life save one of absolute solitude was possible for me.
>
> I had lived over twenty years without the legal right to be alone one hour—to have the exclusive use of one foot of space—to receive an unopened letter, or to preserve a line of manuscript
> "From sharp and sly inspection."
>
> In the later half of the nineteenth century, a Pennsylvania court decided that a husband had a right to open and read any communication addressed to his wife. Living as I did, under this law I had burned the private journal kept in girlhood, and the letters received from my brother, mother, sister and other friends, to preserve their contents from the comments of the farm laborers and female help, who, by common custom, must eat at our table and take part in our conversation. At the office I had received, read and burned, without answer, letters from some of the most prominent men and women of the era; letters which would be valuable history to-day; have, therefore, no private papers, and write this history, except a few public dates, entirely from memory.

Jane's husband would consent to no separation nor would he give Jane any part of her personal property:

> My husband would consent to no separation, and we had a struggle for my separate, personal property or its equivalent; a struggle in which Wm. M. Shinn was my lawyer, and Judge Mellon his, and in which I secured my piano by replevin,[1] Dr. John Scott being my bondsman, and learned that I might not call a porter into the house to remove my trunk. I therefore got my clothing, some books, china and bedding by stealth, and the assistance of half a dozen families of neighbors.

Bitter and disillusioned, Jane decided to leave Pittsburgh. In 1857, taking Henrietta, nicknamed "Zoe," with her, she made the arduous trip to St. Cloud, Minn. She went to live with her sister, Elizabeth, who with her husband, Henry Z. Mitchell, had moved there from Ohio some time before.

The Mitchells and their children were living a quiet life until Jane appeared: to Henry Mitchell must go the martyr's palm for being such a great brother-in-law. Jane had proposed to go and live in a cabin by herself with the baby forty miles from St. Cloud. There would be, said Jane, "No sound of strife. . . but those of waves, winds, birds and insects."

Minnesota was still a territory with marauding Indians, wild animals and raging winter snows. Horrified, Henry vetoed her plan so Jane contented herself with starting a newspaper. Sister Elizabeth took care of Zoe.

The first edition of the "St. Cloud Visiter" (again the Samuel Johnson spelling) came out in 1858. In the first few months the paper lost $2,000 and Mr. Brott, the publisher, and Jane's backers were worried. Jane wasn't and in a few months her paper was the best known paper in Minnesota. Jane's ascent to fame was simple. . . she simply attacked Sylvanus B. Lowerie, the wealthiest and most influential man in Minnesota. He was from Tennessee and owned slaves and wanted Minnesota to be a slave state and that Mrs. Swisshelm would not allow. He was a General and the Governor but neither position mattered much to Jane. At one point Jane's newspaper office was broken into by Lowerie's friends and her type and machinery dumped into the river. However, this move backfired and the good people of St. Cloud, who had been rather apathetic about Jane before, were solidly behind her now. Jane won the day, Lowerie's power was broken and when Minnesota was admitted to the Union in 1858 as the 32nd state, it went in as a free, not a slave, state.

There were other forces at work, of course, but Jane's paper and her abolitionist speeches and her constant agitation really turned the tide against slavery in Minnesota.

Along with her newspaper work Jane had begun giving speeches in Minnesota about women's legal rights which were well received. Her speaking career blossomed and she was very happy. It was on a speaking tour in 1860 or '61. . . Jane said she can't remember which year. . . that she read in the New York Tribune that her husband James was divorcing her.

James remarried later but Jane never did.

In 1862 the Sioux Indians had risen in the Minnesota River Valley and killed many settlers. Thirty-eight of the Indians had been hanged for their part in the uprising but Jane felt the whole tribe should be hung. She toured the state urging death for those Indians but could not generate much enthusiasm for her idea. In 1863, upset by her lack of success at home, she decided to go to Washington, DC and see President Lincoln about having all the Indians hung.

Of all the puzzling enigmas about Jane Grey Swisshelm the strangest is her dislike, even hatred, of Indians. She defended with her pen and with her life everybody in the world from newspaper boys to derelicts but for our native American she had only vitriol.

She only got as far as the Secretary of the Interior who told her she was wasting her time as "Mr. Lincoln would never hang anybody."

Since nobody paid attention to her Indian proposals and the government seemed more preoccupied with fighting the Civil War than with listening to Jane Grey Swisshelm, Jane found herself rather neglected. To take up her time she started to do volunteer work in the hospitals around Washington where the wounded were being dumped at an alarming rate.

Some of Jane's most brilliant newspaper work was done at this time as she wrote to the papers of the scenes and sounds she saw in the hospitals every day. She was very moved by the suffering of the young men who had gone to serve the cause and returned only to die of neglect, dysentery and disease in the hospitals.

Strangely enough, Jane, whose own daughter had seen very little of her and who even now was living with an aunt in Minnesota, requested that the men call her "Mother," and many of them never knew her real name. To hundreds of wounded men Jane was just "Mother."

But Jane Swisshelm could get things done. When told there were no lemons to be had in Washington to give the men to prevent scurvy, Jane appealed for lemons through her newspaper column and lemons came pouring in to Washington from every part of the North. Jane had no use for the Army and their slow way of doing things; she could accomplish more in two days with her newspaper writing than they could in two weeks.

In the course of her nursing career, Jane ran headlong into Dorothea Dix and the two of them, being so much alike and accustomed to each having their own way, detested each other on sight.

Miss Dix was a real nurse and in charge of the Army hospitals and nursing services. She and Jane fought for a long time but in the final crunch, Miss Dix had officialdom on her side and won the day. Jane retired from the field pleading the press of business and returned to St. Cloud. She had been in poor health and she spent some time recuperating.

While Jane was in St. Cloud she met up with an old enemy, General Sylvanus B. Lowerie.

Jane says in her memoirs:

> He called and we spent an hour talking, principally of the war, which he thought would result in two separate governments. His reason seemed to be entirely restored; but his prestige, power, wealth and health were gone. I tried to avoid all personal matters, as well as reference to our quarrel, but he broke into the conversation to say:

"I am the only person who ever understood you. People now think you go into hospitals from a sense of duty; from benevolence, like those good people who expect to get to heaven by doing disagreeable things on earth; but I know you go because you must; go for your own pleasure; you do not care for heaven or anything else, but yourself."

He stopped, looked down, traced the pattern of the carpet with the point of his cane, then raised his head and continued: "You take care of the sick and wounded, go into all those dreadful places just as I used to drink brandy—for sake of the exhileration it brings you."

We shook hands on parting, and from our inmost hearts, I am sure, wished each other well. I was more than ever impressed by the genuine greatness of the man, who had been degraded by the use of irresponsible power.

Jane sold her newspaper, settled her affairs in Minnesota and took her child to Pittsburgh to live with her ex-husband. Then, surprisingly enough, Jane went back to Washington, DC. But this time she did not go into hospital work. Jane had run out of money so Edwin Stanton, an old friend, got her a job clerking in the War Office.

Jane was blunt and outspoken and not in the least political. She placed truth above all else and always telling the truth got her into the bad graces of people who could have done her some good. Jane would never stoop to toady anyone and she never feathered her own nest while doing good, as so many people then and now manage to do. As a result, she entered into her declining years in poor financial shape. She refused to take anybody's charity and insisted on earning her own way.

Jane was not content with her job clerking so in December of 1865 she started an abolitionist paper, "The Reconstructionist," in Washington. She viciously attacked Andrew Johnson and as a result he had her fired from her government position. In her memoirs she notes rather boastfully that she was the first person he had ever dismissed.

The paper was a failure and it lasted only until March of 1866. Jane had sorely misjudged the temper of the times; the nation was anxious to bind up old wounds, not create new ones.

Jane Swisshelm turned again to the ever-helpful Mr. Stanton and in one fell swoop he managed to get her a livelihood and to get her out of his hair. Stanton advised her to go back to Pittsburgh and sue for her share in her recently deceased husband's estate.

This Jane did, successfully, and began living at Swissvale with her daughter, Zoe. Jane had decided that Zoe was to be a concert pianist and made her practice in a specially built room with no windows to distract her. Zoe went to the Pittsburgh Female College and won a gold medal for music and literature. Jane had a whole career planned out but while mother and daughter were visiting friends in Chicago Zoe met, fell in love with and married Henry Allen. She gave up her musical career entirely and never came back to Pittsburgh.

Jane Swisshelm returned alone to Pittsburgh and continued to live in her husband's family home, which no longer exists but was located somewhere near the area of Greendale Avenue in Edgewood.

"Swissvale" Home c. 1882. Carnegie Library of Pittsburgh.

In 1880 Jane Swisshelm wrote her autobiography, "Half a Century" which is now extremely rare and the copy at Carnegie Library in Pittsburgh is kept locked up.

Jane was a rebel whose cause had been remedied. . . She still wrote and published but much of the old fire was gone. Jane was a truly great abolitionist and the Civil War had ended slavery, at least on paper. For a long time Jane and the times had marched together but now the nation wanted to forget the war, get back to business, get on with the new problems and not dwell on the past. Jane no longer had her audience.

The times are always changing. . . there is always something new. . . a new movement, a new crisis, a new invention, a new natural disaster like a tidal wave or an artificial one like war. . . there are always new headlines. Times change, tastes change, stories change. . . but for someone like Jane Grey Swisshelm change was almost impossible. She was formed in granite and would hold true to her beliefs and be a rock that everyone could cling to.

In June of 1884 she visited her daughter in Chicago who now had two daughters of her own. Jane then returned to Pittsburgh and on July 14, 1884 an article she had written entitled "The Bloody Shirt" was published in the Pittsburgh Commercial Gazette. Just one week later on July 22, 1884 a headline in the Pittsburgh Commercial Gazette read:

> Passing Away: a Great Mind Losing It's Hold on Earth. Jane Grey Swisshelm Dying; a sketch of one of the leading characters of the day.
> The news that Jane Grey Swisshelm has laid aside her pen forever will be heard with deep regret by those people for whom she has so often fought with all the vigor of her intense nature.
> Last night she was near the shadowy line that is the boundary of this existence and that which is to come. She was living and that is all, the attending physician said when he left her chambers at 10 o'clock not expecting her to survive the hour of night when the human clockwork reaches its most feeble pulsations.

And Jane didn't.

On July 23, her obituary appeared in the same paper. It was a lovely write-up but it was not on the front page. It was next to an ad for ruffled parasols, which Jane would not have liked at all.

They said she died of summer complaint, which might have been cholera as there was a mild cholera epidemic then. She was 69 years old.

Pallbearers included Judge Mellon, John W. Chalfant, J. G. Seibenick, N. P. Read, S. Schoyer, Jr. and Dr. J. B. McClelland.

Newspapers all over the country carried her obituary and letters of condolence were received from many prominent people.

Jane Grey Swisshelm is buried in Allegheny Cemetery near the Butler Street entrance. Her tombstone is a huge piece of rough granite engraved on one side with:

Jane Grey Swisshelm

Born in Pittsburgh Dec. 6, 1815
Died in Swissvale July 22, 1884
"Speak unto the children of Israel, that they may go forward"[1]

On the other side of the stone is a beautifully engraved picture of her home in Swissvale where she died and underneath is the carved name, "Swissvale."

The stone is larger than any around it and it sits on a little rise. None of Jane's kin are around her. . . no friends are buried nearby. In death as in life, Jane sits alone above everybody, confident of herself and her life.

For many years the numbers three and zero, thirty, scribbled with copy pencil at the end of a newspaper story signified to the typesetter that was the end of the story. . . that there was nothing to follow.

Today newspapers are into computers and we do not use thirty any more. . . the computer would not understand.

But I think it would be appropriate and that Jane Grey Swisshelm would approve. . . to end her story with a thirty.

30

---

[1]The Biblical quotation, which was Jane's favorite, is from Exodus, 14th chapter, 15th verse. For the location of the grave and the source of the scriptural passage the author is indebted to Miss Ellen McKee of Homewood.

Mary Ellen Leigh McBride
Mrs. McBride, a journalist, has worked as a reporter on the **Pittsburgh Sun Telegraph** *and* **Pittsburgh Post-Gazette.** *She has also contributed articles to various publications and worked as free lance reporter. Her early ancestors came to Philadelphia before the Revolutionary War as printers and were the official printers for the state of Pennsylvania for many years. She is a former President of the Women's Press Club. Mrs. McBride received her B.A. degree from Chatham College and received her M.A. degree in English literature from the University of Pittsburgh.*

John A. Brashear as a young man, 1870.

JOHN A. BRASHEAR

by James E. O'Brien

In this book, Wallace Beardsley has a chapter on the famous astronomer and scientist, Dr. Samuel P. Langley. Langley and Brashear were very close to each other—Langley as teacher, Brashear as student. I believe that if John Brashear and Samuel Langley were here today, they would be amazed and pleased with the rapid developments in aerospace technology and solar research in which they both pioneered. It is quite possible that they would be right in there with the late Dr. Wernher von Braun, Dr. Kurt Debus, and others who are investigating the planets and outer limits of our solar system. John Brashear would be a bit handicapped with his six grades of formal education, but he would be burning the midnight oil to keep up with the computers and print-out charts on space science that he helped bring about. Perhaps what would please John Brashear the most, were he alive today, would be the thousands of amateur astronomers with their home-made reflector telescopes, all involved in tracking and reporting the flight of space satellites, such as Echo, Telestar, Early Bird, Tiros and the many Russian-made satellites! While Brashear owed much of his success to rich benefactors like William Thaw, Henry Phipps and Andrew Carnegie, he wished to consider himself as a benefactor to those amateur astronomers of limited means who were struggling to get a practical knowledge of the stellar universe. Brashear's first advertising in *Scientific American* in 1881, written from his little shop on Holt Street on Pittsburgh's South Side, was more of a compromise between business and charity! He listed prices of $135 for a fully mounted 5-1/2 inch mirror-type telescope and $700 for a 12-1/2 inch telescope, but he was careful to suggest that they could build their own at less cost. In the advertising pamphlet he stated, "A working amateur can now own a telescope that was at one time only within the reach of kings. I will ever hold myself in readiness to give advice so far as my time and ability will permit, *whether you choose to get one of my telescopes or not.*"

The life of "Uncle John" Brashear has in this space-age become of particular interest in the Pittsburgh area. It was very fitting that the Pittsburgh Board of Education named their newest high school The John A. Brashear High School. It was one of our board members that suggested this was a proper way to honor one of Pittsburgh's most illustrious citizens, a man who rose from a job of millright and toolmaker to gain world wide recognition as a telescope manufacturer, astronomer, educator and philosopher.

John Brashear was not a rich man who left a lot of money to endow a foundation in his name. Let us take a look at the "Roots" of this man.

John Brashear was born in Brownsville, Pennsylvania on November 24, 1840. The Brashear family were descendants of French Huguenots who had migrated to America in 1658. The Brashear homestead, an old inn in Brownsville operated by his grandfather, Basil "Brown" Brashear, still stands at the eastern end of the new Route 40 bridge over the Monongahela River at Brownsville. The story of his childhood and youth is as interesting as the story of his adult life and rise to fame. John had a very close relationship with his maternal grandfather, Nathaniel Smith, who introduced "Little John" to the skills of photography, gyroscopes, music, clock repairs, and of course the wonders of the celestial constellations. The most significant event of Brashear's childhood was the five cent look through the long, refractor-type telescope of an itinerant stargazer named Squire Wampler in 1849. John got his first look at the planet Saturn, and its colorful rings were to remain a challenge to his destiny for many years after. John's maternal grandfather was a jack of all trades who was also noted as a country preacher and philosopher. No social gathering nor church camp meeting was complete without an address by Nathaniel Smith. He was well known to mix his theology with discourses on the stars, as his grandson was to do thirty or forty years later. John's autobiography gives great credit to his Brownsville boyhood in shaping his whole future outlook on life. In Brashear's autobiography[1] he recalls the Tom Sawyer-Huck Finn adventures on the river; the red brick school house on the Brownsville Commons; and two teachers, Joshua Gibbons and George Wilkinson, who influenced him most. Brashear's father and mother were both lovers of music. Young John played a bass drum in a community brass band organized by his father. On one memorable occasion this band traveled in a gaily decorated horse-drawn bandwagon to Jefferson College at Canonsburg on the old National Pike, a round trip of fifty miles. They played for the college commencement exercise in 1852. Exactly fifty years later, in 1902, Brashear returned to Washington and Jefferson College in Washington, Pennsylvania to receive an honorary degree of Doctor of Laws.

At the age of fifteen, John Brashear went to Pittsburgh to attend Duff's Mercantile College for a period of four months. This was not a pioneering venture because his Grandfather Smith was working in Pittsburgh at the spike factory of Lewis, Oliver and Phillips. When he returned to Brownsville he worked for a short time in a grocery store, then as a "printer's devil" at the local newspaper office, and for a brief time with an auctioneer. While still in Brownsville Brashear landed a job in the engine works of John Snowden and Sons, where he apprenticed as a pattern-maker and part-time bookkeeper. This job required great ingenuity and prepared him for later jobs as a mechanic and millright. In 1859 Brashear set off for Louisville, Kentucky where he worked a short time as a mechanic, building engines for the city waterworks. Here he lived with old friends from Brownsville and though he was only twenty years old, Brashear spent his leisure hours giving bible talks and sermons at the river-front missions. When the Civil War broke out in 1861, he lost his job due to general unrest in Louisville. Brashear then found work making coffins and saved enough to pay his boat fare back to Brownsville.

After a short visit home, Brashear went to Pittsburgh where he found work as a mechanic in the rolling mill of Zug and Painter which was located at a spot just beyond the present P & LE Railroad complex, which we now call "Station Square." Brashear lived with his grandparents for a while on the North Side, using a steam ferry from the foot of Chartiers Street to the foot of Saw Mill Run. The difficulties of winter floods and ice jams caused him to move to a rooming house on the South Side where he met Phoebe Stewart while they both attended choir practice at the Bingham Street Methodist Church (13th and Bingham Streets). John was the choir director. Phoebe's father, Thomas Stewart, was not at all impressed with this twenty-one year old courting his nineteen year old daughter, particularly because John was a boarder in the Stewart house and was earning $10 a week, part of which he sent back to Brownsville. But in 1862, in a simple wedding, John and Phoebe were married at the house of Phoebe's brother, without her parent's knowledge. When the parents were told John and Phoebe were married, they were evicted from the Stewart's house. The couple then moved in with Grandma and Grandpa Smith in Allegheny, where John began again the long ferry trips to and from work. Occasionally he used a borrowed skiff to row back and forth, or he used the new Smithfield Bridge, completed in 1861 by the engineer-designer John Roebling.

Despite the inauspicious beginnings of this marriage it was really molded in firm cement. The very happy union lasted until Phoebe died in 1910 while the Brashears were vacationing at their Canadian home called Isle Urania in Muskoka Lakes. Phoebe and John Brashear never had children of their own, but they adopted a son, Harry, who died of typhoid fever at the age of nineteen; and a daughter, Effie, who married James McDowell. The McDowells remained very close to Ma and Pa Brashear, living with them in the house on South Side and later, on Perrysville Avenue. James McDowell and John's brothers, William and Frank, worked with Brashear and kept the telescope business going while John traveled and lectured around the world.

The first test of the Brashear's enduring marriage and mutual love was a sermon he preached at the Bingham Methodist Church on the South Side. To fulfill the wish of his mother, John Brashear constantly studied the scriptures and completed a course of study qualifying him for a license as a local Methodist preacher. John was asked to substitute one Sunday while the regular pastor was supposed to be away. Well, the regular pastor changed his schedule and was present when John gave a very eloquent talk, well blended with the scientist's point of view on evolutionary creation, similar to the sermons and bible talks given by his model, Grandfather Nate Smith. After the sermon was over, the pastor and most of the congregation were outraged. John was humiliated and disappointed. His wife, Phoebe, comforted John through that heartbreaking experience and encouraged him to pursue other goals.

Shortly after they were married, John and Phoebe rented a run-down house near the rolling mill of Zug and Painter. Before long they created flower and vegetable gardens out of the barren cinder yard that surrounded the house.

While John Brashear was putting in those ten-hour days in the mill, he took the opportunity to develop his interest in astronomy and related fields which had begun years before. Night after night he and "Ma" would go and study the stars, sometimes climbing the South Side hill or going across the other river where they could get a broad view of the sky.

A strike in 1867 caused the mill to close, but John Brashear soon found a position in another South Side mill, that of McKnight, Duncan and Company. This mill, located on Thirteenth Street, was destroyed by fire in December 1871, but Brashear had made himself so valuable as a mechanic and general maintenance man that the owners gave him an important share in building a new mill, which was completed in a year. John received a $300 per year wage increase and a $100 gift for a vacation trip, the young couple's first trip out of Pittsburgh. They went by train to Cleveland and took a boat to Put-In Bay at Sandusky, Ohio.

On May 28, 1870, John and Phoebe purchased two lots on Holt Street (on the cliffside slopes above the present Duquesne Brewery site on South Side). Brashear described it as "pretty steep but a fine view of the hills, the Monongahela River and the busy mills." He picked this spot because it reminded him of his home in Brownsville. John and Phoebe spent every spare moment, with some help from his friends at the mill, building a little cottage of "Steamboat Gothic" design. They cut down a large oak tree on the lot and used it for foundation posts under the house. Two years later John and Phoebe occupied the house. During their first winter there, they lived in three rooms with what was called "paper plastering," a temporary lining to keep them from freezing. Shortly after, a strong March storm knocked the house out of plumb on the wooden foundation posts. Brashear's friends helped him to reset the foundation and eventually he put up a stone wet-wall foundation with a plain dirt cellar floor. If you were to come up Holt Street today it would still be a major accomplishment, even in a car with automatic transmission on a black-top street, because it is a thirty-five degree grade. Consider what it must have been like 105 years ago on plain dirt streets without steps! John and Phoebe enjoyed the life in South Side. They mixed well with the local German choral societies and cantata societies where John taught singing classes and led the church choir.

With encouragement from Phoebe, John diligently pursued his reading and proficiency in astronomy. Without a telescope he could not fulfill this goal, so Brashear ordered a glass for a five-inch lens from a New York outlet of an English manufacturer. There was not much room for a

Brashear's telescope workshop at 4 Holt Street, Southside, 1880.

workshop in his house, so Brashear bought a little 8' x 10' coalshed from a neighbor and hauled it next to his kitchem. Brashear designed a small steam engine, bought a second-hand lathe, and in his words, "we had a pretty fair amateur outfit." When the glass arrived from New York, he and Phoebe went to work at making his first telescope lens with all the zeal and interest of children with a new toy. Brashear would go to work in the mill at 5:30 A.M., arrive home at 6:00 P.M. or later, and then work till midnight cutting, grinding and polishing with tools he had made himself.

After two years of effort, John Brashear had just finished the lens when he dropped it, breaking it into two pieces. If anyone wants to know the slow process of lens grinding, they can drop in at the Brashear Center on South Side any Monday and Wednesday evening to observe the telescope class. With Phoebe around, John could not remain discouraged. They ordered the second glass and a year later Brashear assembled his first nine-foot long refractor telescope. They called in the neighbors, and everybody celebrated looking at the moon and the stars, and especially Saturn with its rings.

John Brashear knew that this telescope was not of the best quality, so he picked up enough courage to write Professor Samuel Langley, head of Allegheny Observatory, asking permission to bring the object glass (the main lens) over for inspection and to receive suggestions on how to improve it. There was an immediate response from Dr. Langley and John found his way by shoe leather express (no street cars ran out Perrysville Avenue) to the old original Observatory late in the evening. He was welcomed by Langley and given the privilege of a look at Saturn through the Observatory's thirteen-inch refractor-type telescope, which Brashear enjoyed very much. He wrote,

> That first visit to the old Allegheny Observatory had a profound effect upon all my life. It was my introduction into the larger world of science and the beginning of my friendship with men who found their greatest happiness in discovering nature's hidden truths in spite of poverty, isolation and increasing work of body and mind.

The Allegheny Telescope Association had been meeting socially for about fifteen years and with the generosity of William Thaw, the wealthy Vice President of the Pennsylvania Railroad, the Association had built this first Observatory at the top of the hill right above Federal Street (now the 1900 block of Perrysville Avenue). Langley had made this Observatory famous by giving accurate time readings to the railroads, similar to Greenwich Mean Time.

After that first visit with Langley, Brashear was advised to make a reflecting-type telescope. Brashear started on a twelve-inch lens with a ten-foot focal length, but this major effort also failed when Brashear, following instructions from a British Science Journal, was silvering the finished product. The unequal heating of the glass surface caused the lens to crack. This happened during the cold winter of 1878, but within two months John Brashear had successfully finished the second mirror using his own formula for the silvering process. The Brashear formula was very successful, so much so that Brashear loaned his telescope to Dr. Langley and to several other noted astronomers at the time. The Brashear silvering process became known in all parts of the world after John sent it to the same English magazine from which he had obtained the first formula, which had caused his mirror lens to crack. From this time on, John Brashear bought books (as he could afford them) and studied more mathematics, physics and astronomy, and he became a closer friend of Langley. All the while Brashear was working in the rolling mill twelve hours a day!

John Brashear inserted his first ad in *Scientific American:*

> Silvered-glass specula, diagonals and eye pieces made for amateurs desiring to construct their own telescopes.

> John A. Brashear
> No. 3 Holt Street
> South Side, Pittsburgh, Pa.

Hundreds of inquiries came, and with the help of Phoebe he worked to fill the orders. In 1881 Brashear became exhausted from overwork and his doctor advised him to give up the job in the mill or the optical business. In a family council meeting which included daughter Effie and her husband James

McDowell, it was decided that Brashear would give up the job in the mill and their combined incomes would keep them alive. McDowell was working in a glass factory in South Side.

John Brashear said, "I am a little afraid that failure would have been our lot had not the Good Samaritan, William Thaw, found us at this turning point in our lives." One evening when John had completed some work for Professor Langley, he was delivering the finished product to the Observatory and Langley introduced him to William Thaw, Sr. Thaw was much impressed by Brashear and had read the Brashear newspaper column on astronomy in the Pittsburgh Evening Chronicle, the Ledger, the Dispatch and Commercial Gazette. Thaw journeyed to the South Side to look over the Brashear workshop which was still just the coalshed in the back yard. Thaw offered to pay off the $800 debt which Brashear owed on his house, and in addition he wrote a check for $3000 for Brashear to build a new workshop. In addition, John got a salary of $600 per year. Soon John Brashear was in business, and with the help of his son-in-law, James McDowell, they took on more orders, and McDowell was able to give up his job in the glass works. The two men performed delicate technical work which included new experiments in polishing rock salt lenses and prisms to help Professor Langley with experiments in measuring radiant energy from the sun, using an instrument called the bolometer spectrograph. Orders for Rowland Diffraction Gratings, another Brashear specialty, came from West Point, Royal Observatory of Dublin, Cambridge University, Turin, Italy, McGill University in Toronto and the University of Paris. (Brashear always sent instructions with all of his products on how to mount them on telescopes.) Several thousand spectrograph plates were made in the Brashear shops, all with very accurate measurements within 1/200,000 of an inch, and one thousand parallel lines to the inch. Through these achievements Brashear became a friend of several famous German astronomers[2] after furnishing them with diffraction gratings. Brashear taught himself to speak and write German. One of his most disappointing experiences was the break he had to make with these men of science during World War I.

Meanwhile, John Brashear became the chief mechanic, draftsman and supplier for Samuel Langley's experiments with the first flying machine. Langley's purpose was not a manned flying machine, but to determine the laws that govern flight. Some weird contraptions were built at the time; one of them, a "whirling table" (wind tunnel, was constructed here in Pittsburgh behind the old Allegheny Observatory). Few people know that Samuel Langley came close to launching the first man-carrying flying machine in 1903 with much skepticism and cynicism from the press and the public. Langley died in 1906 and the Wright brothers pulled the trick in 1907, one year later at Kitty Hawk, North Carolina.[3]

John Brashear quickly moved into the company of the steel barons and gods of the mills. Thaw had urged John to relocate his home shop to Perrysville Avenue next to the old Allegheny Observatory. Thaw built Brashear's new workshop and provided him with a majestic-looking house at 1954 Perrysville

Avenue on the condition that ownership of the buildings would revert to Thaw when Brashear ceased to use it for making telescopes. It was moving from the top of one hill to the top of another. Today at the intersection of Buena Vista and Perrysville, all one can see is a factory building with the name Fletcher Anchors and Printing across from the G. S. Simon's Funeral Home. At this location John joined the Conservatory Club at the Allegheny Commons and soon rubbed shoulders with such men as Henry W. Oliver, Henry Phipps, Robert Pitcairn, Charles Schwab, A. Brian Wall, C. C. Mellor, B. F. Jones, Edward Bigelow, Joseph Woodwell, Thomas Miller and Andrew Carnegie. It was Henry Phipps who arranged John Brashear's first trip to Europe, inviting him to chaperone Phipps' son, also named Johnny. James McDowell was left in charge of the factory while John and Phoebe Brashear made visits to every observatory and scientific society in England, Scotland, Ireland, France, Switzerland and Germany. In each city Brashear's hosts treated him like royalty. Brashear comments in his autobiography about his attendance at the Annual Dinner of the Royal Astronomy Society in London:

> It was certainly a royal event for me, for I was received with great kindness, and I could not help but have an occasional thought that it was only a few years since I was a greasy millright in Pittsburgh. While social lines were drawn very close, science has no boundaries of this kind. I think that scientific men respect the work of enthusiastic amateurs, if that work is done in a conscientious, careful manner.

This was the key to Brashear's success. Those gods of the mills saw much of themselves in John Brashear; most of them had begun as laborers or mechanics or bobbin boys and had moved up into the world of money and business. They were able to satisfy their desires to help humanity by their admiration of John Brashear's accomplishments, although in Western Pennsylvania, historians of the labor strife and trade union movement would claim that Brashear was guilty by association with some of these powerful industrialists. During the 1892 Steel Strike, Brashear was seriously torn between his compassion for the millmen and loyalty to his benefactors.

After Andrew Carnegie paid for John Brashear's second trip to Europe to attend astronomical society meetings and exhibits, there was a move to build a new observatory in Allegheny, and "Uncle John" (as he was known by many) was made chairman of the project. In 1893 Brashear had been granted an honorary Doctor of Science degree from the Western University of Pennsylvania (soon to be called the University of Pittsburgh). Later Brashear received other honorary doctorate degrees from W & J, Franklin Institute, Stevens Institute, Princeton and Wooster College.[4] Brashear served as President and acting Chancellor of the Western University of Pennsylvania, and Carnegie asked him to serve on the Plan and Scope Committee of Carnegie Institute of Technology (now Carnegie Mellon University). Brashear had quite an influence on the plan for Carnegie Tech to become a great technical university to train able young men and women to work in the industries of Pittsburgh. After some delay (during the Spanish-American War and the financial panic of 1893), the $300,000 fund drive for the new Allegheny

John A. Brashear, 1890.

51

Observatory was successful because of generous donations from Carnegie, Thaw, Frick, Porter and Schwab. The Observatory was dedicated in August 1912.

In 1909 Henry C. Frick asked John Brashear to undertake the management of the Frick Educational Commission with an endowment of $250,000. At the time, there was an anonymous endeavor by Frick to provide scholarships and training for Pittsburgh teachers for summer study to improve their learning and capacity for teaching. Speakers were invited to visit the schools and address the students. The beneficiaries of these scholarships organized the Phoebe Brashear Club, named in memory of John's wife who had died in 1910. This club was expanded to include any teachers who wanted to pay the one dollar annual dues, and years later, they in turn were responsible for the expansion of the Brashear Settlement Association as a social agency serving the South Side area.

Before he died in 1920, John Brashear received many marks of distinction, such as being named Pennsylvania's most distinguished citizen, in 1915.

Brashear's precepts speak for themselves. Couched in past century phraseology and biblical spirit, John Brashear's philosophy is best remembered by the quotation on the memorial tablet over his vault in Allegheny Observatory: "We have loved the stars too dearly to be fearful of the night."

"Somewhere beneath the stars is a work which you alone were meant to do. Never rest until you have found it." Brashear was devoted to work and perfection. He saw the personal worth of all human beings based on his deep religious faith and conviction that every man should have educational enlightenment. Brashear accepted the good will of his benefactors with this statement, "Scientific men owe much to men like these for the beautiful spirit they have shown in their generous gifts made not for charity but as a recognition of life work so often done without proper monetary compensation."

In 1917 the Brashear Memorial Association was started as a neighborhood social agency to continue the philosophy and goals of John and Phoebe Brashear. Mrs. John M. Phillips was chiefly responsible for the effort to raise funds to purchase his old homestead and adjoining buildings on Holt Street. John Brashear was still living when the Association was formed and he objected to soliciting of any kind for this purpose. Nevertheless, it was the pennies and nickels from the Pittsburgh school children that provided the funds for the purchase of Brashear House in 1916.

The history of the Brashear Association is another chapter, but we feel that John Brashear would be proud of its accomplishments over the past sixty years.

[1]John A. Brashear, *The Autobiography of a Man Who Loved the Stars*, edited by W. Lucien Scaife, American Society of Mechanical Engineers, New York, 1924 (out of print).

[2]Dr. Schott of Schott and Company; Dr. Kirschensteiner, referred to in his autobiography (1888), first trip to Europe; Dr. Schumann; Dr. Scheiner; and the Repsold brothers.

[3]Langley had successfully launched an unmanned aircraft on a three quarters of a mile flight in 1896.

[4]Can be seen at Brashear Center.

James E. O'Brien

Mr. O'Brien is the executive director of the Brashear Association, a South Side social service agency founded in 1917 as a memorial to John and Phoebe Brashear. After five years of military service in World War II, he attended the University of Pittsburgh and received his master's degree in social work in 1948. Thereafter he worked as program and camp director at the Brashear Association. In 1956 he was appointed executive director of the Associated Neighborhood Centers of Youngstown, Ohio. He later became welfare director of Mahoning County in Ohio. His principal interest is in the South Side. He is a retired Colonel in the United States Air Force Reserve Patrol.

H. J. Heinz at age 21.

H. J. HEINZ

by Robert C. Alberts

In December 1975 I reviewed a book for the New York Times *Book Review*—a biography of Pittsburgh's Charles M. Schwab. The author, Robert Hessen, of Stanford University, said this:

> The trend to de-emphasize or ignore the role of the individual leaders of industry in analyzing the process of industrialization has gone too far. The ambitions and achievement of audacious leaders like Schwab have altered the course of economic development in this country. We should make a systematic re-examination of various myths and misconceptions about the steel industry and its leaders—that the leaders all thought alike, used the same methods, and had the same goals; that their decisions were based primarily on a dispassionate analysis of costs and anticipated profits, with little or no influence of such psychological motives as empire building, anger, jealousy, pride and revenge.

In other words, Hessen feels that the early business barons were individuals, not types. I agree with him—and I feel that H. J. Heinz is an excellent illustration of his point. H. J. Heinz was more of an individualist than most of the other industrialists of his time.

Pittsburgh was a center for coal and coke, iron and steel, aluminum, oil, glass, rails, and heavy machinery. But Heinz, in this unlikely part of the country, specialized in food, in the primary business of feeding people. For fifty years he was a dominant force in developments that changed agricultural practices—the processing of food—and the kitchen habits of the nation.

He founded a giant corporation in a new industry. He carried its products and his philosophy to four continents with a promotional flair that probably has never been surpassed in American business.

Henry John Heinz the First was born in 1844 on Pittsburgh's South Side, of German immigrant parents, the oldest of four boys and four girls. In 1850 his mother and his father, who owned a brickyard, moved to Sharpsburg, up the river from here, the father building his house with his own bricks. Master Heinz got started at the age of eight peddling vegetables from the family garden around the neighborhood in a handbasket.

Harry specialized in freshly grated horseradish roots packed for the first time in clear glass bottles, so that the customers could see for themselves that his product had no adulterants—no leaves, no wood fiber, no turnip filler—only pure horseradish. Horseradish was consumed in great quantities in the nineteenth century because it sharpened the appetite, made dull food palatable, and supposedly had medicinal qualities, especially for grippe and catarrh. Horseradish would not keep unless it was grated and bottled in vinegar—a chore that made the housewives' eyes smart.

In 1869, when he was twenty-five, Harry married Sarah Sloan Young of Pittsburgh. She was, we are told, of a respectable North Ireland Presbyterian family. The same year he started in the food processing and packing business in Sharpsburg with two brothers named Noble. Heinz & Noble Company made a fine success of it for about five years. They even moved into a factory in downtown Pittsburgh, on the south side of Second Avenue near Grant Street. But there was a bad depression in the 1870s; the company had grown too large too fast and it was badly undercapitalized. In 1875 it filed for voluntary bankruptcy with assets of $110,000 and liabilities of $160,000. This event has been kissed off in most articles about the Founder as something mildly unpleasant but rather amusing. The diaries for those years reveal that it was most unpleasant and far from amusing. Heinz went through hardships and a humiliating ordeal that would have broken all but the toughest spirits.

He started up again with his cousin Frederick and his brother John, with a few thousand dollars of capital, and after several very tough years he got on solid ground and began to grow. He paid off all his debts—he carried a list of them around in a pocket notebook with the title "Debts of Honor."

In 1888 he took full charge of the company and began to build the complex of factory buildings on the north shore of the Allegheny River across from downtown Pittsburgh—the ones that are still there today. By 1892 he and Sallie had four children—Irene, Clarence, Howard, and Clifford.

Henry Heinz's diary gives the character and flavor of this man better than anything else I know, and at the same time it gives a social history of the times and a picture of life in Pittsburgh. He was a little weak on spelling, but he could write. These passages from his diary tell us much about him.

> April 13, 1877: Sallie and I for once go to the Opera House to hear Edwin Booth play Richard the Third, a historical play. I do not approve of opera-going, yet my conscience did not dictate to me on this occasion.
>
> August 12: Am reading a book titled "The Successful Merchant."
>
> December 31: Spent happy day at office. At 5:30 our office force and salesmen presented me with a very handsome inkstand (cut glass) and a fine gold pen and pencil combined. I returned heartfelt thanks in a short speech, when we all wished each other a Happy New Year and gave all a jar of pickles.
>
> January 11, 1879: Excellent sleighing, deep snow for the first time. We have no sleigh nor do we care much about it.
>
> May 19: Baltimore. Mr. Ports and I left on the new steamer Virginia for Norfolk at 9 P.M. The boat travels 16 miles an hour which is good time. We slept in bunks below (economy) and overhead there was a number of stomping horses and a lot of Pennsylvania farmers opposite in the same room. *Stateroom next time.*
>
> May 20: Norfolk. Find people are nearly all prejudiced and have southern proclivities. Don't want to live here. They think it's God service to bleed a northern man.
>
> January 19, 1880: I loaned C. A. Sipe, our pastor, $50 today as the church was behind with his salary.

November 2: This is Presidential and General Election Day. General James A. Garfield is the Republican candidate (a good one) and General Hancock the Democratic candidate. Receiving telegraphic returns tonight at Sharpsburg station.

November 3: A glorious victory is announced through all the press. The Pittsburgh *Commercial* heads a column in large type. GLORY BE TO GOD!

January 12, 1882: I had all the wagon salesmen together in my room this 7 P.M.—a talk on temperance. The result—a handshake never to drink while in our employ. Took all to supper.

January 14: The five vinegar salesmen are so warmed up on the subject of temperance that they are about to organize a temperance society.

March 11, 1884: I paid Covodes the last I owed them of the Debt of Honor, $366.88, this being part of the interest.

October 22: Very sleepy and flat this A.M. after dissipating in the way of marshalling the Sharpsburg division of the political parade and on horseback four and a half hours. Will see that some others have such honors in the future.

November 5: Mr. Wood leaves with a nice new span of bay horses, harness and peddling wagon for Cleveland. He drives all the way. It usually requires three days. Such an outfit as the above costs us $1,000, but it pays to start right.

August 13: Clarence (twelve years old) and Howard (eight) go to the city with me to begin to work five or six hours per day in the office and factory instead of all play.

A later entry shows how far Henry Heinz had come from the days when his conscience kept him from going to the playhouse.

May 25, 1889: Saturday. This night closes the greatest musical festival ever held in Pittsburgh in the new Exposition Buildings. Our family attended every other night and other nights we invited our relatives to use our private box. It was a royal treat. Miss Emma Juch and Guiseppi Campanari were among the singers who received $1,000 per night. A success and an introduction to the new Exposition Buildings.[1]

The company began to move into its new buildings on the North Side in October, 1890. The plant very soon became world-famous for its enlightened treatment of employees and its fine physical plant for employee comfort. It received a gold medal, in fact, in 1899 at the great Paris Exposition "for the policy of the firm tending to the improvement of factory conditions . . . and for the sociological features of its business as exhibited by means of photographs." People were especially impressed by the treatment of the women who worked there. There were more than 1,000 of them at the plant in 1900.

Each woman had a private locker with a key. If she handled food, she was given a manicure once a week. She had the free services of a dispensary nurse, a physician on call, and two company dentists. She could read in the reading room after hours, borrow books, attend evening lectures of entertainment in the auditorium for employees. She could take free classes in cooking, dressmaking, millinery, drawing, singing, and training for citizenship. She could use the swimming pool and gymnasium and sun herself on a roof garden on top of the bottling building. There were weekly organ recitals in the

H. J. Heinz Company, Handwrapping Tins, c. 1905.

Auditorium, and concerts given by an employee Choral Society of sixty voices.
Four times each year the chairs were removed from the Auditorium and the
floor waxed for a large dance, generally to Rocereto's sixteen-piece orchestra.
To spare Mr. Heinz's religious feelings, the dances were called "Promenade
Concerts." Several times a year each girl in her turn climbed into a horse-
drawn wagonette with eight other girls and spent a morning or afternoon, at
no loss in pay, being driven through the park and downtown area.

This doesn't sound like such a big deal in this day of television
entertainment and equal pay for women, but it attracted national attention in
1900. My favorite passage in *The Good Provider* describes the working
conditions of that time:

> Immigrant women of all ages came to Pittsburgh by the hundreds of
> thousands. The women who sought employment were terribly limited in
> the work they could do. Teaching and nursing required skills they did not
> have and could not acquire. Most office clerks and salespeople were men. A
> woman could work as a household domestic, or as a scrubwoman, or as a
> prostitute, or at manual labor in some trades—in laundries, in garment and
> glass factories, in stogie factories, in packaged food plants.
> To a girl who had worked for several years stripping moist tobacco
> leaves off their stems, weighing and tying them in pounds for the rollers,
> sitting with her back to a damp wall in a cellar, working by the light of a
> gas jet, eating her lunch off the corner of her workbench . . . to a peasant
> girl from Central Europe who a year earlier had been living in some remote
> village in a cabin with an earth floor, the animals housed under the same
> roof on the other side of the wall, who worked in the fields in all weather . . .
> to such a girl the physical comforts of the Heinz plant, the relatively short
> hours, the pay and the companionship, were a revelation and a delight.

A Heinz girl worked from 7 A.M. to 5:40 P.M., which was the working
schedule in industry in those days. On Saturday she quit an hour early, at 4:40
P.M. She began at the going wage for women, five cents an hour, three dollars
a week, unless she was good at piece work, in which case she could earn up to
$7 or $8. This was half the wage paid to men doing similar work. It doesn't
seem like much, but in 1900 Heinz specialty salesmen began at $12 a week; an
unskilled mill hand earned 15 cents an hour; and the average daily wage was
less than $1. It was a time when a woman's full silk-lined tailor-made suit at
Gusky's Department Store on Market Street, "Fresh From the Best Eastern
Centers of Fashion," cost $15. A hand-made cheviot skirt cost $5. A linen
handkerchief, 5 cents. A pair of all-wool blankets, $2.69. A man's shirt, $1—all
shirts were chemise shirts, the kind you pulled on over your head. Ten bars of
Lily White Floating Soap, 19 cents. A 48-pound sack of white flour, 89 cents.
A pound of Armour's ham, ten and three-quarter cents. A gallon of Diamond
Monogram Whiskey, $3. And so forth.

In my opinion, and in the opinion of others more qualified to make a
judgment, H. J. Heinz has never been surpassed in this country—perhaps
never equalled—as a promoter and showman in the industrial field. He used
the public tours of the Heinz plant, for example, to excite favorable attention
and make people talk. He was the first American industrialist to open up his

plant operations to public view. He used the company stables—the finest in the country—for the same purpose. One reporter called them "equine palaces" and declared with a straight face that the horses actually exhibited pride in their surroundings. The stables were fireproof, heated by steam, lighted by electricity, screened at the windows. The 110 horses were fed, watered and brushed by electrically operated machinery. Their harness, individually fitted for each horse, was carried to and from the tack room on an overhead conveyor. The horses were all jet black except one white mare, and they pulled 65 cream-white wagons with green trim. They appeared in every parade.

He used the Heinz pickle pin, one of the most famous giveaways in merchandising history, to advertise his name, his company, and his products.

And then there was the Heinz Pier at Atlantic City—his costliest, most ambitious and probably most effective promotional undertaking. "The Sea Shore Home of the 57 Varieties," as it was called, was built at the end of Massachusetts Avenue in 1899. It is still remembered with gratitude by thousands of footweary sightseers. It extended some 900 feet into the Atlantic Ocean and had several pavillion buildings. These offered the visitor, free of charge, rest rooms, an auditorium and a concert-lecture series, an exhibition of photographs of Heinz operations; a reading room with up-to-date home-town newspapers, free souvenir cards and stationery, a kitchen, and a glassed-in sunparlor. The sunparlor held a collection of—you can't call it art—curiosities such as an Egyptian mummy, two nine-foot elephant tusks, and a chair that had belonged to General Grant. The kitchen had displays of Heinz products, free samples, cooking lessons, and a counter where one might order "a sample assortment of the choicest of the 57 Varieties, which will be delivered to your home through your grocer at a special price, all charges paid. Only one case sold to any one home." In season, as many as 300,000 visitors used the Pier on a busy day. In the 45 years of its existence, 50 million people visited the Pier, and every one was given the Heinz pickle pin. It was destroyed in the hurricane of 1944.

One of the attractions at the Heinz Pier and elsewhere was a giant painting by an artist named John Mulvaney—12 by 20 feet in size—titled Custer's Last Rally. Heinz bought it for $25,000 in 1898, and the demand to see it was so great that it was constantly circulated around different locations—especially at food fairs.

Another stellar attraction was the first large outdoor electric advertising sign—in New York at Fifth Avenue and 23rd Street. It was six stories high, used 1200 Mazda lamp bulbs, and cost $90 each night. Electric lights were still a novelty in 1900, and everyone who saw it oohed and ahhed.

Heinz got national attention when he moved "The Little House Where We Began" from Sharpsburg to the plant site on the North Side. This had to be done by river, and it was quite an engineering feat. When the building arrived, spectators lined both shores, and 1500 Heinz employees left the plant to watch the event. It was placed on the Heinz grounds. In 1954, it was carefully disassembled, moved to Henry Ford's Greenfield Village, and there put together again.

Henry Heinz traveled a great deal in this and other work—for instance, in overseeing the English company he started around 1900. In the 25 years between 1890 and 1914, Heinz went to Europe every year but four. His wife Sarah died tragically of pneumonia in 1894, and after her death, Heinz's youngest sister Henrietta became his hostess and in charge of his household.

In 1905, at age 61, Heinz incorporated his company with himself as president and a select group of relatives and executives as the only stockholders. He was now head of a company that was the country's largest producer of pickles, vinegar, and ketchup; the largest grower and manufacturer of sauerkraut, pickling onions, and horseradish, the second largest producer of mustard; the fourth largest packer of olives. Heinz was operating nine branch factories in six states, thirty-eight salting houses in nine states, a branch house in London, and agencies around the world. The company employed 2,800 full-time people, 400 of them "travelers," salesmen.

A passage from the good Provider reads:

> Into the Allegheny factory sidings came long train loads from the farms and salting stations. From foreign lands came carloads of produce—raisins and green olives from Spain, currants from Greece, casks of cauliflower from Holland, fresh fruits and sugar from the West Indies, whole spices from the East Indies, mustard seed from England, France, and Italy. From the distilleries came scores of thousands of used oak kegs and barrels, their insides to be scraped clean of charcoal for reuse for kraut and vinegar. (Federal law did not permit a second use of such containers for whiskey).

The company was now being run more and more by its executives, though everything of importance was cleared through the Founder and he had the final say.

Around 1908, Heinz's son Howard began to assume more authority in the company. Howard is remembered today as a formal, conservative man, but in the early days he was somewhat dashing. He had one of the first automobiles in Pittsburgh and certainly the best—a Panhard Levassor that today is in the collection of William Penn Snyder in Sewickley—H. J. Heinz II gave it to him. He drew the speculative eye of the mothers in Pittsburgh who had marriageable daughters, but he married a lumber heiress from Saginaw, Michigan named Elizabeth Rust. Howard and Betty had two sons: H. J. Heinz II, who is the present chairman of the company; and Rust Heinz, who was killed in an automobile accident on the Westinghouse Bridge in 1938.

The Founder was successful, but he felt a deep dissatisfaction at one aspect of his operations. Commercial canning still had a bad name; he was not in a truly respectable business. Commercial food processing and preserving did not enjoy public confidence, and it was under constant attacks from consumers groups, "muck-raking" journalists, and the Federal government. And so Henry Heinz, who had always had strong convictions on the importance of purity and quality in food, called for government regulation of his industry. He felt that the way to earn public confidence was to work in partnership with a federal regulatory agency. Federal regulation, he felt, would make the industry respected and trusted.

He sent his son Howard to Washington with petitions, and he gave his support to Dr. Harvey Wiley and President Theodore Roosevelt in their program to clean up the industry. Naturally, he was not exactly popular with his fellow-food processors.

Congress passed and the President signed the Food and Drugs and Meat Inspection acts of 1906, which ruled that all foods coming within federal jurisdiction must be prepared in a clean manner from pure and wholesome materials and free from any added substance that might render them injurious to health.

The Pure Food Law marked the real birth of the modern food processing industry. It started to grow, to win investment capital and to enter millions of American kitchens.

Heinz was now an elder stateman of his industry. He was active in such Pittsburgh causes as flood control, smoke abatement, and in various charitable undertakings. He was president of the World Sunday School Association. He had bought, four years before his wife's death in 1896, a huge baronial mansion in the Point Breeze section, and there he lived with a staff of servants, various relatives, and assorted visiting grandchildren. He had a conservatory, open to the public, and a private museum, open to school children, that had more than 3,000 art objects, including a famous collection of oriental ivory and 100 antique watches now in Carnegie Museum. He built a settlement house for children on the North Side in memory of his wife. It is still there and is still operating today.

On May 9, 1919, Henry Heinz had his secretary write to his son Howard, who was then in Rumania as Herbert Hoover's food commissioner in the Balkans. Five days later, at age 74, he was dead of pneumonia. He left an estate of $4 million and many charitable bequests to friends, relatives, servants, employees and religious organizations. At his death, the company he had founded 50 years earlier had 6,500 employees, 100,000 acres in crops, 25 branch factories, 85 salting stations, and 55 branch offices and warehouses. It owned 258 railroad cars, a seed farm, factories for making bottles, boxes and cans. In 1971, its sales grossed $1 billion.

One of the finest tributes paid to H. J. Heinz came from Dr. Harvey Wiley when the death was announced. He sent a telegram addressed to Howard Heinz that read:

> I appreciate the loyalty with which your father and all of his staff stood by me in the darkest days of my fight for pure food. I feel that I should have lost the fight if I had not had that assistance.

One of his associates, a member of the family, said, "He was a father to us all. He reared us into manhood, and he guided us with a kind and gentle spirit." Three Japanese leaders who had welcomed Heinz on his visit to the Orient in 1913 sent a telegram: "Your loss, world's loss."

I would like to close with a postscript—with a passage I regretfully had to drop from *The Good Provider*.

Howard Heinz, of course, was in Europe when he received the news of his father's illness, and he started back home at once. His wife had planned to join

H. J. Heinz with his grandchildren before the conservatory at Greenlawn, 1916. H. J. Heinz II is on the left.

him in Europe, changed her passage date, attended the funeral, and returned to New York to sail alone on the Caronia on May 29. She risked the chance that she would pass her husband in mid-ocean, for she had received no acknowledgement from him that he knew she was going to sail. She sat at the captain's table with, among others, Sir Thomas Lipton, "who," she said, "used yachting to sell tea," and William Horlich, "of malted milk fame." Mr. Horlick's wife was unpleasant to her, but he was "a very nice gentleman and immensely amusing, quite a blood and sporty but a boy in spirit and fun." Sir Thomas Lipton had a "delightful burr in his conversation and is quite amusing to talk to for a few minutes, but he is the greatest egoist I ever met. He made the assertion that no man had ever been so poor and needy and risen to such wealth and importance as he. I nearly laughed, it sounded so infantile."

The Caronia sailed into Liverpool at 7:30 A.M. on June 12, and Elizabeth Heinz looked down from the railing to see her husband waiting for her on the dock.

---

[1]Diary of H. J. Heinz is in the possession of H. J. Heinz, II

Robert C. Alberts
Mr. Alberts, a native Pittsburgher, is the author of four biographies on figures in American history: Major Robert Stobo, William Bingham, H. J. Heinz, and Benjamin West. **The Good Provider: H. J. Heinz and His 57 Varieties,** *was published in 1973. He has also published extensively in* **American Heritage** *and other periodicals, and presently is secretary of the Western Pennsylvania Historical Society.*

Stephen Foster, 1859 at age 33.

STEPHEN FOSTER

by Fletcher Hodges, Jr.

This Bicentennial year of 1976 has been an important year, both for our country and for Stephen Foster.

One hundred fifty years ago, on the 4th of July, 1826, Stephen Collins Foster was born in Pittsburgh. The Bicentennial has renewed our interest in our history, and it has been responsible for renewed interest in the works of such American composers as Stephen Foster.

In the lobby of the Library of Congress in Washington, D.C. stands a marble bust of Stephen Foster, the work of the eminent American sculptor, Walker Hancock. The project was sponsored by the University of Pittsburgh, and the funds were donated by a group of American citizens. On the base of the bust is engraved:

> "HE MADE THE SWANEE RIVER
> AND THE OLD KENTUCKY HOME
> IMPERISHABLE SYMBOLS OF
> OUR AMERICAN HERITAGE"

If Foster had done no more than that, his place in our history would be secure!

Harold Vincent Milligan, who wrote one of the first biographies of Stephen Foster, was himself a musician as well as a critic. He has given us a thoughtful and sympathetic analysis of the significance of Foster.[1]

Milligan discusses Foster's place in music as follows:

> Stephen Foster occupies a unique position in the history of music, not only of this country but of the world. No other single individual produced so many of those songs which are called "folk-songs," by which is meant songs that so perfectly express the mood and spirit of the people that they become a part of the life of all the "folk" and speak as the voice, not of an individual, but of all. So completely do the "folk" absorb these songs and adapt them to their own uses, that the individuality and frequently even the name of the originator is completely lost, thus giving rise to the erroneous idea that a "folk-song" is a song created not by an individual but by a community. It is obvious that all things must have a beginning, however obscure, and every folk-song is first born in the heart and brain of some one person, whose spirit is so finely attuned to the voice of that inward struggle which is the history of the soul of man, that when he seeks his own self-expression, he at the same time gives a voice to that vast "mute multitude who die and give no sign." Such a one was Stephen Foster, more fortunate in his fate than that glorious company of nameless poet-souls, whose aspiration after "the fair face of Beauty, haunting all the

world," is preserved in the folk-songs of the world. Surely his name is worthy of at least one volume upon the shelf of history!

It was not a great life, as the world counts greatness. It might even be called a failure, a life sadly out of harmony with its environment. But it has left an indelible impression on the world, and its influence, subtle, indefinite, immaterial but pervasive, is incalculable.

If the philosopher was right who said, "If I may make the songs of a people, I care not who may make the laws," then Stephen Foster's name is worthy of remembrance. Although purists may question their right to the title "folk-songs", his melodies are truly the songs of the American people, while their appeal is so universal that the best of them, "The Old Folks at Home," "My Old Kentucky Home" and "Old Black Joe," are sung the world over.

The day of his birth, July 4th, 1826, was a notable one in the history of the United States. It marked the semi-centennial of the signing of the Declaration of Independence, and great preparations had been made throughout the country to celebrate appropriately the fiftieth birthday of the Republic.

While these celebrations were in progress, two of the nation's founders passed away: John Adams, its second President, at Quincy, Massachusetts, and Thomas Jefferson, at Monticello, Virginia.

Synchronous with the ending of these two great lives, a third life was just beginning, a life destined also to exercise a powerful, though less tangible influence on the human race.

Colonel William Barclay Foster was one of the leading citizens of the frontier community which centered in the thriving young city of Pittsburgh. His home at Lawrenceville, on the hills above the city, was naturally chosen for the celebration of Independence Day. In the assembled crowd were many veterans of the Revolution, as well as survivors of the War of 1812, and of various conflicts with the Indians; the woods back of the house were the scene of a "barbecue," with band music and speeches appropriate to the occasion. Just at noon, as the guns were firing the national salute, a son was born in the Foster home, "The White Cottage." This child was named Stephen Collins Foster.

Stephen Collins Foster, beloved American composer of the middle nineteenth century, has won a permanent place in the hearts of his countrymen. His music is an important part of the nation's cultural heritage. It is also a part of the world's heritage.

Through his genius, Foster caught the spirit of a period in our country's history which is gone, never to return. This period, with its tenderness, sentiment, humor, and tragedy, is crystallized in the music of Stephen Foster.

Foster's fame rests chiefly on his four great songs of the South: *Old Folks at Home, My Old Kentucky Home, Massa's in de Cold Ground,* and *Old Black Joe.* These beloved plantation melodies were simply intended to portray one race of people, one section of our country, and one period in our history. But Foster did more than this. He created songs which have leaped the boundaries of space and time, and express universal thoughts and emotions. Love of home, love of family, homesickness and timesickness—these are the themes of Stephen Foster's immortal melodies.

The best of his sentimental ballads are still sung today. His hauntingly beautiful *Jeanie with the Light Brown Hair,* his tender *Come Where My Love*

Lies Dreaming and *Beautiful Dreamer* recall the charm of an age which is past. *Oh! Susanna* and *Camptown Races* are proof that Foster possessed a sense of humor and could write in a lighter vein. Other songs still heard today are *Old Dog Tray, Old Uncle Ned, Nelly was a Lady,* and *Nelly Bly.*

Foster was a prolific writer who devoted most of his life to music. During his brief career he wrote more than two hundred original songs and compositions. Foster also arranged, adapted, and translated over a hundred other works. About twenty of his best works so combine the qualities of poetry and melody, simplicity and sincerity, that the resulting songs form a remarkable contribution to the music of our country and to all mankind.

The Foster family belonged to the pioneer aristocracy of Pittsburgh. They were prominent in the political, commercial, and social life of the young city. Stephen's father, William Barclay Foster, was active in politics as a member of the Pennsylvania State Legislature and mayor of Allegheny City, now the North Side of Pittsburgh. William was of the rugged Scotch-Irish breed which settled Pennsylvania west of the Susquehanna River. Stephen's mother, Eliza Clayland Tomlinson Foster, was descended from the English stock which settled on the Eastern Shore of Maryland. On both sides of his family, Stephen was descended from men and women who had come to America long before the Revolution.

The Pittsburgh that Stephen Foster knew as a boy was less than two generations removed from the frontier. Of pioneers in the western wilderness, like Stephen's grandfather, James Foster, Sir George Otto Trevelyan, the English historian of the American Revolution, wrote:

> The Scotch-Irish to the west of the Susquehanna resided, isolated and armed, on farms which they themselves had cleared; and they had no defense against a raid of savages except their own vigilance and courage. A fierce and resolute race, they lived not indeed in the fear, but in the contemplation, of a probability that their families might be butchered, and the fruits of their labor destroyed in the course of one bloody night.[2]

These Scotch-Irish forebears of Stephen Foster were not only "a fierce and resolute race"; in addition to their ruggedness and their courage, they also brought with them to their new land a love of music and poetry. In his narrative poem, *Marmion,* published in 1808, the great Scottish poet, Sir Walter Scott, describes his emotions on hearing a Scottish ballad sung in his own country:

> Oft have I listened and stood still,
> As it came softened up the hill,
> And deemed it the lament of men
> Who languished for their native glen;
> And thought how sad would be such sound
> On Susquehanna's swampy ground,
> Kentucky's wood-encumbered brake,
> Or wild Ontario's boundless lake,
> Where heart-sick exiles, in the strain,
> Recalled fair Scotland's hills again!

The Susquehanna region of Pennsylvania, mentioned by Scott, was known personally to Stephen Foster's Scotch-Irish ancestors. Stephen's great-grandfather, Alexander Foster, emigrated to America from northern Ireland about 1725, and settled in what is now Lancaster County, Pennsylvania, about 1728. It was here that Alexander's son, James, was born in 1738. James became a soldier in the Revolutionary War, serving in a Pennsylvania regiment, and was present at the surrender of Cornwallis at Yorktown. After the war, James and his family moved west with the advancing frontier. Through these two men, Alexander and James, as well as his father, William, young Stephen Foster inherited the Scotch-Irish love of music and poetry.

Stephen Foster was among our first genuinely American composers. His songs were American in theme, rather than mere imitations of contemporary English and German music. There were other composers in America during Foster's youth, but most of them lived in the older seaboard cities of Boston, New York, Philadelphia, or Baltimore, where the influence of European-trained teachers was strong. Such men looked across the Atlantic to England and Germany for their inspiration, and composed transplanted English or German music. Not Stephen Foster! Born at the meeting place of North and South, East and West (such was the Pittsburgh of his youth), Foster did not look elsewhere for his inspiration—he found it all about him. He sang of the America that he knew: the American home, the sentimental emotions underlying the superficial practicality of the American temperament, life on the Ohio and Mississippi rivers, slavery, the slumberous plantation life, the red-hot political campaigns, and southern battlefields. Because he generally knew what he was singing about, and felt it deeply, his best music still lives and breathes.

William and Eliza Foster had a family of eleven children. When Stephen's youngest brother died in infancy, Stephen became the youngest member of this large family, cherished and protected by parents, brothers, and sisters. This position of the youngest child in his much-loved family colored Foster's way of life and is reflected in his songs.

William and Eliza could well be proud of their family. Their sons led useful, honorable lives, and were successful in their chosen careers. William, Jr., the eldest son, became a prominent civil engineer. He built canals in Kentucky, Ohio, and Pennsylvania. He was one of the chief engineers in the construction of the Pennsylvania Railroad's main line over the Allegheny Mountains, between Harrisburg and Pittsburgh, which included the Horseshoe Curve, and he eventually became vice president of the company. As Stephen's eldest brother, he played an important part in Stephen's early life.

One of the Foster daughters, Ann Eliza, was active in church work. The Fosters were Episcopalians, and Ann Eliza married an Episcopal minister, the Reverend Edward Young Buchanan. He was the brother of James Buchanan, who became President of the United States in 1857, serving until 1861. Ann Eliza, too, as an older sister, earnest, serious-minded, and deeply religious, affected Stephen's childhood.

The Fosters were a close-knit family, and Stephen had a happy childhood. All the Fosters were interested in music, art, and literature. Stephen's mother and sisters sang and played musical instruments, and it was from these members of his family that the young Stephen early acquired an interest in music and poetry. With their encouragement, Stephen learned to sing, compose, and play, with little or no formal training. The cultured atmosphere of the Foster home helped to compensate for Stephen's failure to complete his formal education.

As a boy in Pittsburgh, Stephen showed early that music was his chief interest, whether taking part in children's neighborhood theatricals, singing in his home, or learning to play various musical instruments. While his family encouraged him in his music, they thought of it simply as an interesting hobby, rather than as a possible life career. There was little opportunity for the serious study of music in the Pittsburgh of Foster's youth. Whatever he learned was largely through his own efforts.

The composer's biographers usually refer to him as Stephen, rather than as Foster, because of the youthful qualities of his personality, which he kept throughout his short life. As a boy, Foster was kind, modest, unassuming, sympathetic, and impractical. His personality did not seem to change with the passing of the years, and in many ways he remained an immature boy to the end of his life.

Stephen's early education was consistent with that of the sons of other leading Scotch-Irish families of the Pittsburgh community. He attended the Allegheny Academy, and received, in addition, private tutoring. Early in 1840, when Stephen was thirteen years old, his family decided to send him to school in Bradford County, Pennsylvania, where his brother William was engaged in the construction of the North Branch Canal along the Susquehanna River. For a year and a half, in 1840 and 1841, Stephen was a student at two Bradford County institutions, the Athens Academy and the Towanda Academy.

Stephen was never very happy in school because he found it difficult to adapt himself to discipline and routine. An intense individualist, Foster preferred to study those subjects which interested him, and his chief love was music, but education in western Pennsylvania in the 1830's and 1840's provided little place in the curriculum for a subject like music, which was far removed from a practical, materialistic existence!

In July 1841, Stephen Foster entered Jefferson College, at Canonsburg, Pennsylvania. His experience with higher education lasted only a week. After a brief struggle with homesickness, Foster returned to his family in Pittsburgh.

The next five years, from 1841 through 1846, were spent in Pittsburgh. Stephen studied with private teachers, learned French and German, and acquired some ability as an artist. Occasionally he found work in an office or warehouse, but he devoted most of his leisure hours to music, for which, his father said, "he possesses a strange talent."

Foster's family was worried about him. He did not wish to return to school, he was not interested in selecting a career, and he held only temporary jobs. At that time, devotion to music did not seem to promise a life's work not even when Foster's first published song was composed. This song, *Open Thy Lattice, Love,* was composed in 1843, when Foster was about seventeen years old. The words were not his; he found the verses in a magazine and set them to music. His song was published a year later, in 1844, and while Stephen probably earned little or nothing from its sale, he had the pleasure of seeing his work in print for the first time. Light, gay, and melodious, *Open Thy Lattice, Love* was evidence of Stephen's growing musical talent.

Commencing in 1845, a group of young men met twice a week at the Foster home to sing under the leadership of Stephen. After they had sung the popular songs of the day, Stephen decided to compose some original music for the group. Among the songs he wrote were *Lou'siana Belle, Old Uncle Ned,* and *Oh! Susanna.* A few years later, while Foster was living in Cincinnati, *Old Uncle Ned* and *Oh! Susanna* were published, and these two songs made him famous.

Stephen was beginning to share his family's concern about his future. He was restless and dissatisfied with his rather aimless existence. Foster did not realize, nor did his family, that his life's work might be found in his music. Attempting to make a decision of some kind, Foster considered making the army his career. At the age of nineteen, using his family's political influence, Foster sought an appointment to West Point. Early in 1846, he learned his application for West Point had been rejected. This was, no doubt, all for the best, for Stephen's personality was hardly that of a professional army officer! A military career for him would have been a disaster as it was for two other nineteenth century American artists—Edgar Allan Poe and James Abbott McNeill Whistler.

His family now urged him to seek permanent employment. Late that year, 1846, Foster left Pittsburgh and went to Cincinnati to become a bookkeeper in a steamboat agency, Irwin & Foster, in which his brother Dunning was a partner.

Stephen spent the next three years in Cincinnati. They were among the happiest and most formative years of his life. Cincinnati was a vigorous and growing young city of the West, populated by New Englanders, Pennsylvanians, Virginians, and Kentuckians. The traditions of the Old South played an important part in the life of the city. To this mingling of the streams of several American cultures, a strong German element added an Old World flavor and an interest in the arts, notably music. Cincinnati's levees were washed by the waters of the Ohio River; it was an important shipping point for both passengers and freight. Southern planters, river men, gold-seekers bound for California, Negro roustabouts, all formed a colorful and ever-changing panorama of humanity along Cincinnati's water front. The city carried on a thriving trade in pork, wheat, and cotton; Cincinnati well deserved the title of Queen City of the West.

From his office on the levee, Stephen could observe first-hand all this activity. His new life was interesting and stimulating. In the friendly environment of Cincinnati, both fresh and mellow, Stephen's genius blossomed. It was there he began to write songs in earnest, and it was there he decided to abandon a business career and to become a professional composer.

While Stephen was interested in the steamboats and the picturesque life along the waterfront, his heart was never in the actual business of the steamboat agency. He was more interested in other phases of Cincinnati life. He made friendships among the musicians, writers, minstrels, and publishers of the city, and these friendships affected Foster's later career.

Foster gave manuscript copies of *Oh! Susanna, Old Uncle Ned,* and other songs, which he had written earlier for his friends in Pittsburgh, to several acquaintances in Cincinnati musical circles without any conception of what the results might be. The Cincinnati minstrels sang them. The Cincinnati public adopted them as the newest songs of the day and the minstrels carried them to other cities. Foster's songs spread like wildfire through the country. Publishers in Cincinnati, Louisville, Baltimore, New York, Philadelphia, and Boston printed many editions of Stephen's songs. Most of the editions were "pirated"—published without his consent—and Stephen earned nothing from their sale. Overlooking the possibility of financial profit, he had failed to protect his own interests through copyright or contract with the publishers.

Oh! Susanna was published in 1848, just after gold was discovered in California. By 1849, thousands of Americans had started for the West to seek their fortunes. These Forty-Niners took unto themselves Stephen's hearty *Oh! Susanna,* made it their marching song across the continent to the gold fields of California, and eventually transformed it into that young state's unofficial anthem. The song spread all over the world. *Oh! Susanna* and *Old Uncle Ned* as well, became national and international successes. Their composer, who had simply been writing songs for the amusement of himself and his friends, found himself famous, if no richer, through his own talent.

Early in 1850 Stephen returned to Pittsburgh to devote himself completely to his music. He was ambitious; he worked hard and his efforts were crowned with immediate and spectacular success. The six years from early 1850 through 1855 were the most successful of his entire life. Songs, compositions, arrangements, and translations—more than one hundred sixty works in all— poured from his pen during these years. Many of these works were of only passing interest; they enjoyed a brief period of popularity and then were forgotten. But Foster's genius was now at its height. In addition to his many works of only moderate quality, Foster was composing songs which would never die. Each year at least one new song was published which added to his present fame; *Camptown Races* and *Nelly Bly* in 1850, *Old Folks at Home* in 1851, *Massa's in de Cold Ground* in 1852, *My Old Kentucky Home* and *Old Dog Tray* in 1853, *Jeanie with the Light Brown Hair* in 1854, and *Come Where My Love Lies Dreaming* in 1855.

Stephen Foster occasionally set the verses of other poets to music of his own composition, as he did in the case of *Open Thy Lattice, Love,* composed in 1843. Few of these songs composed in collaboration with other writers are remembered today. Foster was at his best and most successful when he could wed his own melody to words of his own creation.

Stephen Foster burst like a shooting star upon American music. He burned with a quick, bright, brief flame for a few spectacular years, and then faded away in a dim trail lit only by occasional sparks. Foster's tragedy was that he could not maintain the high standards of his early years. According to some erroneous legends, Stephen Foster was an underpaid genius, starving in a garret while others grew rich from his labors. According to other legends, equally erroneous, he earned great wealth through his music.

The facts are that Stephen made a modest, if not a spectacular, financial success as a composer. There are records which prove that he was paid over fifteen thousand dollars from 1849 to 1860. His heirs received more than four thousand dollars when his copyrights were renewed some years after his death. The total *known* earnings from his music were thus well over nineteen thousand dollars. Since there are no reliable records about the earnings of the songs composed in his early years, or of the songs composed in the closing years of his life when he was living in New York, it is not possible to give accurate figures for Stephen's total income. We know, however, that his income from his first and last efforts was relatively small.

If Stephen Foster were a successful professional composer of the late twentieth century, endowed with the same genius for touching the human heart which he had in the mid-nineteenth century, he would no doubt be a very wealthy man. His work would be protected by national and international copyright. He would be paid for the use of his songs on records, tapes and on the stage; in clubs and restaurants; and in motion pictures, radio and television, and his resultant income would be far greater today than it was in the 1850's. At that time there was only one medium for the popularization of his works—blackface minstrelsy, represented by such groups as the Christy Minstrels. Foster was not paid by the minstrels for the use of his songs, other than occasional small amounts received from the Christy Minstrels for the privilege of being the first to sing certain melodies. Foster's only source of income was from the sale of his published music in the United States. Since international copyright had not yet been established, Stephen derived no income from the large sale of his songs in other countries. International "pirating" of books and music was practiced by publishers on both sides of the Atlantic Ocean. This situation, most unfair to author and composer and bitterly decried by Stephen's contemporary, the English novelist Charles Dickens, himself the victim of "pirating" by American publishers, no longer exists. The work of the writer and composer is now protected by international copyright.

Part II

It is true Foster died in poverty, a failure if judged only by his last works. Foster's tragic end was due to his own mismanagement of his business affairs, and to the decline of his talent in his last unhappy years. But in 1850, when he returned to Pittsburgh from Cincinnati fresh in his youthful ambition, happy in his career, with success ahead, he was entering the most prosperous period of his life. His average earnings during this period were approximately fourteen hundred dollars a year, which was a comfortable income in the 1850's. Stephen felt, therefore, that he could afford marriage, and on July 22, 1850, he married Jane Denny McDowell, the daughter of a Pittsburgh physician. The McDowells, like the Fosters, were of Scotch-Irish pioneer stock and the two families had known each other in Pittsburgh for some time.

The couple's daughter and only child, Marion, was born in Pittsburgh on April 18, 1851. When she grew up, Marion became a music teacher, composed songs, married, and had three children. She lived to be eighty-four years old. Altogether, Stephen and Jane have had many descendants, most of whom are alive today.[3]

The marriage of Stephen and Jane was not always happy and serene. They never ceased to care for each other, but there were many complications. Stephen was sometimes a difficult person to live with. Although he was basically a kind, friendly, and sympathetic man, he was also a genius, with the instability of temperament often associated with genius. He was moody, careless about money and other practical matters, occasionally improvident, and toward the end of his life he began to drink excessively. Perhaps Stephen's place as a much-loved youngest son, his mother's favorite child and the little brother of his family, made it difficult for him to adapt himself to the more mature role of husband and father. It would have taken a saint to put up with Stephen under all conditions, and Jane was not a saint! She was a pretty, high-spirited girl with a will and temper of her own. She, too, came from a family where she had enjoyed a favored place. No wonder that Stephen and Jane had their marital problems—problems which resulted in occasional separations. Yet through all their lives, through periods of calm and through periods of storm, they were always in love. For example, *Jeanie with the Light Brown Hair* was written in 1854, during one of their periods of separation. Stephen was living in New York; Jane and their daughter were living in Pittsburgh. According to family tradition, "Jeanie" of the song was none other than Jane, the auburn-haired girl Stephen married, and into this lovely melody he poured all the affection he had for his young wife. Shortly after the song was composed they were reunited.

Just about the time his daughter, Marion, was born, Foster was working on *Old Folks at Home,* or *Way Down Upon the Swanee River* as the song is often known. Perhaps the great events of love, marriage, and the birth of his child, which he had recently experienced, gave him the inspiration to create his masterpiece. This wonderful song is among the best-loved melodies in the history of the world. Although Stephen never saw the Suwannee River, he immortalized it in song. It was to become a half-legendary stream, encircling the earth. It flows through the soul of humanity. It was to become a symbol of all mankind's vague, lost, wordless dreams; of joys that have vanished; of unattainable longings; of homesickness and timesickness.

The Suwannee River rises in the Okefenokee Swamp of southern Georgia, and flows through northern Florida into the Gulf of Mexico. The nearest Stephen Foster came to Florida was New Orleans, which he visited in 1852, some months after *Old Folks at Home* was published. In 1851 Stephen was simply working in Pittsburgh on a new song about the South for Christy's Minstrels to sing. The first draft of *Old Folks at Home* read: "Way down upon de Pedee ribber . . ." Stephen had the Pedee River of South Carolina in mind, but he was not satisfied with the name. He asked his brother, Morrison Foster, for advice. Morrison suggested the Yazoo River of Mississippi, but Stephen rejected it as unpoetic. Morrison then opened an atlas, and the two brothers studied the map of the United States, searching for a Southern river with a musical, romantic name. At last Morrison found the Suwannee River in Florida. "That's it, that's it exactly," Stephen exclaimed in delight. He shortened the name of the river to "Swanee" and changed his manuscript to read: "Way down upon de Swanee ribber . . ." Thus *Old Folks at Home* was born.

If Foster had become famous when *Oh! Susanna* and *Old Uncle Ned* were published in 1848, his fame was to increase ten-fold with the publication of *Old Folks at Home* in October, 1851. *Old Folks at Home* was sung throughout the entire English-speaking world, and was translated into other languages. The royalties Stephen received from *Old Folks at Home* enabled him to take Jane on a steamboat trip to New Orleans in February, 1852. According to one account, they made the trip to attend the Mardi Gras festival, but there is some evidence that New Orleans did not commence its traditional observance of Mardi Gras until about 1857. This trip down the Ohio and Mississippi was one of the happy events of their marriage. It was also Stephen's only visit to the Deep South.

Occasionally we hear erroneous legends concerning Stephen Foster's association with the South. Some of these legends say that he had close bonds with the South. According to some stories, he traveled extensively through the South, spent much of his life and wrote many of his songs there. It has even been stated that he was a Southerner and that he married a Southern girl. Motion pictures, radio, and television have helped perpetuate these errors.

Stephen Foster had little first-hand knowledge of the South even though many of his songs have that part of the country as their theme. When he was about six years old, in 1833, his mother had taken him on a brief trip to Augusta and Louisville, Kentucky. His trip to New Orleans in 1852 was made after he had established his reputation as a writer of plantation melodies. These two trips are Stephen Foster's only visits to the South about which any reliable information is available. While it seems probable that during his stay in Cincinnati Foster was acquainted with Kentucky, just across the Ohio River from that city, we know nothing definite about any visits he may have made at that time. Nor can any definite facts be found to verify the romantic legends connecting him with Bardstown, Kentucky.

Considering his rather slight acquaintance with the South, it is remarkable that Foster's songs portray that part of our nation with such accuracy and sympathy. Stephen's interest in the South must have increased as a result of his trip to New Orleans, and one of his best songs, another plantation melody, *Massa's in de Cold Ground,* was published in the summer of 1852 after

Stephen and Jane had returned to Pittsburgh. Later that year he started work on *My Old Kentucky Home,* which was published in January, 1853.

This great song is another flawless creation of Stephen's genius. *My Old Kentucky Home* is a gem of poetry, melody, and sentiment. The soul of the person who sings it is released of emotions almost too deep, too intense to be borne.

> "The day goes by like a shadow o'er the heart,
> With sorrow, where all was delight."

According to Kentucky tradition this song was written in Bardstown, Kentucky, at "Federal Hill," the home of Stephen Foster's relatives, the Rowan family. This tradition has not been verified, since definite, factual, contemporary evidence about a visit or visits Stephen may have paid to his Rowan cousins in Bardstown is lacking. We know that other members of his family visited "Federal Hill." Young John Rowan, Jr. made an unsuccessful proposal of marriage to Stephen's sister, Charlotte, when she was a visitor in 1828. It is possible that Stephen, himself, may have been a visitor on one or more occasions. He may even have been inspired by memories of "Federal Hill" to create *My Old Kentucky Home.* But without documentary evidence we can only hope that some day the legends about this beautiful Kentucky estate and its association with Foster's masterpiece will be substantiated.

There is some evidence that Stephen Foster may have been influenced by Harriet Beecher Stowe's famous novel, *Uncle Tom's Cabin.* Mrs. Stowe's book was published in 1852, just before Foster's song was published, and the song reflects certain phases of the book.

According to Stephen's brother, Morrison Foster, the song was written in Pittsburgh. Since Morrison was quite close to Stephen and was familiar with his activities, his statement is of considerable importance in the controversy about this song. But the place and circumstances of the composition of *My Old Kentucky Home* are of less significance than the song itself. The song is dear to Kentuckians, as well as to all Americans, and to the citizens of the world, everywhere. The Commonwealth of Kentucky established "Federal Hill" at Bardstown as a state shrine on July 4, 1923, the ninety-seventh anniversary of Stephen's birth. It is now known as "The Old Kentucky Home." In 1928, the Kentucky legislature selected *My Old Kentucky Home* as the official state song.

Florida has honored Stephen Foster in a similar manner to express its gratitude for the fame he had brought to that state. *Old Folks at Home* was chosen by the Florida legislature as the state song in 1935. The Stephen Foster Memorial Museum has been established as a state shrine at White Springs, Florida, on the bank of the Suwannee River, the stream which he made immortal in song. Dioramas depicting his songs are on exhibit, his music is played, and his name is honored. This magnificent memorial was dedicated on October 4, 1950.

Stephen Foster is the only composer who has written two of our country's state songs. By 1853, after *My Old Kentucky Home* was published, Stephen stood at the very pinnacle of his career. He had fame; he had success; he had an adequate income. Had he been able to maintain the level of his current achievements, to continue writing songs like *Old Folks at Home* and *My Old Kentucky Home,* and to manage his personal and financial affairs, the rest of his life might have been happy; instead, it ended in misery. Foster did not have the strength, the stamina, or the stability to control his own destiny. Little by little the structure of his life began to break. The first indication of trouble was in May, 1853, when Stephen and Jane separated. Jane left him and he went to New York in June to live and work. This separation lasted for several months, perhaps longer. We do not know the exact cause of their difficulties, or who was at fault. Although they were reunited in 1854 and reestablished their home in Pittsburgh, their long separation was evidence of the growing incompatibility of the two young people.

In spite of the satisfactory income Stephen was receiving in royalties from his publishers, it was never quite enough to meet his expenses. It would have seemed that his royalties were large enough for Stephen to have supported Jane and little Marion and himself in moderate comfort, but such was not the case. Stephen had never been a good manager, and as the family expenses increased he found himself with a growing burden of debt. Money problems became a constant source of worry to him.

We do not know exactly when Stephen's chief weakness, his addiction to liquor, became really serious. Up to this time Foster's drinking had been only convivial, and it probably did not get out of control until the late 1850's or early 1860's. But by the mid-1850's he no doubt began to turn to the solace of alcohol to forget, momentarily, his marital problems and financial worries. In 1855 the burden of grief was added to his emotional complications, when both his parents died. This double loss was a blow from which he never quite recovered. As the favorite child in his family, cherished and protected by others, Foster was more dependent than most people on the approval and the spiritual support of his mother and father. He was especially devoted to his mother, whom he worshipped. The next year, 1856, his brother Dunning, for whom he had worked in Cincinnati, died. The disintegration of Stephen's morale increased from this time on.

If you were to ask me about my own knowledge of the biographical facts of Stephen Foster's life, my reply would be that I have had the opportunity, after forty-five years of association with the Foster Hall Collection in both Indianapolis and Pittsburgh, to study the many records on which other biographers have based their own accounts. I think myself capable of discussing the *facts,* where known, or speculating on the *legends,* where the facts are *not* known.

In discussing the *music* of Stephen Foster from the critical and the technical point of view, let us again refer to that able writer, composer, and musician, Harold Vincent Milligan, who says:

> As a composer, Stephen Foster is a paradox. The wonder is that anyone who could write so well, could at the same time write so poorly. Was he a man of mediocre talent, who stumbled almost by accident upon a few

nuggets of pure gold in the midst of much of little worth, or was he endowed with a great gift which remained for the most part mute and found expression only in a few brief moments of song?

He had practically no constructive ability. So far as the first impulse of his inspiration could carry him, he went, but no farther. Judged by the standards of musical composition, nearly all of his [two] hundred . . . songs are on the same level. These songs were written throughout a period of about twenty years, during which time he neither gained nor lost in the power of expression. His death, at thirty-seven, found him as a composer just about where he had been at the beginning of his career. Both melody and harmony are of the utmost simplicity. He could neither develop a melody nor vary his harmony. His melodies repeat themselves monotonously, and he was content with a few simple chords and modulations. And yet when his inspiration is of so pure and exalted a nature as it is in "The Old Kentucky Home," or "The Old Folks at Home," the very limitations of his power become virtues, resulting in a simplicity and directness of utterance which no amount of erudition and sophistication could have equalled in sincerity and potency. He put the best of himself into the composition of these songs, and it is because they are the honest expression of real emotion that they found their way directly and at once to the world's heart.

It may be seriously doubted whether greater technical facility would have improved his music or achieved for him a greater name in history. The general average of his work might have been higher, but his best songs might have lost something of the sincerity and naive charm which are their greatest attribute. Limited as it was, his technical equipment was exactly suited to the production of such a song as "The Old Folks at Home."

It would be futile to compare him with any of the great men of music. The circumstances of his life, the environments of his mind, were so totally different from those surrounding any of the acknowledged masters of the Art, that any speculations of this kind would be idle. He bears some resemblance to Schubert. Who can say what would have been the sum of Franz Schubert's achievements had he been born in Pittsburgh in 1826?

In 1857, in an attempt to solve his financial problems, Stephen Foster sold to his publishers, for cash in hand, outright, all his future financial interests in those of his songs which they had already published. Once more Stephen proved that his judgment in business matters was often poor. Foster evidently had no conception of the real financial value of some of his best songs, the future interest of which he had sold. Never again would Stephen receive a penny in royalties from the songs which had been his chief source of income in recent years—among them *Old Folks at Home, My Old Kentucky Home, Old Dog Tray,* and *Massa's in de Cold Ground.* Stephen assumed that these songs had passed through their period of greatest popularity and that sales would begin to decline. It did not occur to him that the popularity, as well as the sale of these songs, would continue for years to come. Forced by grim necessity to return at once to the only occupation by which he was capable of earning a living for his family, he settled down to work in 1858, and began composing once more. But the old fire was gone. Foster was reasonably industrious in 1858, 1859, and 1860, but he was composing in a plodding, unimaginative, wooden fashion. His songs were lifeless and mediocre, and their sales were light. By the middle of 1860 he was hopelessly in debt. This year was a definite turning point in his life.

During the summer he made a supreme effort and created one of his truly great works, *Old Black Joe*. There was still a spark remaining in Stephen's dying genius, and in the turmoil of his emotions this spark was kindled into flame for the last time. We know that when Foster composed this song it was not written simply to earn money, much as he needed money. There is no record of what Foster earned from *Old Black Joe*. We do not know whether he was paid cash outright, or received regular royalties from its sale. Foster had to write this song to give expression to the intense emotions burning within him. He felt deeply the passing of happy youth and the loss of family and friends. He grieved for those departed forms. He heard the calling of the "gentle voices" of his dead parents, his brothers, and his sister, gone to a shore where he himself now longed to go. These feelings were intensified by his growing sense of insecurity and failure. It is not a blackface minstrel who steps forward on the stage to sing *Old Black Joe*. It is Stephen Foster himself, and he sings to us from his very soul! We know almost nothing about the actual details of the composition of this song. It was probably written in Warren, Ohio, where Stephen was visiting one of his sisters. It was published in November, 1860, just about the time that Abraham Lincoln was elected to the presidency of the United States.

Some time in the latter part of 1860 Stephen Foster moved to New York City, where he spent his four remaining years. It was an unwise move. His was a personality that needed sympathetic, understanding family and friends—without them he was lost. It is futile to speculate on what Foster's life might have been had he remained in Pittsburgh. Perhaps he might have lived to write songs of genuine merit once more. Perhaps he would never again have composed music above the mediocre. But it seems unlikely that he would have experienced the intense loneliness, despair, and final tragedy which proved to be his fate in New York.

In a courageous effort to recover his lost fortunes, Stephen worked with energy. Approximately a third of his life's work, insofar as a mere enumeration of song titles is concerned, was published after he moved to New York. But with one outstanding exception—*Beautiful Dreamer*—the quality of his work ranged from mediocre to poor. The coming of the Civil War in 1861 destroyed the market for the type of song he was best able to write. In that raging conflict, the gentle voice of the man who had sung about the Swanee River and the Old Kentucky Home was no longer heard. Stephen was reduced to writing "pot-boilers"—undistinguished songs for which he was paid only a few dollars each, outright. If his earnings were exceedingly low at this period of his life, the standard of his work was correspondingly low. He composed feeble sentimental ballads. His attempts to take advantage of the war situation by writing patriotic and military songs were failures. He composed a large number of Sunday School hymns, but however worthy their sentiments, their poetry and music were of little merit.

It became evident that Stephen could not earn enough to support his wife and daughter in New York. Jane and Marion returned to Pennsylvania and Jane became a telegraph operator for the Pennsylvania Railroad at Greensburg, near Pittsburgh. Andrew Carnegie, a friend of the Foster family and at that time still an official of the Pennsylvania Railroad before he entered the steel business, helped her to obtain this position.

Stephen stayed in New York, living on the Bowery not far from present day Chinatown. His income was pathetically small in spite of his industry. He knew poverty and hunger, yet he rejected the help which his family tried to offer him. He drank heavily and, according to some accounts, occasionally verged on alcoholism. But through all the misery of his last unhappy days, there is evidence that he still maintained his pride and his courage. Stephen Foster's life ended in tragedy, but it did not end in degradation. Night was closing in around him, but Foster was still capable of finding within himself the power of creation. In the summer of 1863 he summoned his waning strength to write *Beautiful Dreamer,* his best work since *Old Black Joe* had been composed three years before. Stephen seems to have lost himself in his theme, as he did in his happier days in Pittsburgh when he wrote his immortal melodies. We can see how genuine was his sentiment in *Beautiful Dreamer* when we realize his life and environment at this time. Stephen is evidently seeking an escape from the bitter realities of the Bowery and Broadway, and the failure of his life in New York. He longs for the happiness of an earlier day.

> "Sounds of the rude world, heard in the day,
> Lulled by the moonlight have all passed away."

The song was not published until March, 1864, two months after Stephen's death.

In January, 1864, Stephen was seriously injured in a fall in his room on the Bowery. He was taken to Bellevue Hospital, where he died in the charity ward on January 13 at the age of thirty-seven. Jane and his brother Morrison came to New York and took his body back to Pittsburgh, where it was buried in Allegheny Cemetery not far from his birthplace, the White Cottage. His grave has become a shrine for those who love the Foster songs. Many people have visited it to do him honor, during the passage of the years.

When Stephen Foster died he had just thirty-eight cents in his purse, not much to show for a lifetime if money were the only legacy. But with the coins there was also a scrap of paper, bearing five words penciled by the hand that had phrased so many thoughts common to our humanity. The words were these:

> "Dear friends and gentle hearts."

Even at the last Stephen was able to distill sweetness from his own pain. The little pocketbook, with its contents, is one of the most treasured relics in the Foster Hall Collection at the University of Pittsburgh. It is the thing that visitors most wish to see—a touchstone and a talisman.

The five words on the scrap of paper—Stephen Foster's "Last Message"— were no doubt intended to be the theme or title of a song he did not live to

write. They reflect something of the personality of the man himself—his kindness, his friendliness, his gentleness, and his generosity. We can only grieve that he, who brought so much happiness to the world through his "blessed, heaven-sent gift of melody," knew so much unhappiness.

Because of the greater tragedy of the Civil War, a war in which almost six hundred thousand Americans perished, Stephen Foster died almost unnoticed by the American people for whom he had sung with such deep feeling. Neither he nor his contemporaries realized his national significance. But the Foster renaissance of the present is proof that he has now been given the place which is rightfully his in the history of American civilization.

There are many memorials to the composer throughout the nation. One of the greatest honors which was paid him was his election to the Hall of Fame for Great Americans, in New York City, in 1940. A bronze bust of Foster was dedicated at the Hall of Fame, on the Bronx campus of New York University, in May, 1941. Ironically enough, this bust is located only a few miles from the place where he met his tragic end. Like Robert Burns of Scotland and Franz Schubert of Austria, Stephen Foster of America belongs to the world. We Americans can take pride in our composer whose music has become the heritage of all mankind. His songs are a bond between people of different languages and cultures. Stephen Foster made the world a better place in which to live. Let us continue to honor him and to keep fresh his memory.

In January, 1864, shortly after Stephen's death, an article, "The Late Stephen C. Foster," appeared in the *New York Evening Post.* The writer compared Foster with the Italian composer, Gaetano Donizetti, on whose tomb is a modest inscription. These same simple words could well stand as the epitaph of Stephen Collins Foster. We, his fellow Americans who love his songs, will agree that Stephen Foster was, indeed,

"A FINDER OF MANY MELODIES."

Harold Vincent Milligan's words are the tribute Foster deserves.

> Stephen Foster touched but one chord in the gamut of human emotions, but he sounded that strain supremely well. His song is of that nostalgia of the soul which is inborn and instinctive to all humanity, a homesickness unaffected by time or space. It is a theme which has always made up a large part of the world's poetry, and will always continue to do so as long as human hearts yearn for love and aspire toward happiness. Among all the poets who have harped the sorrows of Time and Change, no song rings truer than that of Stephen Foster. We have traced, as best we may, the story of his life from a bright happy childhood into the dismal shadows of failure and death. From the unpromising soil in which he grew, he was able to distill by some strange alchemy of the soul such sweet magic of melody as to win an immortality far beyond his dreaming. These wildflowers of music which blossomed, unwatched and untended, from unsuspected seeds, have found for themselves a spot which is all their own, where they may bloom forever in Fields Elysian.

Opposite: *"The White Cottage" Birthplace of Foster, lot now known as 3600 Penn Avenue, Lawrenceville. Painting by Miller, 1828. Private collection of Mr. Richard K. Foster, grand nephew of Stephen Foster.*

[1] Harold Vincent Milligan, *Stephen Collins Foster: A Biography of America's Folk-Song Composer,* New York: G. Schirmer, 1920.
This pioneer work may be highly commended for the clarity of its prose and for its deep appreciation of Foster's music.

[2] Sir George Otto Trevelyan, *The American Revolution,* Part II, Volume I, London: Longmans, Green and Company, 1903, pg. 151.

[3] These descendants have lived in Pennsylvania, New York, Connecticut, Florida, Arizona, and Hawaii.

Fletcher Hodges, Jr.

Since 1931 Mr. Hodges has been curator of the Foster Hall Collection, at first in its original location in Indianapolis but since 1937 in the Stephen Foster Memorial Hall at the University of Pittsburgh. He is a graduate of Harvard College and holds an honorary degree of Doctor of Literature from the Lincoln Memorial University, Harrogate, Tennessee. He is the author and editorial assistant for several works on Stephen Foster, including a complete edition of Foster's music.

Self portrait, c. 1880. National Portrait Gallery, Smithsonian Institution, Washington, D.C. Watercolor on paper, 13" x 9½".

MARY CASSATT

by Herdis Bull Teilman

As a major artist of the 19th century, Mary Cassatt ranks with the expatriates Sargent and Whistler, as well as Homer, Ryder, and Eakins,—the last a fellow Pennsylvanian whom she greatly admired. But even though Cassatt's career developed abroad, her lifestyle was decidedly American, and this is reflected in the mood and subject-matter of her paintings. Arriving in Paris during the early years of the Impressionist movement, she became stimulated by new artistic concepts, and before long was associating with the most advanced painters of the time. It was not unusual in the 1890's for French critics like Andre Mellario to consider Cassatt, along with Whistler, as America's most distinguished artist. It is of equal significance that she was highly regarded by her colleagues. Encouraged by her mentor Edgar Degas, Mary Cassatt turned to the mother and child theme with which her name is uniquely identified. Even so, Adelyn D. Breeskin, the leading authority on Cassatt, estimates that portraits and figure pieces comprise about two-thirds of her total output. It is also important to keep in mind that Cassatt's subject-matter dating from the mid-1870's to the nineties is considerably varied, and that she had already achieved a personal style of her own before motherhood themes became predominant.

The many facets of Cassatt's life and intellectual interests, political and feminist, as well as cultural, cannot be dealt with here. Certainly the appreciation of Impressionism in this country was greatly due to her earliest efforts. One could emphasize Cassatt's influential role as an advisor to collectors; or as the devoted daughter of a Victorian family whose demands and expectations often interfered with her career. But most important was Mary Cassatt, the artist. Her spirited and enlightened pursuit of an original artistic expression, marked from the beginning by a strong sense of professionalism, made possible her achievement as our greatest woman painter up to that time.

Cassatt's sympathy with the aims of the Impressionists, opposed to juries and official exhibitions, is evident in her correspondence. The artist Julien Alden Weir received a letter in 1878, in reply to an invitation to exhibit with the Society of American Artists in New York; which even reflects a concern somehow prophetic of artistic developments at home, though at a more distant future. We are also afforded a glimpse of her forceful personality:

> Your exhibition interests me very much. I wish I could have sent
> something. I am afraid it is too late now. We expect to have our annual
> Impressionist exhibition here and there are so few of us that we are each

required to contribute all we have. You know how hard it is to inaugurate anything like independent action among French artists, and we are carrying on a despairing fight and need all our forces, as every year there are new deserters. I always have a hope that at some future time I shall see New York the artist's ground. I think you will create an American school.[1]

Though elected a member of the Society two years later, Cassatt consistently refused prizes and honors, except for a Gold Medal received in 1914 from the Pennsylvania Academy of Fine Arts.

Our concern is primarily with Cassatt's formative period, including her association with the Impressionists until shortly after their last group exhibition in 1886. During these years she painted her most impressionist works.

On May 22, 1844, less than a year before the great Pittsburgh fire, Mary Stevenson Cassatt was born across the river on the North Side, then called Allegheny City. At that time, the family lived in the house built by her father, Robert Simpson Cassatt, on Rebecca Street (now Reedsdale Street). Two years later, he became mayor of the town, and then president of the Select Council. Of French Huguenot and Dutch descent, the Cassatt family had come to America by way of Holland in 1662. The name, originally Cossart and changed to Cassat around 1800, acquired a second "t" in the 1840's.

Before long, the Cassatts moved back to Pittsburgh, where they had once lived, later acquiring a country estate near Lancaster. In 1849, when Mary Cassatt was five years old, her parents Robert and Katherine Kelso Johnston departed for Philadelphia with their five children.[2] Robert Cassatt was a moderately successful stockbroker and speculator in real estate, though not especially ambitious. On the whole, he preferred farming, horseback riding, and traveling. Accordingly, when Mary was seven, the family went abroad for four years to live in Paris, Heidelberg, and Darmstadt; and it was there that her older brother Alexander studied engineering. Eventually, he became vice president and president of the Pennsylvania Railroad.

After their return to Pennsylvania, the Cassatts lived in West Chester at their country home near Philadelphia, and soon acquired a brick house in the city, where they lived until the Civil War. By 1860 Mary's dream was to return abroad to study art, but for the time being, she enrolled the next year at the Pennsylvania Academy of the Fine Arts, where Thomas Eakins was a fellow student. For four years she drew from antique casts, the live model, and made copies after paintings in conformance with academic instruction of the time, all of which soon proved unequal to the challenge she sought.

There were no great public art collections in America as yet. Little did Cassatt know that her decision to study the old masters in Europe would enable her to play a key role in reversing this situation. It was there that she became the influential advisor to the H. O. Havemeyers, the Potter Palmers, and other Americans who first established major art collections. In 1866 Cassatt obtained permission to go to Paris, where a sheltered life with family and friends remained in keeping with her conservative background. Nevertheless, for a woman to strike out on her own to study art was an act of true courage. In her day it was inconceivable that a well-bred American woman could pursue an artistic career. Fortunately for American art, Cassatt's convictions and power of persuasion overcame the obstacles which would have prevented exposure not only to the great art of the past, but also to the most advanced contemporary painting.

After studying briefly in Paris with the artist Charles Chaplin, Cassatt, again disenchanted with academic methods, became largely self-taught.

During the Franco-Prussian War, Cassatt returned to Philadelphia and in the fall of 1871 visited relatives in Pittsburgh. Her brother Alexander Cassatt, then living in Altoona, later moved with his wife Lois Buchanan, niece of the President, to Philadelphia. Mary Cassatt returned to Europe by way of Italy, and in 1873 went to Spain, where she became impressed by Velazquez and Goya. Inspired by these masters was a contemporary French artist whose work she had probably seen at the Paris World's Fair of 1867: Edouard Manet. Both Manet and another great Realist painter, Courbet (who influenced Cassatt's early work), had exhibited unofficially during the Fair. Indeed, her first painting in the Paris Salon of 1872, done in Rome, is reminiscent of one of Manet's Spanish subjects. Cassatt's *On the Balcony during the Carnival*[3] was signed with her middle name "Stevenson," probably because of sensitivity to family disapproval of her career. Another work close to Manet, painted in Seville and accepted the following year, was also sent later to the National Academy of Design, New York. *Torero and Young Girl*[4] shows a girl vivaciously offering panal, a sweet drink, to a bullfighter. The representation of contemporary subject matter derives from Courbet and Manet, while the strong highlights and the foreshortening of the girl, whose animated pose is unusual in Cassatt's oeuvre, reflect the study of seventeenth century baroque painting. The influence of Manet can also be seen in the broad, vigorous brush strokes and the use of black to offset the colorful costumes, an interest of Cassatt's at this time. Men rarely appear in the later works, except for family and friends.

According to Adelyn Breeskin, very few of Cassatt's paintings from the early years of study abroad have been located; several were lost in the Chicago fire of 1871. The only surviving copy was painted in Holland a few years later, a freely interpreted sketch after a group portrait (in Haarlem) by Frans Hals.[5]

Clearly, Cassatt regarded the study of old masters as essential for her development, but she was keenly aware of new trends and receptive to innovative ideas. No sooner did she settle permanently in Paris, than a group of advanced young artists around Manet including Monet, Pissarro, Renoir, Sisley and Morisot, organized an independent exhibition in 1874, apart from the official Salon; they became known as the Impressionists. Like them, Cassatt had begun to paint outdoors before her sojourn in America. Her own work of 1875, refused by the Salon as the color was considered too light, was accepted the next year when she darkened the background. Cassatt's swift response to the bright palette and broken brushwork of the Impressionists is revealed in a small spontaneous painting, *Picking Flowers in a Field,* from a private collection of the same period. One of her few landscape subjects, it was painted out-of-doors, and shows two women in a sunny field and a child picking flowers in the foreground. The composition, with its high horizon line, recalls works by Renoir and Monet, particularly the latter's *Wild Poppies,* 1874 in the Musé e du Louvre. The figures are relatively small, and seem to blend with the landscape in a manner seldom repeated in Cassatt's later work.

One of the organizers of the first impressionist exhibition was Edgar Degas. Since her return to Paris, Cassatt was known to flatten her nose against the window of a dealer to see Degas' pastels and, in her words, "absorb all I could of his art." She became a close friend of Louisine Waldron Elder, and persuaded her to buy a Degas pastel for $100. Thus, at the age of seventeen, the future Mrs. Havemeyer initiated her famous collection with an impressionist work, the first to enter an American collection. For his part, Degas commented on a Cassatt painting seen in the 1874 Salon, realistic portrait influenced by Courbet: "that is genuine, there is someone who feels as I do." When they finally met in 1877, Degas, who was ten years older than Cassatt, invited her to join the Impressionist group.

At thirty-three, Cassatt welcomed the opportunity to depart from the Salons, and told her biographer Achille Segard, "I accepted with joy. At last I could work with absolute independence without considering the opinion of a jury. I had already recognized who were my true masters, I admired Manet, Courbet, and Degas. I hated conventional art. I began to live."

Cassatt is known to have completed only two self-portraits, both on paper. The first, done about this time, was once owned by Mrs. Havemeyer, who had met the artist in 1873. A colorful gouache in the impressionist manner, it reflects Degas' influence in the informal pose of the figure. The other, reproduced here, is the charming *Self Portrait,* 1880, acquired in recent years by the National Portrait Gallery in Washington, D.C., which shows a self-confident Cassatt in her mid-thirties, apparently seated and at work. She is characterized as having "wide apart, kindly, but intense grey eyes. . . a tightly compressed mouth, and, most marked of all, a long pointed chin."[6] The white of the paper lends itself to the sparkling freedom of details, such as her bonnet, the contour of the chair, and the drawing board suggested at the lower right. This bright, spontaneous watercolor sketch communicates admirably the vitality of the artist and her serious dedication to painting. During this period described by Adelyn Breeskin as a happy one, Cassatt turned to a subject she had encountered in the form of Correggio's Madonnas when a student in Parma—that of mother and child. By now, as we shall observe, Cassatt is working in an assured style in a number of important compositions and attracting the favorable notice of such critics as J. K. Huysmans and Emile Zola when they were shown in the Impressionist exhibitions.

A major work of Cassatt's early career, *Little Girl in a Blue Armchair,* 1878 (National Gallery of Art, Washington, D.C., lent by Mr. and Mrs. Paul Mellon) shows the direct influence of Degas, as is known from a letter to her dealer Vollard. Cassatt was greatly upset when this painting was not accepted for the American section of the Great Exposition that year, especially because Degas had thought so well of it that he had advised on the background.

Probably he painted the effect of light coming through French windows, and was responsible for the gray floor between asymmetrically arranged, blue upholstered chairs. The configuration of the floor area, whose abstract design creates a positive element in the composition, has parallels in Degas' ballet scenes. The influence of Japanese prints and of photography is evident in the arbitrary cropping of the picture by the frame, permitting a casual view as in a snapshot. The little girl sprawling on the chair in the foreground is indicative of Cassatt's future interest in the portrayal of children. Sleeping nearby is the artist's Belgian griffon dog, who often appears in her paintings.

Degas and Cassatt worked together on a periodical called *Le Jour et la Nuit,* for which they prepared a number of prints, but the project was never realized. In a masterful etching with aquatint by Degas, *At the Louvre: La Peinture,* c. 1879, Mary Cassatt and her sister Lydia, holding a catalogue, are partially obscured on the left by a marble doorway through which they are seen in a picture gallery. The striking representation of Mary's standing figure as a graceful silhouette viewed from the rear, was derived from Degas' study of Japanese woodblock prints, and, as Frederick A. Sweet has observed, it may actually be inspired by Hokusai's *Manga.*[7] Japanese depictions of the everyday "fleeting moment," in which forms are often overlapped, seen from a surprising angle, or asymmetrically from a high vantage point, had an important effect on modern art. The author describes Cassatt, leaning elegantly on an umbrella: "Here we note her slender, erect figure, neatly tailored, and her crisply unfurled umbrella all conveying to us something of her tense, energetic character." In other versions by Degas in prints, drawings and pastel, the same expressive posture conveyed by the silhouette and the angular gesture of her arm extended by the umbrella, evoke Cassatt's personality, self-confidence and concentration on works of art in the Louvre. Also shown alone, her face is averted in variations of the theme based on an initial drawing, seeming to illustrate a point made by Edmond Duranty that "with a back we can discover a temperament, an age, a social position."[8] This statement has special significance when one considers the qualities sought by Degas and Cassatt in their art: simplicity, directness, and objectivity.

Cassatt was apt to pose when an attitude Degas had in mind was too difficult for models to adopt, as for instance, the customer trying a hat in *At the Milliner's (Miss Cassatt),* a later pastel of 1882. Although Cassatt never formally studied with Degas, her patience was amply rewarded by being exposed to his unique pastel technique and other important innovations during this period. Fashion seems to have been one of many interests they had in common. During her years in Paris, Mary Cassatt frequented couturiers to seek out fashionable clothes for her models. These contribute to the contemporaneous effect, the color and lively patterns of her work.

From the first, Degas acknowledged a basic rapport between Cassatt's pictorial approach and his own. Though regular exhibitors with the Impressionists, both were unorthodox in their methods and, in fact, referred to the group by its original name of "Independents." To be sure, their perception of reality accorded with the impressionist aim of recording a passing moment, but rather than intensifying transience by dissolving forms in a luminous atmosphere, they sought a more controlled expression through a formal structure which emphasized draftsmanship. Primarily figure painters, both Degas and Cassatt were influenced by Manet more than by Monet. Morever, Degas preferred artificial light to sunlight. Though Cassatt often worked out of doors, she painted few purely impressionist works.

Many of the works of both Degas and Cassatt reflect their cultural and economic background. Degas' father was a French banker, his mother was a Creole and his two brothers whom he visited in 1872, lived in New Orleans. This shared American experience probably strengthened the bonds of friendship between the two artists. Though its full extent is not known, it is generally believed their relationship was closer in the artistic than romantic sphere, even though after Degas' death Cassatt burned the letters he had written to her. Despite his cynicism, Degas admired Cassatt's artistic integrity, as well as her wit and independent nature. He also benefitted greatly from her understanding of his art, her loyal support and promotion of his work among collectors. Though like Degas, Cassatt was single and financially independent as well, her life was complicated by the care of her invalid sister and mother. This situation, no doubt, took its inevitable toll and may explain Cassatt's comparatively limited artistic output. Despite her intellectual compatibility with Degas, occasionally their strong personalities clashed. Degas could be ruthlessly sarcastic, especially when frustrated by failing eyesight. Mrs. Havemeyer's *Memoirs*[9] relate how Cassatt once commented on getting along with Degas, "Oh, I am independent, I can live alone and I love to work. Sometimes it made him furious that he could not find a chink in my armor, and there would be months when we just could not see each other, and then something I painted would bring us together again. . . but he was magnificent. And however dreadful he was, he always lived up to his ideals." Although in later years their association diminished, after attending Degas' funeral in 1917, Cassatt wrote to the artist George Biddle[10], ". . . His death is a deliverance but I am sad, he was my oldest friend here and the last great artist of the 19th century. I see no one to replace him."

Within a year after she had met Degas, Cassatt's parents and sister Lydia came to Paris to live with her. Hereafter, models were readily available to pose for compositions in which the artist's conception counted for more than an individualistic portrayal. Cassatt's unconventional attitude as to subject is revealed in several impressionistic interpretations of her older sister, such as the *Portrait of Lydia Cassatt,* 1878, (Joslyn Art Museum, Omaha, Nebraska). Here, Lydia reading a newspaper, is wholly absorbed in her mental activity, unaware of the spectator.

A similar approach can be seen in a large oil of the following year, *Woman and Child Driving,*[11] 1879, reproduced here, which portrays Lydia on an excursion with Degas' niece Odile Fevre in the Bois de Boulogne. They are accompanied back to back by the Cassatt's young groom, whose appearance is humorously anonymous, and seem just to have come into view. The idea of continuous action is implied by the close-up depiction of the carriage, only

Woman and Child Driving, 1879 Philadelphia Museum of Art, The W. P. Wilstach Collection. Oil on canvas, 35¼" x 51½".

partially revealed, and the pony, whose hindquarters remain visible on the left. However, the groom faces inactively out of the picture in the opposite direction from the pony, tending to counteract the effect of motion. The arbitrary emphasis upon the linear design of the harness and wheels, the asymmetrically grouped figures on the right and the apparent lack of communication between them, are elements derived from Degas. Moreover, the tilted carriage lantern echoing Lydia's gesture of holding the reins is an effective device used by Cassatt as a central focal point to create tension in the composition. The subject of a woman intently driving a cart is rare for the period, and may well be the only example of its kind.[12] Horses were popular with the Cassatt family, and the artist herself enjoyed riding until an accident in 1888 ended her horsemanship.

Around 1879 Cassatt, inspired by Renoir and Degas, began her outstanding impressionist creations of young women at the theater and opera. Characteristic of these works is the warm coloring due to Renoir's influence. The influence of Degas is apparent in the bold composition of the figures in off-centered loges which, partially cut by the frame, are brought close to the beholder. Pastels of the same theme were acquired by Degas and Gauguin, who remarked that compared to Berthe Morisot, Miss Cassatt had as much charm but more force.

Most important is Cassatt's vivid portrayal of *Lydia in a Loge, Wearing a Pearl Necklace* (Private Collection, Pennsylvania), her first painting exhibited with the Impressionists in their fourth group exhibition of 1879. During this period Cassatt's paintings show a free handling of form and her occasional painterly use of black, similar to that of Manet, Degas, and Renoir. She is also most effective in her use of white; in the latter she may be compared to Whistler.

In *Mother About to Wash her Sleepy Child,* 1880 (Los Angeles County Museum of Art, California), a subtle harmony of white with accents of blue shadows is apparent in the clothes and the basin at the lower left. Cassatt often used children as models after her brother Alexander's visit to France in 1880 with his family. Included in the fifth Impressionist exhibition, this is among the earliest of the maternal subjects representing Cassatt's major effort, particularly after 1900. Her later, almost exclusive concentration on a single theme was marked by great variety and originality, and soon earned her a reputation as the foremost painter of this genre. With family and friends available to pose, it was not necessary to aim for an exact likeness, and the artist was free to consider purely pictorial concerns. Cassatt wanted to capture in a unified composition that intimate rapport which exists between mother and child. This is expressed by the spontaneous pose of the robust baby, who sprawls with sturdy legs across the mother's lap, looking up at her in contentment. Their momentary poses are enhanced by the loose brushwork and scintillating reflections of Cassatt's impressionist style. The firmly modeled forms seen close-up are monumental within the vertical, compressed space of the picture. The composition is held in balance with an objectivity characteristic of Cassatt's best renderings. It was this special gift of expressing the relationship between mother and child without sentimentality and with directness, that Adelyn Breeskin feels certain "Degas urged her to perfect."[13]

Cassatt, like Monet and Renoir, often portrayed individuals in moments of leisure in their own comfortable bourgeois setting; or in the artist's home. A sense of calm detachment pervades these works; in the contemplation of observed reality she approached the spirit of Degas.

An outstanding example is Cassatt's painting, *Lady at the Tea Table,* reproduced here, completed in 1885. The Canton tea service displayed on the table was a gift, following the Cassatt's visit to England, from the daughter of Mrs. Robert Moore Riddle, who was the subject. Cassatt was not interested in attaining exact likeness, and therefore did not do many commissioned portraits, preferring to limit herself to people she knew. Yet this arresting image of her mother's cousin as well as two portraits of Mrs. Cassatt in the same decade, particularly the earlier masterpiece *Reading "Le Figaro,"* 1883 (Philadelphia Museum of Art), reveal the artist's skill and her perceptive rendering of character. Though the portrait of Mrs. Riddle was done as an act of gratitude, she and her daughter did not care for its less sympathetic aspects; they decided the nose was too large, and did not appreciate the rare quality of this work. Stored therefore in the artist's studio, it was retrieved years later by Mrs. Havemeyer, and exhibited in 1914 at Durand-Ruel's. The portrait was a great success, and later given by Mary Cassatt to the

Lady at the Tea Table, 1885. The Metropolitan Museum of Art, New York, Gift of the artist. Oil on canvas, 29" x 24".

Metropolitan Museum of Art, New York, where most of the Havemeyer Collection is now located.

Mrs. Riddle's austere appearance, emphasized by the erect posture and plain dress, is relieved by her white lace cap and clear blue eyes which seem to reflect the glistening Japanese porcelain below. The domestic activity is not stressed; rather, the figure is monumentalized by its simplified outline which forms a pyramidal silhouette against the rectangular paneling of the light wall.

Cassatt's interest in formal, geometric design at this time may have been inspired by Japanese prints in this early use of flat, linear pattern. Moreover, the horizontal disposition of the china in the foreground recalls similar arrangements by her friend Manet, who died in 1883, the year this picture was commenced.

Girl Arranging Her Hair, 1886 (National Gallery of Art, Washington, D. C., Chester Dale Collection), shows a continuing concern with formal aspects of composition, but in a more complex manner. Certainly among Cassatt's most consummate works, this was in the eighth, or last, Impressionist exhibition of 1886. Also exhibited then was a series of Degas' pastels of women bathing and combing their hair—the inspiration for Cassatt's theme. This painting was apparently intended to refute an insinuation by Degas that women knew nothing about style. Cassatt's version of a girl at her morning toilet must have achieved the desired goal, for he enthusiastically acquired this work for his own collection. The girl coiling her hair before a washstand indeed corresponds with Degas' own point of view, that a subject should be rendered as though it were unobserved in a natural, everyday activity. An awkward unposed attitude can reveal new relationships of inherent beauty between the figure and its surrounding space. Although Cassatt's model is more individualized than Degas' subjects, her form is integrated with the background by means of the arms stretched in a diagonal "s" curve from one raised elbow to the other, which is lowered. The audacious design is conveyed by the neckline of the white gown and the hair held in both hands. (Limbs, a significant factor in Cassatt's figure composition, are often arranged in parallel or opposing directions). Here, the physical reality of the girl is heightened by the firmly modeled head and neck. Her plain features are of a peasant type preferred by the artist. Among the models that Cassatt used often after her sister Lydia's death were her housekeeper Mathilde Vallet and her cousin Susan.

Since 1879 Cassatt had been an active member of the Impressionists. We note that around the mid-eighties the artist began to rely less on broken brushwork and spontaneous effects, seeking instead a sense of greater structure and permanence. Coinciding with a similar development among the Impressionists, this tendency away from a concern with purely optical sensations of light, culminates in Cassatt's work of the following decade. It is evident in variations on the maternal theme such as the superb *Emmy and her Child,*[14] 1889, reproduced here.

The greatest impetus in the new direction of Cassatt's style was her visit with Degas and Morisot to the large 1890 exhibition of Japanese prints at the Ecole des Beaux-Arts. Acquiring several of these woodcuts long known to her, Cassatt found that upon closer study they now held a fresh inspiration. She adapted their decorative qualities of linear design in large, simple planes of color, and created the following year a series of color prints that are among her most creative works. These aquatints, unique in terms of style and technique, were included in her first solo exhibition at the Durand-Ruel Gallery. One called *Woman Bathing* is said to have elicited a compliment from Degas, "I will not admit that a woman can draw that well." The bold structural clarity of

Emmy and Her Child, 1889. Courtesy Wichita Art Museum, The Roland P. Murdock Collection. Oil on canvas, 35⅜" x 25⅜".

Young Women Picking Fruit, 1891, Museum of Art, Carnegie Institute, Pittsburgh, Pennsylvania. Oil on canvas, 52" x 36".

major paintings during the most prolific period of the nineties, such as *The Bath*, 1892 (Art Institute of Chicago), is based on a completely personal interpretation of oriental principles of design and perspective.

A project incorporating Cassatt's significant experiments with color prints, was her mural decoration on the theme of Modern Woman executed for the Woman's Building of the 1893 Chicago World's Exposition. Commissioned by Mrs. Potter Palmer, the mural (now lost) was painted at Chateau Bachivillers, Cassatt's summer residence. Correspondence with the Chicago patroness reveals that Cassatt wanted the mural not only to be contemporary in spirit, but "bright" and "gay." This intent is borne out by paintings related to its central panel which was called *Young Women Plucking Fruits of Knowledge and Science.* Pastoral in mood, independent works include *Young Women Picking Fruit*,[15] 1891, reproduced here (exhibited eight years later in the Carnegie International) *Baby Reaching for an Apple,* 1893 (Virginia Museum of Fine Arts, Richmond) and a lively oil sketch for the mural, in a private Paris collection. These light-filled orchard scenes depict women and children interrelated through carefully measured gestures; their hands and limbs play a role equivocal with still life. Imposing in scale, the corporeality of the figures is reinforced by their strong contours. Cassatt's realistic adherence to solid, three-dimensional form despite the flattened backgrounds and impressionist high-keyed color, is a distinctive characteristic which shows a greater affinity with American rather than French Impressionism.

Cassatt purchased the Chateau de Beaufresne, near Beauvais. Some of her paintings of this period such as *The Boating Party,* 1893-94 (National Gallery of Art, Chester Dale Collection), use a bold patterning and broadly contrasted areas of brilliant color most reminiscent of Gauguin. Subsequently, Cassatt's style shows a partial return from normal to impressionist precepts. The painterly loosening of forms is symptomatic of her later work, partly as a result of a greater use of pastel.

Cassatt was prone to seasickness and returned only twice to the United States after the death of her parents; once in 1898 when she visited her younger brother Gardner in Philadelphia, and did some portrait commissions, and again in 1908. By then most of Cassatt's efforts for the past several years were devoted to forming the Havemeyer Collection and advising her brothers and other collectors. Her astuteness is exemplified by acquisitions such as Simon Vouet's *The Toilet of Venus,* c. 1640, purchased for J. Gardner Cassatt around 1905 and given by his daughter Mrs. Horace Binney Hare to the Museum of Art, Carnegie Institute, in 1952. Preoccupied with these and other concerns, Cassatt's own work is, on the whole, less imaginative and limited mostly to portraiture and maternity subjects. However, she achieved vigorous effects with pastel which, in her last works of 1913-14, became her only medium. After a trip to the Near East in 1910, ill health and oncoming blindness forced Cassatt to give up painting. She survived her parents and her brothers and spent the war years mostly in Paris and Grasse, near Cannes. In 1921 Cassatt returned north to the Chateau de Beaufresne, where she died five years later at the age of eighty-one.

A legendary figure in her later years, Cassatt had received her first recognition in France; in 1904 she was made Chevalier of the Legion of Honor. Though she had been represented since the late seventies in exhibitions in Philadelphia, Boston and New York, Cassatt was still not widely known in the United States at that time. Like many of her French colleagues, Mary Cassatt's impressionism appears to have been to all but a select few, too advanced for the public. Nevertheless, one-woman shows in 1895 and 1903 in New York, organized by her dealer Paul Durand-Ruel, assured Cassatt a clientele and the respect of artists who benefited from her example and advice. A few years later, she was invited to participate in a mural competition to decorate the new Pennsylvania State Capitol Building in Harrisburg, but withdrew before completing the project.

In an article on the Second Annual Exhibition of the Society of American Artists held in 1879, William C. Brownell perceptively expressed his regret ". . . that she should keep her countrymen in comparative ignorance of the work she is doing."[16] Probably for the first time, an impressionist work had been publicly shown in America, even though Cassatt's contemporaries were exposed to the new idiom as students in Paris. Only after Durand-Ruel's important 1886 exhibition of French Impressionism in New York, which represented Cassatt and Degas, did the movement make headway among such artists as Theodore Robinson and the Ten American Painters (Weir, Hassam, Chase, Dewing, Twachtman, and others). Ironically, American taste for Impressionism preceded that of French collectors, but with few exceptions Americans still felt culturally insecure in relation to older traditions abroad, and therefore favored the purchase of French instead of American paintings.

Despite Cassatt's modernity and her precedence as an American participant in one of the most revolutionary art movements, she did not favor avantgarde 20th-century trends. Yet, unknown to her, she was represented in the Armory Show of 1913 which introduced Fauvism and Cubism to the United States. By then Impressionism, widely practiced in this country, had largely become an academic formula in the hands of followers. Furthermore, in the decade or so after 1886, Cassatt's own artistic direction corresponded in its formal concerns and an increasingly personal use of strong, arbitrary zones of color with aspects of later and Post-Impressionist painting.

Lincoln Johnson wrote that Manet, Degas, Morisot and Cassatt, who together "catalogued what Baudelaire had called the heroism of modern life . . . were themselves heroes, for in addition to finding a unity with the past and apotheosizing the mundane reality of their present, they were helping to create the future by daring assults on contemporary preconceptions. In effect they were redefining the concept of the picture."[17] Cassatt's significance in this respect can be gauged by the fact that her color prints were included in the progressive 1892 exhibition of the group of painters called *Les XX* in Brussels, along with works by Seurat, Pissarro, Maurice Denis and Toulouse-Lautrec.

Although Cassatt was associated with the French Impressionists, her activities contributed to the gradual appreciation and acceptance of younger American compatriots. However, Theodore Robinson and other artists during the mid-eighties and nineties were, like Sargent, inspired by Monet, instead of Manet and Degas. In the realization of a modern vision, Cassatt's conceptual approach allied her fundamentally with Whistler, and even John Twachtman, an American Impressionist who was greatly influenced by him. But their art, like that of Prendergast (whose art essentially belongs to this century), tended toward greater abstraction than Cassatt's depictions of a feminine world. The romantic landscape evocations of Twachtman contrast with Cassatt's objective clarity, the solidity and weight of her figures—indicating the range of American Impressionism. Furthermore, an analytical interest in geometric structure combined with a genuine sense of humanity, relate Cassatt with the indigenous tradition of respect for the fact, so greatly exemplified by the sober realism of Homer and Eakins.

Mary Cassatt was a strong individualist. She came from a family of means, and had the foresight to embark on a career in France, where opportunities were traditionally most favorable for women artists. That no one succeeded in discouraging her ambition may partly be due to her mother, who was a highly cultivated person with a special interest in French culture. Though by the turn of the century Mary Cassatt was recognized by the land of her birth, it was only after death that her paintings began to acquire the significance they have today. Mary Cassatt was not only the outstanding woman painter of her time, but remains a force in American art today.

[1] Frederick A. Sweet, *Miss Mary Cassatt, Impressionist from Pennsylvania* (Norman, Oklahoma), 1966,
   p. 48.

[2] Lydia, Alexander, Gardner, Mary, and Robbie.

[3] Philadelphia Museum of Art

[4] Sterling and Francine Clark Art Institute, Williamstown, Mass.

[5] Frans Hals, *Meeting of the Officers of the Cluveniers-Doelen*, 1633

[6] Sweet, p. 10.

[7] Sweet, pp. 50, 115; Katsushika Hokusai, 1760-1849, "The Strong Woman of Omi Province" 1814, in Theodore Reff, "Degas: A Master Among Masters", *Bulletin*, The Metropolitan Museum of Art, New York, XXXIV, no. 4 (1977), il. 76.

[8] Edmond Duranty, *La Nouvelle Peinture*, 1876, in Jean Sutherland Boggs *Drawings by Degas* (City Art Museum of St. Louis, 1966), pp. 134-36.

[9] Louisine W. Havemeyer, *Sixteen to Sixty, Memoirs of a Collector* (New York, 1961),
   pp. 244-45.

[10] Sweet, p. 193

[11] Philadelphia Museum of Art

[12]Susan Fillin Yeh, "Mary Cassatt's Images of Women," *Art Journal*, XXXV/4, (Summer 1976), pp. 362-63.

[13]Adelyn D. Breeskin, *Mary Cassatt, A Catalogue Raisonné of the Oils, Pastels, Watercolors and Drawings* (Washington, D. C., 1970) p. 12.

[14]Wichita Art Museum, Kansas, Roland P. Murdock Collection

[15]Museum of Art, Carnegie Institute, Pittsburgh

[16]William C. Brownell, "The Young Painters of America," *Scribner's Monthly*, July, 1891, pp. 321-34.

[17]Baltimore Museum of Art, *Manet, Degas, Berthe Morisot and Mary Cassatt* (1962), p. 21.

Selected References

Breeskin, Adelyn D.
> *The Graphic Work of Mary Cassatt: A Catalogue Raisonné.* New York, 1948.
> *Mary Cassatt: A Catalogue Raisonné of the Oils, Pastels, Watercolors and Drawings.* Washington, D.C., 1970.
> *Mary Cassatt.* Washington, D. C., National Gallery of Art, 1970.

Bullard, E. John
> *Mary Cassatt: Oils and Pastels.* New York, 1972.

Hale, Nancy
> *Mary Cassatt.* Garden City, New York, 1975.

Ségard, Achille
> *Mary Cassatt, un peintre des enfants et des meres.* Paris, 1913.

Herdis Bull Teilman

Miss Teilman is the former curator of painting and sculpture at the Museum of Art, Carnegie Institute. She was educated at the University of Oslo, the Institute of Art and Archaeology of the University of Paris, Barnard College, and the Institute of Art, New York University. Before coming to Pittsburgh in 1970 she was a curator at the Newark Museum.

Dr. Jackson at age 21 from The Life of Chevalier Jackson, An Autobiography, *The MacMillan Company, 1938.*

DR. CHEVALIER JACKSON

by Harry L.Wechsler, M.D.

Chevalier Jackson, inventor of the bronchoscope and esophagoscope, has to be regarded as one of the major contributors to the development of modern medicine. As one becomes familiar with his work, it is obvious that his achievements were not accidental. His heritage and family life influenced him greatly. He was the youngest of four sons, born November 4, 1865, to William Stanford and Katherine Ann (Morange) Jackson in their home that was located on Fourth Avenue in downtown Pittsburgh.[1,2] His father of English descent and of moderate means was a stock raiser, a veterinarian by training, an avid reader of Huxley and Darwin, and a tinkerer with a microscope. His mother, a dutiful housewife, satisfied her inquisitiveness by reading medically oriented books. Jackson attributed his talents as a cook and artist to his maternal grandfather, Jean Morange, who as a ten-year-old lad left his native France employed as a cabin boy aboard a sailing vessel. After an apprenticeship as a machinist in Dedham, Massachusetts, Morange emigrated to Pittsburgh to work as a tinsmith. Chevalier's early happy years in Pittsburgh ended abruptly; when due to financial reverses, the family moved about six miles from Pittsburgh to Idlewood nearby Crafton.

As Jackson was a very sensitive and perceptive lad, he was appalled by the mundane, unsavory ways of those who lived about him. He had a great distaste for fisticuffs—a usual way of settling disputes by neighboring coal miners and teamsters. Emotionally upsetting to him was the maiming of animals by cock and dog fights, favorite pastimes of the laboring class at that time. He was disturbed and frustrated when he watched unskilled drivers unmercifully beating horses hauling awkward coal-laden wagons bogged down in muddy roads. What was most distressing to Jackson was parental abuse of his peers—the children. One day he saw a shocking accident. A young friend of his was acting as a brakeman perilously perched on the rear of a wagon that the boy's father was recklessly driving downhill. Constantly jogged up and down the young boy lost his footing, was thrown under the wagon and crushed to death when run over by one of the wheels. Jackson, in his autobiography,[3] recalls the father's seemingly unremorseful state and callous response to his son's fatal accident. Undoubtably this was to haunt him during his early years of medical practice, when he witnessed all too frequently, the evidence of child abuse. Jackson himself was mistreated by his schoolmates.[4,5] It was more important in those days for children to work with their parents than to attend school. Consequently, many of Jackson's classmates were older than he and quite envious of him. These older, less endowed boys taunted him, stole his lunches, destroyed his school papers, and physically abused him. What was unusual was Jackson's response. He suffered in silence, never complaining to his parents or teachers. On one occasion tied, gagged and left abandoned in an old mineshaft by his classmates, he was accidentally discovered by a disgruntled miner who pursued his dog into the shaft. The miner planned to punish the disobedient animal—not realizing that the dog was following Jackson's scent. A consequence of this experience was a serious bout of pneumonia.

During these early years Chevalier developed his artisan ability. He made fine wood carvings that he distributed to members of the family at holiday time. His talents were invaluable to his family. In order to bolster a faltering income, his father turned the house into a summer tourist retreat. Chevalier served as maintenance man. The skills that he developed repairing the plumbing and heating systems were later to serve him well in developing the bronchoscope. He also added to his earnings during employment as a decorator of glass pottery in a china shop. With these funds he attended the University of Western Pennsylvania (now known as the University of Pittsburgh) from 1878 to 1882. He was an excellent student, but did not participate in any extracurricular activities. After classes he immediately returned home by train to help with family chores and to continue working in the china shop. Apparently the frequent appropriation of his lunch by his bully schoolmates in grade school days and the need to conserve money, enabled him to develop Spartan eating habits. A pretzel sufficed for lunch. Rarely did he eat food that his mother insisted upon packing for him. He usually offered it to classmates whose appetites were less satiated. There is no record at the University of Pittsburgh that Jackson received an undergraduate degree.[6]

After finishing college in 1882, Jackson apprenticed to Dr. Gilmore Foster. Once again he moonlighted in a china shop to obtain funds to attend medical school. He entered Jefferson Medical School in Philadelphia in 1884. Due to his limited resources he continued his austere ways.[7] Jackson lived in meager quarters, ate no lunch, and was sustained through the day by a distasteful lingering taste due to a rancid codfish ball eaten during breakfast. During the summer he sold medical textbooks in the Boston area and also served as a cook on a fishing schooner. The crew and captain were so appreciative of his culinary talents that they voted him a share of the profits. Unfortunately by this time his parents were in such dire financial straits that they were unable to attend his graduation in Philadelphia!

While at school Jackson became fascinated with laryngology.[8] He was greatly influenced by the very able Professor J. Solis-Cohen. To pursue studies in this field under Sir Morrell Mackenzie in London, Jackson returned to Pittsburgh to earn money working in a china shop. These funds were supplemented by a $50 advance from a bachelor guest at the family's hotel. The man suffered from chronic laryngitis and for his financial help, Jackson promised to treat him gratis for life. This money was just enough for a ticket, steerage-class, on a trans-atlantic steamer. On the ship the young physician endeared himself to the ship's doctor by caring for seasick steerage-class passengers during a severe gale. Later Jackson was moved to more livable quarters, though it meant total isolation and confinement, to care for one of the travelers who had smallpox. In London he enriched his knowledge of laryngology under the tutelage of Sir Mackenzie. There is little doubt that the first concepts of endoscopy were ignited by Mackenzie's demonstrations, but Jackson was dismayed at the cumbersome instrument Mackenzie used. Jackson blamed English antivivisectional laws for preventing experimentation needed to develop a more useful esophagoscope.

After a short stay in London, Jackson returned to Pittsburgh in 1887 to practice laryngology. He rented an old tailor shop on Sixth Avenue off Penn Avenue and partitioned it as an office. Dr. English, a colleague and also a professional singer, became a source of many referrals after Jackson successfully treated him for laryngitis. However, Jackson's income was still a meager one.[9] Most patients were poor families without funds. Those few who were able to pay, Jackson charged inadequately, and when Jackson's father died penniless in 1889 Jackson was unable to satisfy the many creditors.

Of all his patients, Jackson's greatest interests were children. This deep concern was undoubtedly a sequela of his early childhood experiences.[10] Jackson tried to treat those children chronically ill with tonsillitis, the cause of high absenteeism in the schools. Although his services were offered free, it was only after pressure was brought by Chris Magee, a political ward boss, that the parents consented to have tonsillectomies done on their children. In this age of antibiotics such a procedure would be deemed unnecessary. However, in Jackson's day, tonsillectomy was a most effective form of treatment.

Using his talents as a craftsman and calling upon his old knowledge of pipes, Jackson successfully devised a hollowed tubular structure in 1890 to insert into the esophagus, which enabled him to recover foreign bodies lodged there. News of these achievements brought him much notoriety and he was besieged with innumerable requests to remove buttons, coins and whatever else people swallowed. The most distressing problem was development of strictures in children who accidentally swallowed lye from unmarked bottles. Such incidents embarked Jackson on what seemed to be an endless campaign to have such bottles labeled as poison. For thirty years he lobbied relentlessly in medical societies, state legislatures and congressional committees and finally Congress in 1927 passed the Federal Caustic Poisoning Labeling Law.[11-14]

1899 was a most eventful year. Jackson married a patient's sister, Alice Bennett White, who became an invaluable partner during his early struggling years and an indispensible confidante throughout his long illustrious career. This was the same year that Jackson developed a bronchoscope that could be passed through the larynx to visualize the respiratory tract. A year later at age thirty-five, he became chief of laryngology at the Western Pennsylvania Medical College. Dismayed by his colleagues' inappropriate and injudicious use of the esophagoscope, Jackson began attempts to refine the instrument. His success was achieved by adapting Max Einhorn's suggestion in 1902 to attach a light-carrier to the far end of the scope.[11-15]

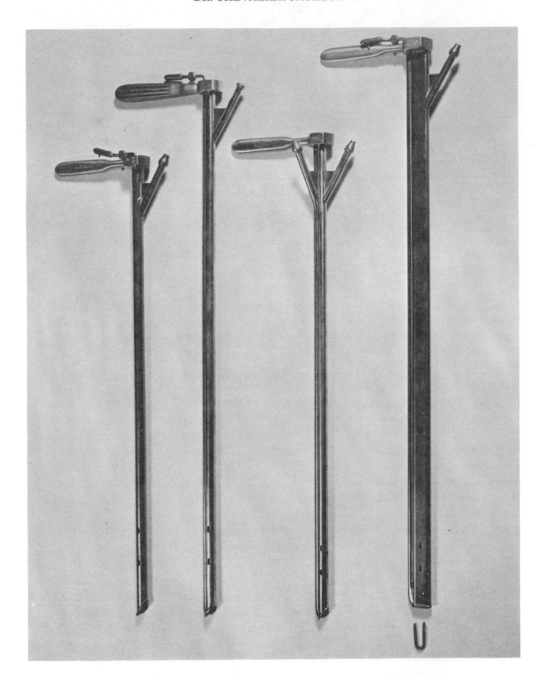

Dr. Chevalier Jackson's Bronchoscopes, c. 1900 College of Physicians of Philadelphia.

Esophagoscopy and bronchoscopy now became practical and relatively safe procedures. Though Jackson was considered a pioneer in bronchoscopy, he never failed to credit development of the bronchoscope to those who preceded him.[16]

All instruments used by Jackson were built after hours by him and his friend, Andrew Lascher, a machinist, in the latter's shop in Pittsburgh's Strip District.[17] Much of his clinical and investigative work was done at the Western Pennsylvania Hospital. Dr. J. R. Johnson,[19] a nonagenarian and beloved physician who recently moved from Pittsburgh to Carlisle, Pennsylvania, told me about Jackson's days at Western Pennsylvania Hospital. He would arrive along with his assistant, Dr. Ellen Patterson,[20] in a chauffeur-driven black Ford touring car. Bronchoscopes were removed from the back seat and carried into the hospital. Dr. Bernie Marks, who doubled as football coach at the then Carnegie Tech, assisted by holding the heads of patients as bronchoscopy and esophagoscopy were performed.[21] Jackson never attempted to do a procedure if he had not perfected it previously, first on mannequins then on cadavers and live animals. In fact, Jackson would not endanger a dog until he was successful using mannequins and cadavers. Another collaborator, Dr. I. Hope Alexander, former Pittsburgh Health Director, stated that Jackson removed foreign bodies faster than he could stuff them down an animal's throat. Dr. David P. McCune, Jr.,[22] of McKeesport, who died October 10, 1976, in his ninety-third year, said while interning at Western Pennsylvania Hospital one of the orderlies named "Barney" willed his body to be used for medical investigation. Jackson would call McCune to get "Barney" ready for a demonstration when foreign and out-of-town physicians arrived to observe Jackson's work. McCune never minded this. When the visiting dignitaries saw how much work the young intern went through to set up the demonstration, they frequently tipped him with $5 and $10 bills.

During these early productive years, misfortune struck. In 1911, Jackson was restricted to bed with pulmonary tuberculosis. After a short rest and unfortunate relapse there followed a two-year convalescence during which he wrote one of his most important texts, "Peroral Endoscopy and Laryngeal Surgery." It was translated into French, then into many other languages. When most of us would be resting on our laurels and reflecting on our accomplishments, Jackson at age 51 chose to move on to new surroundings. In 1916 he accepted the chair of laryngology at Jefferson Medical School in Philadelphia. This new position afforded him the opportunity to develop a bronchoscopic clinic which he was anxious to do. Apparently and most unfortunately this opportunity was denied him in Pittsburgh.[23] In 1918 cordial letters of regret and best wishes were passed between him and Chancellor S. B. McCormick upon his resignation from the faculty at the University of Pittsburgh.

In Philadelphia Jackson was warmly received by his colleagues. His fame was international. Patients rich and poor came from all parts of the world to be treated by him. Stacks of drawers forming part of a Jackson exhibit in the museum at the College of Physicians in Philadelphia are filled with the foreign bodies he recovered from hundreds of patients. In 1919 Jackson was appointed to the chair of bronchoesophagology at the Graduate School of the University of Pennsylvania. Then there were a succession of appointments at the University of Pennsylvania, the Women's Medical College, and Temple University; so that in 1930 Jackson held simultaneous appointments at five medical schools, an accomplishment never achieved before or since.[25] Not one of these appointments offered any compensation. Jackson continued his work in Temple until his retirement in 1938 at the age of seventy-three. He was succeeded by his son, Dr. Chevalier Lawrence Jackson. Dr. James Dill,[26] an obstetrician in McKeesport, who attended Temple during the early forties, reports that there was great excitement in the anatomy laboratory when a young first-year student would pluck a safety pin or a button from the esophagus or a bronchus of a cadaver (evidence of Jackson's doings). Jackson now became financially successful as his practice included prominent and affluent people, but he was never absent or derelict in attending free bronchoscopic clinics that he established at the various medical schools. To all this work Jackson added the responsibility of becoming President of the Women's Medical College of Pennsylvania from 1935 to 1941. Jackson ceaselessly championed the acceptance of women in the field of medicine and chastised his colleagues when they failed to do so. He fought for Equal Rights long before the Bella Abzugs, Gloria Steinems, Betty Fords were born. He said, "I hope that I contributed a little to bring about the breaking down of the old prejudice against the woman physician."[27]

Jackson was in much demand as a lecturer and speaker. He travelled throughout the country and across the seas to fulfill these engagements not becaused he wished it, but felt it was his obligation to spread the gospel of bronchoscopy wherever he could. He composed many of his talks and papers en route, usually while riding a train. Jackson never read from a manuscript while lecturing, enchanting his audiences by ambidextrously drawing illustrations on blackboards with pastel crayons. Jackson was a prodigious writer who published over 250 papers, 12 textbooks and contributed chapters to many others.[28,29] During these years he received numerous national and international awards including the French Legion of Honor, and in 1938 he wrote his autobiography.

Chevalier Jackson was a man of unusual peculiarities and marked eccentricities. He shied away from all social engagements; he considered them to be a great waste of time. He always wore silk gloves, even in summer, compulsively protecting his hands. He preferred the Oriental bow to avoid injury and bacterial contamination of the hands. Jackson opened doors by putting his hands into his pockets so that he would not have to touch the doorknobs. Jackson was a tee-totaler—undoubtably a consequence of his early childhood experiences. It has been said that Jackson was without intimate friends, but he was devoted to the well-being and development of children and he held women in high regard—particularly extolling the latter for their unheralded acceptance of household responsibilities and their tireless devotion to their families. His retirement years were spent with his devoted wife in their

Dr. Chevalier Jackson, age 60. College of Physicians of Philadelphia.

country home, "Old Sunrise Hill", thirty-nine miles from Philadelphia, a distance that Jackson traveled daily to his clinics in the city for so many years. In these later years he did what he liked most—cooking, painting, wood carving and sketching. In 1958 when Chevalier Jackson was ninety-two he died.

Jackson's life spanned the development of medicine from its simple past to the highly sophisticated science that we know today. He saw the advent of modern anesthesia, the introduction of chemotherapy by Ehrlich, the evolution of the entire field of microbiology including the entire spectrum and study of bacteria, fungi and viruses; the discovery of magic drugs such as penicillin and cortisone, and the development of complex surgery and medical techniques.

Jackson was that rare man who, according to philosophers, transcends time and generations. His was a lifetime of frugality, judiciously conserving all the precious moments, utilizing his talents to the fullest and who constantly probed his prodigious mind to conceive unique and daring ways to improve the health of his patients and improve the practice of medicine.

[1]Chevalier Jackson: The Life of Chevalier Jackson. An Autobiography, NY, The MacMillan Company, 1938.

[2]S. L. Shapiro: Chevalier Jackson: A notable centenary. Eye, Ear, Nose and Throat Monthly, pp 100-104, 1928.

[3]Jackson.

[4]Shapiro.

[5]Louis H. Clerf: Chevalier Jackson. Archives of Otolaryngology, 83:124-128, 1965.

[6]There is no record in registrar's office of the University of Pittsburgh that Jackson received an undergraduate degree. This was not necessary to enter medical school.

[7]Jackson.

[8]Shapiro.

[9]John J. O'Keefe: The development of bronchoscope at Jefferson. Transactions and studies of The College of Physicians of Philadelphia, 32:171-174, 1965.

[10]Jackson.

[11]Ibid.

[12]Shapiro.

[13]Clerf.

[14]Emily Lois Van Loon: Dr. Chevalier Jackson: President of the Women's College of Pennsylvania, 1935 to 1941. Transactions and studies of The College of Physicians of Philadelphia, 33:49-51, 1965.

[15]Shapiro.

[16]Jackson

[17]Personal communication to the author by Andrew Lascher's daughter.

[18]Horace Green in 1869 demonstrated tracheal intubation. Joseph P. O'Dwyer applied this concept for treatment of diphtheria victims by insertion of a silver tube to prevent stricture of the larynx during the acute paralytic phase of the disease. Gustav Killian demonstrated that a rigid tube could be inserted into the bronchus through a tracheotomy to remove a foreign body.

[19]Dr. James R. Johnson interned at the Western Pennsylvania Hospital 1913-1914.

[20]Emily Lois Van Loon notes Jackson's preference for women physicians as assistants: "He repeatedly stated that a woman's sensitive fingers were particularly adapted to the delicate nature of endoscopic manipulation."

[21]The Pittsburgh Press' story of Jackson's death, August 17, 1958.

[22]This story told to me by Dr. William W. McCune as told to him by his father Dr. David P. McCune, Jr., who interned at Western Pennsylvania Hospital 1907-1908.

[23]Pittsburgh Press.

[24]Letters exchanged between Dr. Jackson and Chancellor McCormick, August 5, 1918, and August 8, 1918 in Maurice and Laura Falk Library, University of Pittsburgh School of Medicine.

[25]Clerf.

[26]Personal communication to the author.

[27]Clerf.

[28]Chevalier Jackson: Curriculum Vitae in Library of College of Physicians.

[29]Clerf.

Harry L. Wechsler, M.D.

Harry Wechsler, of McKeesport, is a dermatologist and professor of medicine, a member of four local hospital staffs, and a fellow of the College of Physicians of Philadelphia. He is also one of Pittsburgh's eminent book collectors, specializing in Jeffersoniana and Mediciniana. A past president of the Pittsburgh Bibliophiles, he is a member of the Pittsburgh Junta, and a member of the Grolier Club in New York.

Philip Murray, c. 1950. United Steelworkers of America

PHILIP MURRAY AND CLINTON GOLDEN

by I. W. Abel

My purpose is to sketch the broad outlines of activities in which two men had a principal part . . . activities which left a deep and lasting imprint on Pittsburgh and its environs. They are Philip Murray, founding president of the United Steel Workers of America, and Clinton S. Golden, one of its first vice presidents. Both are important to Pittsburgh because they helped shape the destiny and economic well-being of this city and its people.

The growth of our Nation spurred industrialization but this, in turn, brought with it some new evils which accompanied the factory system. The objective of the owners was to obtain the largest amount of work with the smallest possible outlay of wages. Then to achieve more profit, despite human suffering, employers began filling their mills and factories first with immigrants and then with women and children. The history books are filled with accounts of sweated labor, women and under-age children working long hours under unbelievable sanitary and health conditions.

The Steel Industry was centered in Pittsburgh because of the accessibility of needed natural resources; its river system; and its labor pool. It was in this city, at a fraternal hall called Emerald Place—today located in the shadow of the towering corporate headquarters of U. S. Steel—that five small craft unions met 100 years ago—in August of 1876. They were the Roll Hands' Union, the Heaters' Association, the Boilers Union, the Nailers Association, and the Sons of Vulcan, and at that meeting they founded America's first steel union—The Amalgamated Association of Iron, Steel and Tin Workers.

That organization, whose centennial we in labor commemorate this year 1976 along with the bicentennial of our country and the 40th Anniversary of the United Steelworkers of America—was, by the early 1890's, the largest affiliate of the American Federation of Labor and considered the strongest among the unions in the emerging industrial sector.

By that time, too, however, those in control of the American Steel Industry had become determined to keep anything resembling a union off their properties.

It was in the strike of 1892 at Homestead, Pennsylvania, that one of the classic confrontations of U.S. Labor history took place. On July 6, under cover of darkness and fog, two barges with 300 armed Pinkerton guards were brought up the Monongahela River from Pittsburgh, on orders from Henry Clay Frick. Mill owner Andrew Carnegie had gone off to his native Scotland for the period in which the struggle was to be waged and had assigned Henry

115

Frick to cut wages and break the union which three years earlier had won a contract at Homestead. The "Siege of Homestead" raged for 12 hours that day, and when the battle ended, three Pinkerton detectives and 10 steel workers had been killed. Under protection of the state militia, scab labor gradually reopened the mills there.

On the eve of the 1892 strike in Homestead, the Amalgamated Association had almost 300 lodges and a dues-paying membership of over 24,000—almost one-tenth of the membership in the American Federation of Labor. But with the collapse of the 1892 strike, it was a rapid slide downhill for the Amalgamated Association, which by 1910 had workers under contract in only one small open hearth plant.

The formation of the Carnegie-Illinois Steel Corporation in 1901 concentrated the economic power which shaped and dominated the anti-union policies of the industry, bringing about a reversal in relations between employer and employee in the industry. In the late 1800's, there had been a national union which dealt with individual employers, but now there was one great corporation whose negative action practically fixed the standards for the whole industry.

Although another attempt to organize steel took place in 1919, in which Clinton Golden was involved, the United States reached the thirties in the hopeless frustration and privation of the Great Depression. It wasn't until 1935, that the Wagner Act helped balance the scales of labor-management justice which had long been tilted in favor of industry.

Phil Murray and his father came to America from Scotland in 1902, with the rest of the family not far behind. They cleared through Ellis Island on Christmas Day and set out for the bituminous coal fields of Pennsylvania, carrying international coal union transfer cards in their pockets. Two years later, while at work for the Keystone Coal and Coke Company in the Westmoreland County coal town of Madison, Phil Murray was involved in an incident that perhaps more than any other made him a confirmed unionist.

One night, when he came out of the pit, he stopped at the Weighman's office to complain about the money he suspected he and the other miners were losing every day by having their coal shortweighed. Words let to a knock-down, drag-out fight, and the next morning, Murray, was fired for "engaging in a brawl on company property." The whole work force of 600 miners immediately laid down their picks and shovels to join Murray in a fight to get a checkweighman—someone paid by the miners themselves, who could watch the scales with the company man to "check" the weight of coal mined and see that the miners get an honest count.

A strike meeting was held, and Murray's father, who had joined in the walkout, helped elect the young man president of a local unit of the United Mine Workers of America. When hunger ended the strike after four weeks, Murray, surrounded by deputy sheriffs, was taken by train to Pittsburgh and told not to return.

Phil Murray would always say that this episode at the Keystone Coal and Coke Company determined what he wanted to do with his life. In Pittsburgh,

Murray rose rapidly in the United Mine Workers District 5, the Pittsburgh District, and by 1912 had been elected an International Board Member. In 1916 Murray became President of District 5—"the fighting 5" as it was called—in an election that proved his personal popularity. Four years later, in 1920, Phil Murray became an International Vice President of the United Mine Workers. John L. Lewis was the president.

During the next terrible ten years, the UMW was fighting for its life against economic demoralization and the actions of the Coal and Iron police. Murray and Lewis worked together closely. The two complemented each other nicely, with Lewis a far-seeing strategist and master of psychological warfare, thundering and blustering and threatening the coal operators, and Phil Murray then moving in with his solid array of economic facts. A first-rate negotiator, it was Murray often who consolidated the gains won by the wide-flanking efforts of Lewis.

In a sense, then, Murray played infantry to Lewis' cavalry and he still continued to do so after Lewis had knocked big Bill Hutchinson of the Carpenters to the floor at the AFL 1935 convention and marched off to found the Congress of Industrial Organizations, the CIO.

Determined to organize on an industry-wide rather than a craft basis, the CIO began an all-out drive in major American industries. One of its targets, of course, was the Steel Industry which had shown itself to be the citadel of business resistance to labor organization in America. To head the steel organizing drive, Lewis chose Phil Murray, to whom Pittsburgh, the Industry's center, was home.

Phil Murray chaired an historic meeting of the SWOC (Steel Workers Organizing Committee). On June 17, 1936, twelve men sat down in Pittsburgh at this first meeting. They knew well what they were up against. They were aware not only of the futile organizing campaigns of the past, the strike-breaking of the past, but they faced what the industry felt was an insurmountable bulwark against unionism.

And among the dozen men present was one Murray had specifically sought out to assist in the steel organizing drive—Clinton Golden. Golden, as the eastern regional organizer for SWOC, had full responsibility in key geographical steel districts of the heavily industrialized east.

Quaker, pacifist, humanitarian, intellectual, and small-d democrat, Golden was also a tough-nosed union administrator, who had been active in the labor movement as far back as the 1910s. First active with the Machinists, he left that union after unsuccessfully challenging its leadership, and became an advisor to Pennsylvania Governor Gifford Pinchot.

Under the Wagner Act, the National Labor Relations Board was established and the first regional director of the NLRB's sixth region was Clinton Golden. It was a post he held from July of 1935 to June of 1936. Upon leaving the NLRB, Golden became a regional Director of the new Steel Workers Organizing Committee.

With steel organizers now stationed in vital steel areas throughout the country, the industry again girded for union war. The American Iron and Steel

Institute threw down the challenge in full-page advertisements in 375 metropolitan newspapers, at a cost of about $500,000—equal to the entire SWOC budget. To a large degree the industry depended on its control of local governments and local police forces, to crack down on union men. Another tactic of the Steel Industry was to ferment racial and nationality hatreds among the workers themselves.

However, the lessons drawn from the bitter strike of 1919, helped guide the CIO and SWOC to success. The union stressed the need for solidarity to counteract the companies' pattern of division and repression. The same type of multi-language appeal employed by the company in 1919 to urge workers to go back to their jobs was used this time by the SWOC to urge workers to "join the union." The committee, too, successfully mobilized support among a large group of sympathetic community organizations. Murray was a deeply religious Catholic and he thus was able to line up church support for the union drive from his many friends among the liberal Catholic hierarchy.

In 1936, the industry again resorted to strike-breaking, industrial espionage, and private police systems, but this time, there was something new—an arsenal of industrial munitions. A Congressional Committee, the Senate LaFollette Committee, began to investigate violations of the right of free speech and assembly. It later reported, and I quote from its findings, that "the purchasing and storing of 'arsenals' of firearms and tear-and-sickening gas weapons is a common practice of large employers of labor who refuse to bargain collectively with legitimate labor unions . . ."

By the end of 1936, SWOC Chairman Murray announced that 125,000 workers had joined the Union and that 154 local lodges had been established. The Union's growth and the CIO's demonstrated organizing power made a strong impression on Myron C. Taylor, chairman of the board of the Carnegie-Illinois Steel Corporation, now U.S. Steel. It was on March 2, 1937, without need of a strike, that the largest steel company in the world agreed to sign a contract with SWOC—a one-year pact for over 200,000 employees. The gains were modest but included $5 a day in wages, time-and-a-half for overtime, a 40-hour week, and the beginnings of a grievance and seniority system. The historic document was only six paragraphs long—a far cry from the agreements of today.

Another crucial breakthrough came a month later, in the form of a narrow 5-4 U.S. Supreme Court decision upholding the constitutionality of the Wagner Act. The case involved 54 steel workers who had been fired by J&L Steel at the Aliquippa (PA) Works during a 1936 organizing drive. After a hearing that year by the NLRB of District 6, where Clinton Golden served, the board ordered the reinstatement of the workers—a verdict the court upheld. It was at that plant and J&L's property in Pittsburgh, involving a total of 25,000 workers, that the SWOC undertook its first major strike on May 12, 1937. Thirty-six hours later it was over, with the Company agreeing to a Labor Board election and a signed contract if the Union won. That election—the first major NLRB election in the Steel Industry—produced these results on May 20: For the SWOC, 17,028; against, 7,207.

Clinton S. Golden, c. 1942. United Steelworkers of America.

Yet, strong pockets of anti-union resistance still faced the SWOC. Before that month in 1937 had run its course, more lives were to be lost; the ugly side of some companies' tactics again surfaced. A combination of so-called "Little Steel" companies—Bethlehem, Republic, Inland and Youngstown Sheet and Tube—refused to recognize the Union and rebuffed every effort to negotiate. The companies, in effect, forced a strike that stretched across seven states.

During a Memorial Day Union parade and meeting in a field near the Republic Steel Plant in Chicago, 1,000 or so workers were peacefully demonstrating. A holiday spirit prevailed that day until Chicago police confronted the paraders with drawn clubs and hands on revolvers, ordering the workers to disperse. A moment later, on signal, the police attacked—using guns, clubs and tear gas. Ten men were killed from gunfire—all of them shot either in the back or on the side. Thirty others, including a woman and three children, were wounded by gunfire, and 28 more were beaten so badly they required hospitalization.

The incident is known as the 1937 "Memorial Day Massacre", and rightfully so. A newsreel film of the event was so shocking it was suppressed, but was later subpoenaed by the LaFollette Committee. Six SWOC members also lost their lives on Union picket lines in Massillon and Youngstown, Ohio and Beaver Falls, Pennsylvania, during this bitter strike.

Although SWOC lost its efforts to organize the "Little Steel" companies in 1937, victory did come later, after the LaFollette Committee's exposé, extensive NLRB hearing, and the winning of some personal damage suits. By 1942 contracts were signed with all four companies. It was in 1942, also, that the union met in Cleveland, Ohio, to dissolve SWOC and give constitutional birth to the United Steelworkers of America on May 22.

Over the next 34 years of the USWA's existence, the Union established many 'firsts' in American labor—often on the collective bargaining front, but in the courts and the legislative halls as well.

It was the United Steelworkers of America, for example, that blazed the trail to gain pension programs for American workers—winning first, in the late 1940's, the right to bargain for Retirement Benefits which Management resisted.

The struggle to establish this as a legitimate subject for collective bargaining was achieved through an NLRB ruling that was upheld in the courts, including the Supreme Court of the United States. This landmark gain was won under the leadership of Murray and Golden.

Phil Murray served on many government boards and advisory agencies. A strong believer that political democracy was essential to the process of free collective bargaining, he won a medal of Merit for his outstanding leadership of American labor in the all-out production effort of World War II. By this time, Murray had become president of the CIO. The eventual reunification of the American labor movement did not take place until the AFL-CIO merger in 1955, but during the wartime years, the two labor federations worked together in several areas. . . for the first time since the 1935 split. Murray and AFL President William Green appeared together at the Syria Mosque here in

Pittsburgh on April 7, 1942 to pledge, (temporarily at least) labor peace. During the war and for 24 years, Phil Murray served on the Pittsburgh School Board, indicating his strong belief in making better education available to all.

Named as assistant to Murray at the first Constitutional Convention of the USWA, Clint Golden two years later became a vice president of the Union. During the war years, Mr. Golden also served as an administrator of the War Manpower Commission, which had responsibilities for training workers in skills needed in war industry and to teach techniques for handling industrial disputes.

Like other high honors he declined in order to remain closer to working people, Golden turned down an offer from President Truman to become Secretary of Labor. He left the USWA late in 1946, but not before Penn State University somewhat grudgingly agreed to the first USWA-Penn State summer institute. Mr. Golden had been a pioneer in labor education in an effort to see that the stated purpose of the Morrill Act of 1862, the promotion of "the liberal and practical education of the industrial classes," was implemented.

Accepting a position with the government to assist in the reconstruction of war-ravaged Greece, Golden later returned to the United States and became head of the Harvard Trade Union Fellowship Program. But he continued his participation in USWA affairs, virtually until his death on June 12, 1961. Golden had been stricken while discussing the problems of automation before a USWA District 20 Conference in Beaver Falls.

Phil Murray and Clint Golden well may be best remembered for their leadership roles in the great organizing drives and the fight for union recognition of the thirties—the "turbulent years", as they've been called. But their legacy went beyond this. Through their efforts they preserved the Steel Workers Union . . . and it was to this task that Murray devoted the last years of his life.

Both Murray and Golden understood the importance of *Union Responsibility* if the organization was to consolidate its gains. I well remember, for instance, the time that Clint took the train to Canton, Ohio specifically to chew out a guy named Abel, who had helped take Timken workers out on a wildcat strike although we had signed a contract with that company. I was told in no uncertain terms that when the Union puts its name to a labor contract it means what it says . . . and that the same was expected of other parties to such agreements. Golden stressed that discipline was a key to the building of a solid and lasting relationship upon which collective bargaining can be based. And the Timken workers' respect for Clint is best represented in the fact that the local union there—Local 1123, my home local— calls itself the "Golden Lodge", in his honor.

Responsibility is the thing that built this union," Phil Murray emphasized in the last speech before his unexpected death. "We pledge, we commit, we contract—and thereafter we carry forward out Commitments," he told delegates to a District 38 Conference in San Francisco on November 8, 1952— the night during which a heart attack took his life at the age of 66. In working within the framework of our system, it is the function of the union movement, said Murray, "to use the constructive, intelligent strength of the organization to promote the well-being of the members of the Union and their families. By so doing", he continued, "We promote the well-being of the nation. That has been the prime purpose of this union since it was founded, and it must be our purpose in the future".

Since its inception, American labor has been in the forefront of the efforts to institute free public education to improve and seek the highest educational standards. As I have indicated, this cause was very dear to the hearts of Phil Murray and Clint Golden. They both understood the vital role of education in uplifting the masses of people from ignorance and poverty and for integrating into one society and one nation the people of many tongues and cultures who came to the United States in search of freedom and economic opportunity. Free public education was the major plank of the first Workingmen's Party formed in 1829 and labor throughout its entire history has championed quality education for all.

AFL-CIO support was vital to the passage of the groundbreaking Elementary and Secondary Education Act of 1965, the Higher Education Act of 1965, and the GI education measurers, among others.

Organized labor has served as a people's lobby for social and economic progress on all fronts. The unions were the principal force behind FDR's New Deal program which lifted America out of the Great Depression and put it back to work. The labor movement has been guided by the view that economic security and equal opportunity are the cornerstones of a democratic society. Its legislative efforts have not been limited to protecting its own members but advancing all working people. It strongly backed the anti-poverty legislation of John F. Kennedy and Lyndon Johnson and fought for Federal Minimum Wage Laws which benefit mainly unorganized workers. Labor supported the equal employment acts to provide equal opportunity for blacks, women, and other minorities.

Labor constantly has worked for improvements in our Nation's Social Security system and, by so doing, has aided millions of Americans in all occupations, organized and unorganized, to maintain their dignity and to have a measure of economic security in their old age. Our Union particularly, with the active support of the AFL-CIO, was instrumental in achieving Congressional enactment of a new pension security law that includes government reinsurance of private pension plans, so that our older workers will no longer experience the tragedy of broken pension promises when they reach the age of retirement.

Passage of the Occupational Safety and Health Act, we feel, is another recent monumental accomplishment of our Union and the labor movement.

The views of Murray and Golden were important in setting the Union on a political and social course that seeks to promote the well-being of all Americans. These leaders provided the philosophical backdrop for the kind of relationship between union and management that recognizes the parallel economic interest of the parties and is designed to avoid confrontations of the type so common in the past.

In many areas then, I believe our Union's founding fathers would be proud of what their Union has accomplished, the democratic principles it has upheld, the contributions it has made to a free society.

Two centuries ago, the founding fathers of our Nation demonstrated a deep and abiding faith that "We, the People" would sustain both the bid for freedom and the noble experiments in federalism and economic and political democracy that followed independence. Today, our country needs to extend— at home and abroad—the basic principles of social and economic justice that were projected so well by Murray and Golden in the thirties.

I. W. Abel

From 1965 through 1977, I. W. Abel was international president of the United Steelworkers of America, a union of 1,400,000 members. This was the climactic position for a man who began organizing the steel industry in 1936, in collaboration with Phillip Murray, and who in the intervening years had held many posts of increasing importance. At the same time, after 1956, he became first a vice-president of the AFL-CIO, then president of its Industrial Union Department. In the course of his career he received numerous citations from union councils, public service agencies, as well as a number of honorary degrees. In September 1976 a chair in chemical ecology was established in his honor at the Weizmann Institute of Israel, and shortly thereafter he received the highest civilian honor given by the United States Government, the Medal of Freedom. In September 1967 he was named alternate representative of the U.S. delegation to the United Nations. Mr. Abel is now retired and living in Arizona.

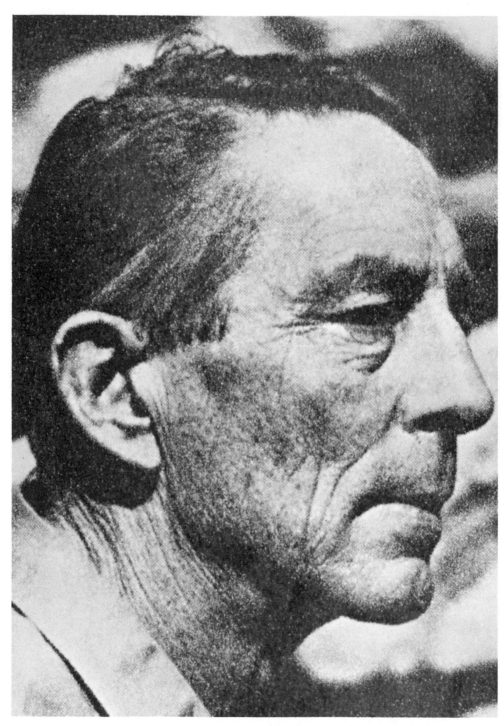

Robinson Jeffers, c. 1932 Carnegie Library of Pittsburgh.

ROBINSON JEFFERS

by Sara Henderson Hay

I should like to present a composite portrait of Robinson Jeffers, the poet and the man, made up on the one hand from the philosophy reflected in his poems, on the other from the personality expressed in his letters. It has always seemed to me somewhat of a miracle, that the letters which an individual writes during a long lifetime, those fragile, perishable bits of paper scattered like leaves before the wind over the world, could ever be tracked down, assembled, arranged and finally published. Luckily, it has happened again and again; we have the correspondence of composers, musicians, actors and dramatists, the voluminous letters of novelists and other authors, and particularly the letters of poets, who, it would appear, could frequently forsake poetry for epistolatry, even though many of them vehemently protested that they hated the process. Byron evidently enjoyed it, to judge from the enormous mass of his letters; so did the most private of poets, Emily Dickinson, who wrote exhaustively to people whom she declined to confront face to face. Edna St.Vincent Millay claimed to suffer from what she diagnosed as epistolaphobia, and so did Robinson Jeffers, who was constantly apologizing for being a wretched correspondent.

But write they did, and these ephemeral and informal documents lend invaluable perspective to the personalities of their authors. It is especially enlightening to read letters along with poems, and surprising, often, to discover how widely the artist's personal life is at variance with the philosophy expressed in his verse. Robinson Jeffers is a sterling example of the dichotomy between person and poet, and we have as evidence an admirable volume, *The Selected Letters of Robinson Jeffers*, edited by Anne S. Ridgeway and published by the John Hopkins Press of Baltimore, Maryland, in 1968. Miss Ridgeway writes in her Preface:

> When I first proposed to assemble Robinson Jeffers' correspondence, I was warned that it was his wife, Una, who wrote most letters, in order to assure her husband time to write poems. I soon discovered that, no matter how much Jeffers disliked answering mail, no matter how ruefully he admitted his vice of procrastination, no matter how scant he thought it, his correspondence was none the less considerable. There are nearly 500 letters in University and public libraries and private collections. They provide some interesting details about Jeffers' life and work, as they might be expected to, but what is more important, they declare a personality not commonly known.
>
> Little is here of the stereotype which has been drawn from his poetry. No hawks wings shudder these pages, and whatever granite they contain

proves remarkably sentient. The man who wrote these letters was a
loving suitor, a devoted husband and father, a courteous friend, a grieving
widower. He was a man dedicated to a life of personal and artistic
excellence, a man who spent his life to poetry. There are the letters of a
gentle, detached, devout and humourous man...

Like most readers who never knew Jeffers personally, I also gathered my
impression of him from his poetry, from the verse narratives with their
nightmare violence and inhuman brutalities, and from the shorter poems,
hardly less negative in their view of life. From the poetry, one gathers that
to Jeffers, humanity is a malign organism in the great body of the universe,
a destroyer, a despoiler, corrupting and proliferating. "There are no fences,"
he cries in desperation, "man will go anywhere . . ."

Louis Untermeyer sums up the idée fixe which runs through all of Jeffers'
volumes:

> Life is malefic. Love, as we practice it, is inverted and incestuous; not
> one self-adoring man in a million expresses outward-going passion.
> Death is the beautiful capricious Savior, 'the gay child with the gypsy
> eyes'. Civilization is a transient sickness. Were the world free of this
> botch of humanity, this walking disease of consciousness, it would be a
> cleaner place, one in which the noble, impersonal elements would be at
> home. In a few thousand years, this may well happen, and life will no
> longer be a torture for the living. Meanwhile our nature 'ignoble in its
> quiet times, mean in its pleasures, slavish in the mass' can, in its
> stricken moments, occasionally 'shine terribly against the dark
> magnificence of things'. Meanwhile we can learn from hawks and
> headlands, we can learn to bear, we can learn to endure . . . .

From the poems one gathers that to Jeffers, consciousness is the great
curse of mankind. He praises the unthinking, enduring ultimates of earth:
rocks, cold stars, granite mountains, depths of ocean, things that have their
being without ambition, without hope, without the curse of mind with its
ancient, never-healing wound.

He pictures, perhaps, an earth which like a tired horse would at some
time shudder its hide and shake off the gadfly of man, and after a while be
restored to its wholeness and beauty, calm under the eternal stars. He lived
into the 1960's and he knew of the atom bomb, and he was appalled in his
latter years by the nightmare of man's ability to blow himself to bits, but
he never, I think, envisioned a holocaust so complete that the planet itself
would be destroyed, a blackened cinder lost in space. He continued, to his
comfort, to believe that nature would somehow survive the pox of man, that
trees and rocks and granite cliffs, like his Carmel coast, would endure when
man had done his worst and departed.

So the *poet* cried doom, and disdained the illusions which made life
endurable: love, joy, the forlorn hope of peace. But the *man* the letters show
was gentle, courtly, a generous and sympathetic friend to his few intimates,
a devoted husband, father and grandfather, a planter of a thousand
cypresses, a builder of walls, a lover of nature's splendour and beauty, a
man kind to animals and birds, a reclusive, shy man who valued and clung
to his privacy. He wrote to a friend:

> "I am set here like a stone in cement. There are many reasons, but I suppose they come in the end to preserving our serenity and getting work done, if possible. For me to see more than two or three people in an evening would mean a month's quarrel with the whole race . . ."

John Robinson Jeffers was born in Sewickley, PA on January 10, 1887. His father, William Hamilton Jeffers, was Professor of Theology in Western Presbyterian Seminary. Apparently the family was well off, as they travelled extensively in Europe and during the early years of Jeffers' life lived abroad for long periods of time; he went to school in Switzerland, England and Scotland, and probably for short periods in Germany. In 1902 they returned for a while to Sewickley, and the young Jeffers attended for a brief time the University of Western Pennsylvania now the University of Pittsburgh. The following year, 1903, the family moved to Long Beach, California, and Jeffers never returned to his native Pennsylvania, except for fleeting visits. He graduated in 1905 from Occidental College, in Los Angeles, and started Graduate studies at the University of Southern California. And here he met the women he loved all the years of her life, and his, Una Call Kuster, a fellow student. They were immediately attracted to one another, but Una was married, and they did their best to attain to what Emily Dickinson called "that piercing virtue, Renunciation." Jeffers took himself off to Zurich, where he attended the University, but returned within the year to enroll as a medical student at USC. Again, he and Una found their deepening relationship a problem. Jeffers departed Los Angeles and his fledgling medical career to study Forestry at the University of Washington, in Seattle; Una, in an attempt to distract herself from the situation, went to Europe for a year. But when they met again, almost by accident on the street in San Francisco on Una's return in 1911, the original passion which had never really died flared anew, and led eventually to the Kusters' divorce. Jeffers and Una were married on August 2, 1913, seven years after their first meeting, and were never again parted until her death in 1950.

The first years of their marriage were spent in La Jolla and Los Angeles, where their first child, a daughter named Maeve, was born but lived only a day. They had planned to go to England in the latter part of 1914, but the war intervened, and Jeffers wrote a friend:

> The August news turned us to the village of Carmel, instead, and when the coach topped the hill from Monterey and we looked down through pines and sea fogs on Carmel Bay, it was evident that we had come, without knowing it, to our inevitable place.

They rented at first a small house on the headland, and there in 1916 their twin sons Donnan and Garth, were born. In 1920 Jeffers wrote a friend:

> We have builded us a little house on the seacliff here; it is just a year since we came to live in it. A delightful place, we think, cormorants on the grey sea rocks in front of us, and pelicans drifting overhead; a most graceful hill range to the south across a neck of water. It is a

> promontory, with water on three sides of us. The house and garage and
> walls are grey granite, sea boulders, like the natural outcrop of the hills.
> In foolish frankness it is the most beautiful place I have ever seen. We
> have two and a half acres; I hope we shall be able to afford more in the
> course of time.

They eventually had five acres. When Jeffers said "we have builded" he
meant it almost literally. He had begun a schedule which lasted his lifetime:
he spent his mornings writing, and his afternoons as a stone mason, hauling
granite rocks from the cliffs, cutting and shaping them with his own hands
to build on to the existing structure which became known as Tor House,
and later to build, with the help of his sons, the stone tower, medieval in its
massive impregnability, called Hawk Tower. He had, fortunately, a small
legacy, the gift of a Pennsylvania cousin, which enabled them to live
modestly and for him to devote himself to his poetry, to which all other
professional and creative efforts were secondary. It was an ideal life for a
poet: the privacy and uninterrupted time which he needed, enough money to
keep at bay the basic economic demands, and most fortunately, a wife who
not only complemented him emotionally but was, as he acknowledged, his
bulwark against the world, the person without whom he could not have
become the powerful and uncompromising poet that he was.

Poetry was, of course, the thing to which he dedicated his being. For all
his sporadic gestures toward other careers—medicine and forestry—he was
never really interested in anything else. He had written poems since his
early youth; his first book, *Flagons and Apples,* appeared in 1912; his
second *Californians* in 1916. According to critical estimates, they were not
particularly distinguished or original. But in 1925, *Tamar and Other Poems*
was published, and that, as the saying goes, was something else again.

Tamar, taking its title and part of its theme from the Biblical story of
Tamar, the daughter of David, who was forcibly violated by her brother
Amnon, was a narrative poem whose theme of incest, sexual violence and
fiery death rivaled Greek tragedy in stark and terrible drama. It was an
overnight sensation. Some read it for the sheer excitement and power of its
story but missed the underlying philosophical meaning which Jeffers
intended and which he continued to defend; others were repelled by the
violence but fascinated by the psychological and Freudian implications. It
was savagely denounced by some critics, as fiercely defended by others. It
was studied by scholars, analyzed and interpreted. Whatever arguments
there were about its morality, there was, as Louis Untermeyer says, no
denying the elemental power of Jeffers' verse. The giganticism of his
settings, catastrophe piled upon catastrophe, the exaggeration of lust and
violence, the inhuman brutalities, were redeemed by the sheer poetic
eloquence, the magnificent vitality, the vivid imagery and sweeping
rhythms of his long lines. As librettos of operas, implausible when read in
resumé are transformed by the music, so Jeffers' over-sized Greek
tragedies, brought up to contemporary times and set on the California coast
instead of Thebes, are lifted into high art by their poetic power.

Explicit though it was, the sexuality in Jeffers' work was never what could be called "of the gutter". There were no four-letter obscenities, no gratuitous vulgarities, no salacious details. It was elegant in its eroticism, classic in the sense that Biblical eroticism is classical. Also, while the settings of most of his narratives were contemporary, the rural coastal country of California, and his characters the simple working people of the region, most of the dialogue is not unlettered and colloquial. When he did attempt the vernacular, the results were artificial and clumsy. Perhaps it requires a willing suspension of disbelief to accept the articulate eloquence and the poetic rhythms of his protagonists' speech, but it suits Jeffers' style.

Attacked by critics and even by friends and fellow poets for the theme of incest which he introduced in *Tamar* and which he continued to use in successive narratives, Jeffers wrote to George West:

> "To defend the theme of *Tamar*: Of primitive motives—hunger, fear of death, etc., sexual desire is surely the most poeticized and dramatized in the normal consciousness, and therefore the readiest for use in a poem. Of environments the family is the most familiar and universal. So the theme that combines these elements ought to reach rather deeply into peoples' conciousness. The theme of incest isn't worn out with use like so many others. It has got to be handled seriously or it is a little too abhorrent. I never had a sister and perhaps for that reason felt the more free to use it."

If Jeffers' formula for a super-effective combination, i.e. sexual desire plus familial environment, brings to mind the famous *Lincoln's Doctor's Dog* surefire best-seller,[1] in any event it worked. *Tamar* was reprinted the following year with the addition of another long narrative poem, *The Roan Stallion,* which became equally controversial because of its quite monstrous theme. And these two remain Jeffers' best known works, those most often associated with his name. They were followed by *The Women at Point Sur,* another Greek tragedy set on the Carmel coast, again incorporating in its blood-spattered story the theme of incest. In a letter to James Rorty, a friend and fellow writer who had been instrumental in bringing the manuscript of *Tamar* to its publisher, the embattled Jeffers wrote, again defending and explaining his stance:

> "The theme of *The Women at Point Sur* is an attempt to uncenter the human mind from itself. There is no health for the individual whose attention is taken up with his own mind and processes; equally there is no health for a society that is always introverted on its own members, as ours becomes more and more. I use incest as a symbol to express these introversions . . ."

He was extraordinarily prolific during these years of the mid twenties. It might seem paradoxical that while Jeffers continued to turn out horrific tragedies, his personal life was eminently serene and happy. He was surrounded by the landscape he loved, and he had his beloved family; he had the time he needed to write, he had never had any of the usual difficulties a poet faces in finding a publisher; he had, also, an apparently inexhaustible inner source to draw from, as well as an intense responsiveness to external and local stimuli—the sight of an abandoned cabin in the hills, a deserted and rock-strewn quarry, an Indian woman and her white husband whom he saw driving through the village in a ramshackled buggy, a grisly episode observed of a woman and her sons torturing a horse.

The Women at Point Sur was followed by *Cawdor and Other Poems.* Of it Jeffers wrote:

> "I think of *Cawdor* as making a third with *Tamar* and *The Women at Point Sur.* But as if in *Tamar* human affairs had been seen looking westward against the ocean, in *The Women at Point Sur* looking upward, minimized to ridicule against the stars, *Cawdor* looks eastward against the earth, reclaiming a little dignity from the association. Where not only generations but races drizzle away so fast, one wonders the most urgently what it is for, and whether this beautiful earth is amused or sorry at the procession of her possessors. . ."

He was writing, in addition to these longer works, many shorter poems, not lyrics so much as rhythmical statements and observations, compressed, usually unrhymed, though he could, and did, occasionally write sonnets and poems in strict metrical pattern and rhyme. One of these infrequent examples I have always found very beautiful, the sonnet

Promise of Peace

The heads of strong old age are beautiful
Beyond all grace of youth. They have strange quiet,
Integrity, health, soundness; to the full
They've dealt with life and been attempered by it.
A young man must not sleep; his years are war
Civil and foreign, but the former's worse;
But the old can breathe in safety now that they are
Forgetting what youth meant, the being perverse,
Running the fool's gauntlet and being cut
By the whips of the five senses. As for me,
If I should wish to live long, it would be
To trade those fevers for tranquillity,
Thinking though that's entire and sweet in the grave,
How shall the dead taste the deep treasure they have?

Regarding his feelings about metrics, he wrote to his friend George Sterling:

> I think two essential qualities of poetry are, first that it be rhythmic, and not in the sense in which we talk about rhythmical prose, but with fairly regular recurrences, metrical and other, making at least a tidal regularity; and, secondly, that it deal with things and emotions which are permanent or capable of perpetual renewal . . .

Jeffers' poetry is not easy reading. It is not, on the whole, the lyrical melodic verse which one commits to memory, to quote for pleasure or for solace. Its impact is in the large, not in the individual memorable phrase or stanza, and the underlying philosophy, so clear to Jeffers, is difficult for the general reader. He was, however, becoming more and more celebrated as a powerful and significant voice in American poetry. He was besieged with letters and

inquiries about his poetic theories, his tastes and interests in poetry, the
influences upon his work, his methods of writing, etc. In spite of his aversion
to letter writing, he answered a good many of these, courteously, as in all his
dealings, to some of the trivial, painstakingly and conscientiously to the
serious questions of students. His kindliness in this regard is in sharp contrast
to the habits of some eminent fellow poets. Thomas Hardy, I have heard, never
returned any of the copies of his books sent to him with requests that he
autograph them, he simply put them on his own shelves. Edmund Wilson had
a printed notice, which he sent to those who enclosed stamped, self-addressed
envelopes, stating curtly, in effect "Mr. Edmund Wilson does not answer
questions about himself or his work and he does not give autographs."

To Jeremy Ingalls, a young poet working on a thesis, Jeffers wrote:

> I am a wretched answerer of letters, but your questions seem few and
> simple. 1. Poets and poetic forms most satisfying: Shelley, Wordsworth,
> Yeats, Milton, Tennyson. Forms: Greek tragedy, Greek lyric. 2. English
> poetry has more significance for me than American, that is, poetry of the
> past. 3. What poets in early reading or personal contact most influenced
> my style or philosophy? None by personal contact. I read and imitated at
> various times all those named above, besides Swinburne, Rossetti and who
> knows how many others. My philosophy had little to do with any reading
> of poetry but came, such as it is, from life and prose, science and the like.
> Perhaps a gleam from Lucretius on one side, and Wordsworth on the other.
> I used to read a good deal of German and French poetry, having been to
> school in Europe and attracted at various stages by Heine, Baudelaire,
> Hugo, but I think neither excited nor influenced me, nor by Latin either
> which my father crammed into me at an early age. No doubt I should have
> mentioned Shakespeare and the King James Bible. Poe captured me when I
> was young; Emerson interested me, Whitman never did."

To Sister Mary James Power, a nun who wrote inquiring about his religious
beliefs:

> As to my religious attitudes; you know it is a sort of tradition in this
> country not to talk about religion for fear of offending; I am still a little
> subject to this tradition and rather dislike stating my attitudes except in
> the course of a poem. However, they are simple. I believe that the universe
> is one being, all its parts are different expressions of the same energy, and
> they are all in communication with each other, influencing each other,
> therefore parts of one organic whole. The parts change or pass or die,
> people and races and rocks and stars, none of them seems to me important
> in itself, but only the whole. This whole is in all its parts so beautiful and is
> felt by me to be so intensely in earnest that I am compelled to love it and to
> think of it as divine. It seems to me that this whole, alone, is worthy of the
> deeper sort of love, and that there is peace, freedom, I might say a kind of
> salvation, in turning one's affections outward toward this one God, rather
> than inward on one's self, or on humanity, or on human imagination and
> abstrations. I think that it is our privilege and felicity to love God for his
> beauty without claiming or expecting love from him. We are not important
> to him, but he to us. I think that one may contribute, ever so slightly, to
> the beauty of things by making one's own life and environment beautiful,
> as far as one's power reaches. This includes moral beauty, one of the
> qualities of humanity, though it does not appear elsewhere in the universe.
> But I would have every person realize that his contribution is not

important; its success not really a matter for exaltation nor its failure for mourning; the beauty of things is sufficient without him. An office of tragic poetry is to show that there is beauty in pain and failure as much as in success and happiness.

To Mrs. Hugh Bullock, founder of the Academy of American Poets, who asked him for a statement regarding his feelings about poetry, he wrote:

> Like the other arts, poetry is a source of high and lasting pleasure but more than most of the others it is capable of affecting life directly; it sharpens the perceptions and emotions, and it can reconcile man to his environment, or inspire him to change it. And poetry enriches life, adding overtones of significance and nobility to common things, as for instance wine, honey, horses, gold, bread, are more valuable for the sake of their even half forgotten poetry associations. England is inestimably more beautiful because Chaucer and Shakespeare and Wordsworth wrote; it is almost humourously obvious that Scotland is dearer to her people because Burns made songs.

His reputation continued to grow. Bibliographies of his work, studies of his poetry, as well as critical articles and essays about him appeared. His books, in spite of the demands upon the reader, were issued in edition after edition. He was invited to lecture, which he declined to do, to serve on committees, which he almost always gracefully avoided except when pushed into a corner, and from which he then extricated himself as speedily as possible, as when he acted for a brief time as one of the judges of an important award sponsored by Harriet Monroe's Poetry Magazine of Chicago. Miss Monroe was considerably irritated by Jeffers' desultory decisions. He did not read much contemporary American poetry, except those books written by his friends or bestowed upon him by editors and others. With the best will in the world he could not bring himself to take time from his own work to read the spate of new poetry, and to tell the truth he was not an awfully good judge or critic. Strict with himself, he was apt to be uncritical in considering other contemporary poetry; he was either too kind, or too disinterested. And a number of times when forced to choose between two candidates, he chose the wrong one. He finally begged off Miss Monroe's committee, as he did also from acting as Chancellor of the Academy of American Poets, an honor which he appreciated but an office to which he felt he could not give proper time to the duties involved.

In 1929 Jeffers and his family made the first of several trips to Ireland and the British Isles. Una Jeffers' family heritage was Irish, and they both found the country and the people congenial. They stayed in rural communities with simple peasant families, they bought a car and drove about the countryside, 5000 miles, Jeffers reported proudly. He was much interested in the Gaelic mythology, and worked on a long poem and several shorter ones inspired by Irish legendary heroes and folk lore; Una kept a Journal of their experiences, a record which was posthumously published, edited and with a Foreward by her husband.

Jeffers felt a great affinity with the coast of Northern Ireland, with its crags and cliffs and wild rocky beaches; he wrote to the poet Mark Van Doren, his great friend:

> Ireland and Northern Scotland and the Hebrides were even more beautiful than we had hoped. England is beautiful too, but the people so tired and the earth so tame, except on the remote edges. And wearily fluffy with trees. There is nothing like travel to narrow the mind!

In 1933 Jeffers published a collection of poems called *Give your Heart to the Hawks.* These particular birds, and other wild and free wings which soared the skies over Tor House and over the sea crashing beneath the cliffs were favorite subjects of his, and one of his most characteristic and most frequently anthologized poems is the one entitled "Hurt Hawks." The poem sprang, as did many of Jeffers' poems, from a specific and literal incident, this being a wounded Red Tail hawk which he and his sons found and vainly tried to nurse back to health. Jeffers was forced to deal it a merciful death.

Hurt Hawks

The broken pillar of the wing jags from the clotted shoulder,
The wing trails like a banner in defeat,
No more to use the sky forever but to live with famine
And pain a few days; cat or coyote
Will shorten the week of waiting for death; there is game without talons.

He stands under the oak bush and waits
The lame feet of salvation; at night he remembers freedom
And flies in a dream, the dawns ruin it.
He is strong, and pain is worse to the strong, incapacity is worse.
The curs of the day come and torment him
At distance, no one but death the redeemer will humble that head,
The intrepid readiness, the terrible eyes.
The wild God of the world is sometimes merciful to those
That ask mercy, not often to the arrogant.
You do not know him, you communal people, or you have forgotten him.
Intemperate and savage, the hawk remembers him;
Beautiful and wild, the hawks, and men that are dying remember him.

I'd sooner, except for the penalties, kill a man than a hawk, but
    the great Red Tail
Had nothing left but unable misery
From the bone too shattered for mending, the wing that trailed under
    his talons when he moved.
We fed him six weeks, I gave him freedom.
He wandered over the foreland hill and returned in the evening,
    asking for death
Not like a beggar, still eyed with the old
Implacable arrogance. I gave him the lead gift in the twilight.
What fell was relaxed
Owl-downy, soft feminine feathers; but what
Soared, the fierce rush; the night herons by the flooded river
    cried fear at its rising
Before it was quite unsheathed from reality.

The years between 1933 and 1948 were productive for Jeffers in spite of many interruptions of his customary regime. He and Una made a second trip to Ireland and several times they visited Mabel Luhan and her Indian husband in Taos, New Mexico. He wrote in 1937 "Thurso's Landing," another grim narrative, and "Such Counsels you Gave to Me," with its title taken from the bloody old English Ballad, "Edward, Edward . . ." And in 1941 among other works, "The Tower Beyond Tragedy," a re-telling of Aeschelus' Greek tragedy which was adapted as a dramatic production, with Dame Judith Anderson, a great admirer of Jeffers, in the role of Clytemenestra. This new turn in Jeffers' interests, the dramatic adaptations of his work, resulted in several productions, notably "Dear Judas", produced in New York in 1947, and his most famous dramatic work, the free adaptation of Euripides "Medea", in which Judith Anderson again starred, and which continues to be performed on stage, and most recently on national television.

The war years gravely distracted Jeffers. Not only did he deplore, as he had from the beginning, the inhumanity of man, his capacity to destroy and despoil, but he worried personally about his son Garth, who joined the Marines and saw active service in Germany. Fortunately Garth returned home safely, with a German bride, at the war's end. Jeffers emerged from his seclusion during this time to serve as an aircraft spotter; Una did Red Cross work.

He was also persuaded at this time, because of some financial pressures, to give a few lectures and readings of his poetry. He was evidently a good speaker, and he was a handsome and attractive man, but he disliked the business of publicity and only with the utmost reluctance left the seclusion of his sea-girt promontory and his satisfying occupations. He wrote to the poet Arthur Davison Ficke:

> If anyone was ever bored, which is incredible, let him get five acres and grow a wood on them, and produce a stone house, and twins, and a book of verses.

His place in American letters was by now assured. Academic and critical interest continued, his works were translated into German, French, and even Czech, and his publishers happily brought out his poems as they appeared, year after year. In 1948 he and Una made their third trip to Ireland and Scotland, but while there Jeffers was hospitalized for a brief time and could not attend the Edinborough production of "Medea", to which Una went alone. In spite of his illness, he completed in the hospital another verse drama, "The Cretan Woman." They returned, somewhat earlier than they had planned, to Tor House, where both sons, now married, were living with their families in what amounted to a family compound. Later Garth moved to Washington state where he took on the profession of forestry, but Donnan and his wife and two children remained with his parents. In spite of increasing age, life was very good.

But 1949 and 1950 brought tragedy, for Una, after a year of painful and debilitating illness, died in September of 1950. It was a crushing blow to Jeffers; his sense of loss was overwhelming. It had been a dreadful time for him, as he had early been told that his wife's illness was terminal, and he had kept the knowledge from her at who knows what cost in self control and heroic dissimulation. She had been his bulwark against the world, she had spared him the distractions of correspondence and of most business and economic matters, but most importantly, they had had a union of the most profound congeniality and never-flagging devotion for the thirty-seven years of their marriage. "There is not a day" he wrote "that I do not think of her and miss her."

Jeffers tried in the years following Una's death to sustain the regular pattern of the life he had led while she lived; writing in the mornings, in the afternoons hauling and cutting stones, tending his trees, walking on the beach. He managed to carry on. A group of poems in the January of 1951 issue of Poetry Magazine brought him the Eunice Tietjen Memorial Award, and in 1952 the Union League and Civic Arts Foundation honored him. With the help of his son Donnan he worked on the annex of Tor House, and his daughter-in-law helped somewhat with his correspondence, even more ruthlessly neglected by him since Una's death.

He was as reclusive as ever, probably more so, but he began some correspondence with his German translator regarding a German version of the stage production of the "Tower Beyond Tragedy." *Hungerford and Other Poems* appeared in 1954, and won the Borestone Mountain Poetry Award. Strangely enough, in spite of his stature as a poet and the significance of his influence on American poetry over some thirty years, Jeffers never was given the National Book Award, nor the most prestigious of awards, the Pulitzer Prize. It may have been because the anonymous judges of the Pulitzer considered his voice too negative, his philosophy too bleak, even though, to quote Untermeyer again, he achieved a startling paradox in that he sang Death with such fervor that his bitter darkness shone more vividly than most surrounding sweetness and light. He wrote during the year 1954 a few prose pieces, and he edited and wrote the Foreword for Una's Irish Journal, published in that year.

It was sadly true, also, that as so often happens with aging poets, in his latter years he became repetitious and pontifical, and fashions in poetry change. His seclusion and his disinterest in contemporary literary movements meant that he drew more and more exhaustively upon the inner springs of his inspiration, and they did not have their pristine vigor.

In 1956 he once again travelled to Ireland and England, but returned home to protest the City of Carmel's project to convert part of his property for use as a public park. In view of Jeffers' lifelong battle against the incursion of the human race upon the privacy and sanctity of nature as a whole, one can only imagine his outrage at this personal invasion. He won his case and averted the condemnation, but his anger and despair at the increasing violations, not only of his own beloved acres but of the planet, obsessed the themes of his later poems.

In 1958 the Academy of American Poets elected him as Fellow; he had long been a member of the distinguished National Institute of Arts and Letters, and of its even more prestigious adjunct, the American Academy of Arts and Letters. In 1961 the National Poetry Society gave him the Shelley Memorial

Award. But his health was failing and on January 20, 1962, at the age of 75, he died at Carmel, and was buried where he longed to lie.

"My address remains Carmel" he had written in a letter long ago, "and I expect it always will."

Sara Henderson Hay

Miss Hay, a poet, is a native of Pittsburgh and lives there at present. She began writing early, and was first published at the age of 10. Her first book of poems, **Field of Honor,** *received an award in 1933, and her subsequent books have won a number of awards including the Bollingen Prize for poetry and much critical praise. One reviewer said that she offered the novel and refreshing experience, in her time, of "verse with clean line and penetrating thought precisely expressed." Her late husband was Nicholas Lopatnikoff, the distinguished Russian/ American composer. She is active in several cultural associations, and gives many readings of her poetry before the public. She was named a Distinguished Daughter of Pennsylvania in 1963.*

Rachel Carson at age 44, at Woods Hole, Massachusetts, 1951. Photo courtesy of Mrs. J. Lewis Scott.

RACHEL CARSON

by Joseph B. C. White

To my mind, Rachel Carson may be the most important woman to have lived thus far in the twentieth century. In fact, one could go further and say she is the most important person in the century because she may have affected every living and future living creature with her words of warning and prophecy. This splendid woman struggled and endured much for us and for all the living environment. Her gift to society was life and she wrapped it in lyrical words.

Rachel Carson was born in Springdale, Pennsylvania, just up the Allegheny River from Pittsburgh. We claim her in Pittsburgh of course, but Springdale was her home and her homestead is still there, protected lovingly by the Rachel Carson Homestead Association. She was born May 27, 1907, the daughter of Robert and Maria Carson. Rachel's father was a farmer of sorts; her mother a quiet, frail woman whose thirst for knowledge infused itself in Rachel, and more than any other person, Rachel's mother guided the mind of young Rachel on the path of inquiry and observation which later became the source of accuracy and detail in Rachel Carson's writing.

It is curious that Pittsburgh, with its parade of powerful minds and industrial figures, would also be the origin of this quiet, studious, shy and retiring writer whose words shook the entire world. She emerged in her final years as strong and as tough as any steel that was ever forged in Pittsburgh. She was tried in the furnace of adversity, faced torrents of abuse which would have felled others and maintained a serenity and singleness of purpose in spite of awesome opposition.

While her father is not prominent in her early life, his choice of occupation gave Rachel the opportunity to be close to the natural world that became her love. The farm was a living book from which she read. In those fields and woods of her childhood, she roamed sometimes with her mother and sometimes alone, drinking in every nuance of movement and change.

Her early years were filled with books and quiet introspection. In what seems to be an over-zealous solicitude for her health, Rachel's mother kept her home from school frequently, tutoring her and laying the foundation for a mind that would later require stern discipline in study and careful preparation. It was also the foundation of a personality which could operate with freedom from typical social relationships which would have sapped her energies and weakened her drive for perfection. Yet she was fully human as her letters to her friends so clearly demonstrate. Rachel Carson brought to her few trusted friends a solid warmth and enthusiasm, which balanced the tough-minded discipline of her life as a scientist and scholar.

Rachel entered Pennsylvania College for Women, (now Chatham College), as an English major. She had fanned a spark of desire to be a writer from the time, at the age of ten, when St. Nicholas magazine published a story she had written. She received a silver badge for the work, but later, another magazine picked up the story and paid her for it at the rate of a penny a word . . . almost three dollars!

Along the way, Rachel had that marvelous experience that is reserved for so few; she met a great teacher in the person of Miss Mary Scott Skinker. Beautiful, well-dressed, intelligent, Miss Skinker made a profound impression on Rachel and others as well. She was a scientist and opened a whole new world of nature that had been so much a part of Rachel's childhood. Rachel changed her major to biology and began to dream of a life as a scientist. Miss Skinker encouraged, guided and loved Rachel. She recognized the love for learning and the discipline that would make this student special, one who stood out from all the rest. Then Miss Skinker moved on in pursuit of her doctorate and was replaced by a teacher who knew less about the subject than her students! As a result, Rachel changed her major again, to zoology, and was graduated magna cum laude in 1928. The following year she entered Johns Hopkins University where she earned her master's degree in zoology and taught there briefly as she did at the University of Maryland.

Rachel Carson did research at Woods Hole, the oceanographic Institute run by Johns Hopkins University, then in the mid-thirties, she entered the U.S. Fish and Wildlife Service of the Department of the Interior as a staff writer. She needed the job as her father had died and she was now supporting her mother. Later on she would add to her responsibilities two nieces, and still later she adopted her nephew, Roger.

In 1936, Rachel Carson wrote a piece she called *Undersea.* It was published in the Atlantic Monthly in 1937. Later she was to say that some of the inspiration of her writing about the sea came from her childhood reading of the works of Joseph Conrad. Miss Carson went far beyond Conrad, for in her words she showed that she was a scientist who understood the functions of the sea and its minute organisms. Her outside reading as well as her research gave her a solid and almost unique combination of science and lyrical imagination which saw fruition in the beauty of her prose. And those who later accused her of unscientific approaches, had only to examine the precision of her facts.

In Rachel Carson's writings, she was creative, innovative, practical and clear. She was asked to do some written programs for radio and was told they were too literary. One of those articles was *Undersea!*

William Beebe, the naturalist and author, chose *Undersea* for an anthology he was preparing. Beebe thought Rachel's work was marvelous and gave her much needed encouragement. In addition, Quincy Howe, a distinguished journalist and publisher, and Hendrik Wilhem van Loon, author, asked Rachel "Why don't you do a book?" That was the beginning of *Under the Sea Wind.*

Paul Brooks, later Rachel Carson's editor and friend at Houghton Mifflin, writes in his book *The House of Life, Rachel Carson at Work* that she was a slow writer, virtually slaving to put her books together, writing in longhand, often at night with only her two cats for company. She re-wrote her sentences painfully, trying to perfect each phrase and working until finally she was satisfied.

Unfortunately, *Under the Sea Wind* appeared in 1941 and few persons were then interested in the lyrical beauty of the sea and the environment it embraced. Americans were too busy riveting ships of steel to put the Japanese empire under the sea to be concerned with the nature of the sea itself. So at the time Rachel Carson's book was largely forgotten.

During the war, Rachel continued her hard work, writing about nutrition (especially the use of fish for war diets), but as she did so, she was assembling the great background of factual material that was not purely scientific but was an understanding of a total environmental attitude that later would be woven into a tapestry of beautiful and sensitive descriptions.

In 1951, as a result of a contract with Oxford University Press, she finally published another masterpiece, *The Sea Around Us.* It became an almost instant best seller. *New Yorker* magazine had decided to publish selected chapters of the book in advance of the publication date. Whether it was the exposure of her beautiful writing to the intellectual readers of America or a combination of influence, snob-appeal, income and attitude, the *New Yorker* reader brought Rachel Carson into the circle of success.

At last, after years of costly struggles to take care of her family which had kept her constantly in debt, Rachel Carson was financially independent. It is a tribute to the people of post-war America, when we were supposed to be a cynical and materialistic nation, that thousands of us were led by this frail lady into the surf and tide pool to marvel at the tiniest of organisms, the slightest drop of salt spray.

Until she became famous with *The Sea Around Us,* Rachel Carson was desperately trying to find a job to meet her increasing financial obligations. She tried the National Audubon Society, the National Geographic Society and dozens of other environmental groups which later would have begged her, just for a public mention. None would hire her.

Rachel lived in a personal world in which her life had been guided or dominated by women. Her mother was the early and continuing dominating force. Rachel went to a girls' school where she was influenced by strong woman teachers. She knew from personal experience and observation the difficulties of women invading the intellectual aspects of science and more than that, the many serious obstacles she faced when looking for employment. Rachel Carson was repeatedly the victim of anti-female moves and attitudes, passed over and ignored.

In the 1950's she was suffering physically, and by the time she finished *The Edge of the Sea* in 1956, Rachel Carson's struggles increased because her aged mother was ill. Rachel herself had a mastectomy in 1960, but she was not told about any malignancy. She suffered sinus infections and had staph infections so severe that she was unable to walk for three weeks. Yet, later she would spend hours in icy surf observing small organisms with water over her knees, so cold that men who were with her could not stand it. But always Rachel

Carson was checking, learning, adding to her storehouse of ideas and facts.

In the period of the 1950's, Rachel was aware that attitudes regarding the environment were going awry. But it was a letter from a lady in Massachusetts calling attention to a large number of birds which had been found dead following a spraying project using DDT for mosquito control, which prompted her to write *Silent Spring.* The stage was set. All the years of preparation and study had led her to this gigantic task of piecing together those widely divergent aspects of the total environment. It was almost as if this was the task for which she had been born. At this time period Rachel Carson was being treated for cancer and she knew that the time she had left was limited. She began massing the material she would need and started her painfully time-consuming effort to trace down each elusive aspect. Rachel Carson did not change her pace; in spite of pain, she went ahead. In checking her material with doctors, scientists, research specialists and ecologists, she knew that she was working on an important book.

New Yorker magazine agreed to run selected chapters before the book appeared in 1962. "Readers Digest," which had a contract to publish any of her writings in condensed form, backed out when it learned about the controversial nature of the new book's content. It was controversial all right. It was the biggest explosion in the field of science since Darwin's *Origin of Species* had cracked the establishment in the nineteenth century.

Essentially, Rachel Carson's new book, *Silent Spring,* warned of the indiscriminate use of chemical pesticides and the long lasting or irreversible effect they may have upon the whole environment, including and especially, the uppermost levels of life—man. Rachel Carson did not call for the total ban of pesticides, only their wise use and the elimination of those which were lethal, and the need for more adequate testing of new pesticides under development. But most of the minds who heard her message or parts of it or inaccurate versions of it, did not wait to examine the facts. Darwin had challenged the established church. But he was a man in an age of growing enlightenment and increasing understanding of science. Rachel Carson was a woman and she had dared to attack or question the basic irresponsibility of a scientific and technological society.

In 1962, we were a people who have given an almost religious respect to science. We were, and are, a trusting, somewhat gullible people. We were sons and daughters of men and women who had come across the seas to subdue the wilderness and extend western civilization. We trusted the institutions we had created.

The public reaction to *Silent Spring* when it appeared in 1962 was caught up at once in disbelief, confusion, ignorance and fear. What Rachel had tried to tell us calmly was that each one of us occupies a spot on the many-stranded web of life that makes up the total environment and that we, occupying the top of the food chain and with the power to alter the environment, must understand the power we have and exercise care in its application.

Criticism came from many areas. *Time* magazine said that she was totally irresponsible, that her statements were untrue and unprovable—in 1962.

Rachel Carson talking with children. Alfred Eisenstaedt. Life Magazine, © *1962, Time, Inc.*

Later, in 1969, when *Time* jumped on the ecological bandwagon and started a section called "Environment", the editors ran a picture of Rachel Carson and talked about the evils of pesticides and how they could be both a blessing and an enemy of our lives.

The chemical industry, mainly through its associations and its captive university scientists, began to lash at Rachel, seeking, curiously, to villify her personally. More than one spokesman from the chemical industry, agriculture, food processing or related field appeared on radio, television or in print to defame her book and yet admitted that he had not really read *Silent Spring*.

In this writer's opinion much of the outrage was visited on Rachel Carson simply because she was a woman. Perhaps if Dr. Rachel Carson had been Dr. *Richard* Carson the controversy would have been minor and the book would not have had half its impact. At that period, anti-female fear lay at the base of a great portion of this controversy. The American technocrat could not stand the pain of having his achievements deflated by the pen of this slight woman.

Slowly, steadily, the truth began to overcome the lies and the fears. One hesitates to say the exoneration was sweet, for the last thing in the world Rachel Carson would have wanted was revenge. She did live long enough to receive accolades from important segments of the public, government and the press. She was responsible for the White House Conference on pesticides because President Kennedy read her book.

Scientific findings began to substantiate her claims line by line. For example, it was shown that there was DDT in the polar ice and the fat of penguins and also in human mother's milk.

What is important for us to remember is that Rachel Carson succeeded in doing what she set out to do: to alert the public to the danger of pesticides and to light a fire under government agencies to provide proper controls. How many of us can say that we have achieved or even set such goals for our lives?

Rachel Carson left us a legacy. Hers was a new way of looking at the natural world. We had moved through the waves of conservation since 1900, first to save the forests, then to save wildlife, then in the fury of nature's eruptions in the dust bowl days, to save the soil. But we were always after one resource at a time, tunneled in our view and blind to side effects. Rachel Carson taught us to look at the entire interwoven fabric of the nature world and to see ourselves as part of it.

Rachel Carson died of cancer in 1964, but her works remain as a legacy of beauty and concern for human life . . . all life.

Joseph B. C. White
From 1955 until 1978, Mr. White worked in Pittsburgh. Beginning at Alcoa in the public relations department, he became, in 1963, educational director of the Western Pennsylvania Conservancy. There he was responsible for developing environmental educational programs, nature centers, and publications in the Conservancy's 26-county area. In 1970 he became superintendent of the Bureau of Conservation in the Allegheny County Department of Parks, Recreation and Conservation. In 1979 he moved to Newark, Ohio, where he is director of the Dawes Arboretum.

Samuel P. Langley, c. 1885. Courtesy Allegheny Observatory.

SAMUEL PIERPONT LANGLEY

by Wallace R. Beardsley

AS A YOUTH—an overwhelming interest in things mechanical, an above average ability to fashion tools, gadgets, and devices of all kinds. He was fascinated by birds in flight, and by the sun, the source of all energy. AS A YOUNG MAN—brimming so with enthusiasm for astronomy that Professor Joseph Winlock, Director of Harvard College Observatory, hired him on the spot. AS A RENOWNED SCIENTIST—Dr. Langley was an imposing man, over six feet tall and weighing two hundred pounds or more, possessed a dignified speaking manner, and he impressed his audiences as "very authoritative." And yet, Dr. Langley was a lonely man, starved for friendship, in need of congenial people to share his interest in science, philosophy, and the fine arts. AS A PERSON—unsatisfied with anything less than perfection, impatient, expecting everything to be accomplished immediately; yet a person who possessed an abiding affection and patience with children. It was he who inaugurated the Children's Room in the Smithsonian Institution, over the entrance to which are the words, "Knowledge Begins in Wonder."

Born August 22, 1834 in what is now the Roxbury section of Boston, Massachusetts, Samuel Pierpont Langley could count among his ancestors such luminaries as the Reverend Increase Mather, a President at Harvard College, and author of the first American treatise (1683) on astronomy; the Reverend Cotton Mather, member of the Royal Society of London; and the Reverend John Cotton, author of nearly 50 books. Even at an early age Samuel displayed a strong attraction to mathematical and astronomical science. His father owned a small telescope, and Samuel, with his brother, John William Langley, spent long hours studying the heavens. While still a student in high school, young Sam would visit the studio of the painter and optician Alvan Clark, where he gained a knowledge of optics.[1]

Then, even as today, jobs in astronomy were scarce. From the time of his graduation from high school in 1851 until 1864 Langley worked as an architect, draftsman, and civil engineer in Boston, Chicago, and St. Louis. This training was to prove of great value in many of Samuel Langley's future scientific studies. In 1864 Langley returned home, as did his brother John after three years of active service as a surgeon in the U. S. Navy. Once again the two brothers turned their attention to astronomy and telescope building. They decided to build a reflecting-type telescope seven inches in aperture with a focal length of five feet. For three years they labored, guided only by an early Smithsonian Institution monograph on telescope construction written by Henry Draper in 1864. With the advice of Alvan Clark all optical and mechanical work was done by their own hands. The brothers tried about twenty mirrors, found them unsatisfactory, and either scrapped or ground and polished once again. When at last Samuel was satisfied, the telescope was an instrument capable of being used for professional scientific observations.[2] Such stress on precision and accuracy became an important characteristic of Samuel's later researches.

Samuel and John traveled to Europe in 1864 and spent nearly a year visiting observatories, scientific institutions, and art galleries, absorbing much knowledge in the process. Upon returning to Boston in 1865, Samuel learned of an available job opening at the Harvard College Observatory. Professor Joseph Winlock was impressed by the obvious enthusiasm of the applicant and his experience in telescope making. Assuming the duties of Observatory assistant, Samuel's astronomical career had begun.[3] (Many years later Langley would be offered the Lawrence Professorship of Physics at Harvard;[4] at the same time, he was offered the position of Assistant Secretary of the Smithsonian Institution which he accepted instead).

Professor Andrew Dickson White, speaking at the Langley Memorial Meeting on December 3, 1906, commented that in 1865. . .[5]

> Langley had not published anything of note; had not made himself known in the universities; had made no popular addresses; had not pushed himself into notice in any way; yet there was in him something which attracted strong leaders in science, inspired respect, won confidence, and secured him speedy advancement.

In 1867, as Assistant Professor of Mathematics at the U. S. Naval Academy, he was in charge of the small observatory there. It was in August that year that Langley was called to Pittsburgh as Director of the Allegheny Observatory and Professor of Physics and Astronomy at the Western University of Pennsylvania (now the University of Pittsburgh).

Langley's first years at Allegheny Observatory were not happy years. The aggravations and the frustrations were almost too much to bear. Only the intercession and the soothing pacification of a very remarkable individual, William K. Thaw, enabled research at the Observatory to proceed. He persuaded Langley to remain despite an attractive offer from Lehigh University in Bethlehem, Pa.[6] When Langley arrived in 1867 the Observatory, aside from the great refractor telescope, was an empty shell. Of vital auxiliary instruments, necessary to make the telescope a useful research tool, there were none. Of furniture, there was only a table and three chairs.[7] The Director's residence was a small dilapidated house on the property which predated the Observatory, having served at one time as a school house.[8] The University classrooms were downtown, a considerable journey in that day. Consequently, teaching left little time for research. The Observatory Committee with William Thaw, chairman, absolved Langley from teaching duties so that research could proceed. The University faculty immediately asked, "Why is the University paying this man a salary when he does no teaching?" The Chancellor demanded he pay rent for the Observatory residence, and evidently tried to replace him with the Observatory assistant C. L. Parker.[9] Harassment

Original Allegheny Observatory in 1886. Built in 1869, demolished 1955. Courtesy Allegheny Observatory.

occurred, for under the date of September 1 the following note in Langley's handwriting appears in the Allegheny Observatory Journal for 1869, upon his return from observing an eclipse of the sun at Oakland, Kentucky:

> Returned. Found a bullet had been fired through the dome, entering at the side turned toward the N. W. about 4 ft. above the ring and going out near the upper panel opposite. The ball must have been from a gun discharged within two rods of the building (probably less) and passed nearly centrally through the dome and about two feet from the object glass.

Little wonder that on March 12, 1874 Langley wrote these words to William Thaw:

> In March 1871 I had been here some four years, the early part of which I do not like to remember. . .

Perhaps the most climactic frustration of all occurred July 8, 1872. In the darkness of the night, thieves entered the Observatory and stole the great lens, removing it right from the telescope. This lens, 13 inches in diameter, was at that time the third largest lens in the world! Langley's own account of the theft appears in his report to the Observatory Committee for 1872-3:[10]

> On the evening of the 8th of July last I returned from a journey, and being fatigued, retired at about 9 P.M., after having passed through the building to see that all was secure before leaving. Between this hour and day-break, a robbery of a kind almost unprecedented was committed, the building having been entered by forcing open the north-east window of the Transit room, and the Object-glass removed from the Equatoreal. It would consume undue time to rehearse the circumstances which made the motives of the theft, at first doubly obscure. We were not very long in learning that a part of them at least, had been to extort money by an offer to return the glass for a reward, and I was authorized by your chairman to say that none would be offered for its return unaccompanied by a conviction of the criminal. The glass was finally recovered, but neither through the exertions of the police, nor by a composition with thieves, (who are believed to have fled,) and recovered without cost to the Observatory.
>
> While the singular nature of the robbery received notice not only from our own, but from European journals, and the Observatory met condolence from its scientific and other friends, from no class more than the former did hearty approval come of the resolution not to jeopardize the safety of this, and all similar property in future, by offering terms to the robbers. It is gratifying to recollect that this resolution, which was adhered to under the temptation of an offered surrender of the glass, for a comparatively slight sum, has been rewarded by its subsequent gratuitous recovery.
>
> The glass was considerably, but not fatally injured, and by the donation of the requisite amount from W. Thaw, Esq., I have been able to put it in the hands of the well known opticians, Messers. A. Clark & Sons, who now report its actual condition as nearly perfect, with the exception of certain scratches, which it has not been thought advisable to incur the expense and risk of grinding out, as these chiefly affect its external appearance.

Referred to here is the same Alvan Clark, by this time the greatest lens maker of all. One can imagine the special care he took to restore this lens for his old friend, and though the remaining scratches alluded to still appear on the lens surface today, it remains an exceptionally good telescope for visual observation.

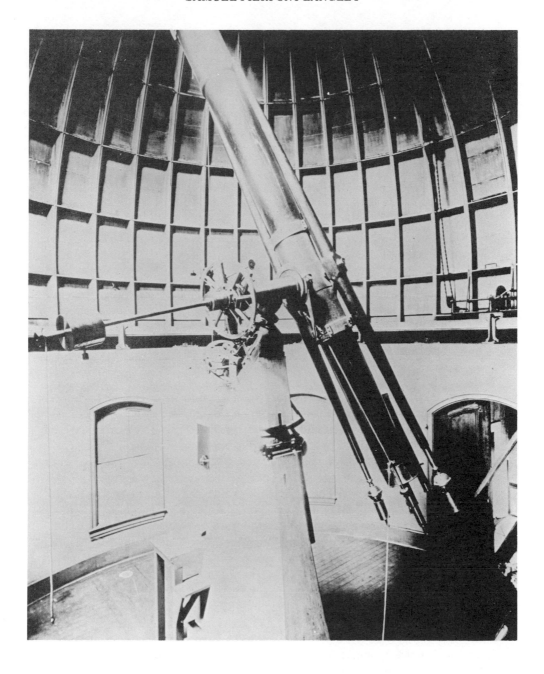

13" Fitz Refractor used by Langley c. 1892. Courtesy Allegheny Observatory.

Langley's scientific accomplishments were many. Between 1869, when Langley first proposed Railway Time-Service, and 1891, the List of Principle Memoirs and Articles on Scientific Researches conducted at the Allegheny Observatory contains more than 80 entries, far too many to dwell upon in this brief description. Holden summarizes Langley's early work in this way:[11]

> The situation of his observatory at Pittsburgh, where dense clouds of smoke and dust and dirt obscure the heavens, and the meager state of his instrumental equipment, almost forced him to take up the study of the sun, which has light enough to penetrate even a Pittsburg fog. Fortunately, this study demanded very few auxiliary pieces of apparatus: the telescope has to be directed upon the sun, its motor-clock keeps it constantly pointed upon the same spot and the observer has to follow, with infinite diligence and patience, the elusive details which the moments of best vision may allow him to glimpse. Two very important and rare qualifications are also necessary. The observer must be entirely unprejudiced and impartial; recording that which he sees, whether it is expected or not, and recording nothing which he does not see, no matter how firmly he may be convinced that it ought to be visible. This is the first qualification—one of unusual mental constitution; and the second is one of unusual manual skill. The observer must be able to delineate the most extraordinary and complex details justly and correctly. Both of these unusual qualifications Professor Langley possesses in a marked degree. His well-known and most beautiful drawing of a "Typical Sun-spot" illustrates this. This has since been copied in very many places, and it has received the very highest praises from all competent judges.

In subsequent researches Langley described the minute detail of the surface of the sun. He was able to measure the intensity of the heat and light radiation received from the entire sun, including the invisible infrared rays about which little was known. He also did this for different portions of the sun's surface. To accomplish this difficult task he had to invent the instrument he needed. This was a very delicate platinum wire detector which changed its electrical resistance in accordance with the amount of radiation falling upon it. This instrument is known today as the bolometer. Langley's greatest desire was to measure the Solar Constant, that is, the amount of radiation received by the earth from the sun at the top of the earth's atmosphere. To do so, in 1881, with the aid of the U. S. Signal Service (then responsible for weather forecasting and research), he led an expedition to the top of Mt. Whitney in California. This work did much to increase Langley's stature as a scientist.

In 1876 Langley was elected to the National Academy of Science; in 1878, elected Vice-President of the American Association for the Advancement of Science, serving as President in 1886-7. In 1882 he received an invitation to address the British Association for the Advancement of Science, and in 1885 he lectured to the Royal Society, London. Honorary degrees were conferred upon him by the Stevens Institute of Technology, the University of Wisconsin, the University of Michigan, and in 1885 by Harvard University. Langley became the first recipient of the Henry Draper medal of the National Academy of Science a year later; and in 1887 he received the Rumford medal from the Royal Society, in London.

Some time during these busy years of solar research at Allegheny Observatory his thoughts turned actively to the possibility of man flying through the air. This was, of course, a general topic of the times, much like space flight is today. It was a dream that Langley had nurtured since boyhood when he would lie in the meadow watching the birds in flight.[12] During the next few years Langley often mentions the valued help of his assistant Frank W. Very. Very was a man of broad scientific interests. One of the strongest of these was nature study.[13] Thus, as Langley deliberated more and more about flight, Very was called upon to conduct detailed examinations of the wing structures of many species of birds. Fifty species of the hummingbird alone were part of this work. Langley[14] theorized that a flying bird, weighing nearly a thousand times as much as the air it displaced, had to be sufficient evidence that heavier-than-air flight could not be impossible.

Thus the problem was really what sort of body would best take advantage of the air's sustaining properties, and how much power would be necessary to sustain and propel any such object.[15] These were scientific problems; to them Langley brought a scientific approach.

Today such a scientific approach involves wind tunnel testing of aerodynamical structures. But in 1887 the wind tunnel concept was virtually unknown. Langley devised what he called a "Whirling Table," similar in concept to one used by Cayley.[16] By performing his experiments at the ends of a long rotating arm, Langley discovered it was possible to simulate air speeds of up to 70 miles per hour. On July 14, 1887 an anemometer to record wind velocity was installed[17] and aerodynamical experimentation at Pittsburgh's Allegheny Observatory began. On September 21 Very conducted the first test of the Whirling Table.

The year 1887 must have been a hectic one at the Observatory. On January 12 Langley accepted the position of Assistant Secretary of the Smithsonian Institution in Washington, D. C. Continuing as Director of the Observatory, he spent half of his time in Washington and the other half in Pittsburgh. But in August the Secretary of the Smithsonian Spencer F. Baird died and three months later Langley was named Baird's successor. Still Director of Allegheny Observatory, Langley had to spend more and more time in Washington. It was Langley's assistant, Very, who conducted the daily affairs of the Observatory, who performed the experiments on the Whirling Table according to Langley's wishes, and who reported to him weekly by letter. In the three years that followed, Very proved to be an indispensable and valuable assistant to Langley. In August, 1891, Langley resigned as Director of the Observatory. The Whirling Table experiments were completed, the University was inaugurating a new Chancellor, William J. Holland, and Langley's friend and benefactor, William Thaw, was dead. The Observatory was about to embark on new directions in astronomical research under James E. Keeler, the new Director. And under Keeler, Frank E. Very now became Adjunct Professor of Astronomy.

Among the research findings of Langley[18] is "Langley's law", that thin planes consume less power for support at high speeds than at low speeds. Thus the higher the speed the less need be the angle of inclination (wing angle) to sustain a given weight. Langley's ultimate aim was to prove the feasibility of heavier-than-air flight. Since the Whirling Table served only to define the scientific principles involved, the next step had to be the practical application of these principles. And so Langley went on into the field of flying where so many before him, lacking basic scientific knowhow, had failed.

Langley's first experiments involved model airplanes powered by rubber bands, similar to what many of us did as children. Gradually, Langley developed the necessary estimates of power requirements dependent on weight and wing area. As he scaled up the size of the models, Langley also set to work building smaller and smaller engines (at first choosing steam over gas engines for practical reasons), seeking maximum horsepower output per unit weight. This itself was a formidable task, and the results he obtained were at the forefront of engineering achievement. At last it became possible to combine engines and models into heavier-than-air flying machines. Langley named them "Aerodromes." Successive models were built and tested, only to fail. But each failure suggested necessary changes; the changes would be made, the model rebuilt and tested again. Failures, Langley reasoned, were the necessary steps leading to success. Finally, on May 6, 1896, Aerodrome No. 5 flew not once but twice, each time soaring gracefully for over a half of a mile over the Potomac River, and climbing to a height of nearly 100 feet. A witness to the event was Langley's close friend Alexander Graham Bell, and it was Bell who announced the result to the world. Later that year Aerodrome No. 6 flew nearly one mile and remained aloft nearly two minutes. Langley was satisfied. He had proved his point; he had succeeded in what he had set out to do. The feasibility of heavier-than-air flight was now assured. Manned flight would come in due time, but others might pursue the ultimate glory.

But fate travels along strange paths. The United States was soon at war with Spain, and one of the most distinguished scientists of the day, Dr. Charles Doolittle Walcott, visualized a futuristic dream. Walcott, a paleontologist and geologist, was a strong advocate of government support for aviation, and it was he who eventually succeeded Langley as Secretary of the Smithsonian Institution. He presented Langley's experiments with heavier-than-air flying machines before President McKinley, pointing out to him the value of airplanes in military operations. Thus, at President McKinley's insistence, Langley agreed to begin the development of a manned Aerodrome, backed by the support of the War Department.

Again there were no engineering precedents. Engines were needed with even greater horsepower to weight ratios. It was Langley's brilliant assistant, Charles Mathews Manly, who succeeded where no engineering concern could. Manly built the world's first radial cylinder gasoline engine; a five cylinder machine weighing only 2.4 pounds per developed horsepower. (The lightest machine previously built at that time weighed twelve pounds per horsepower). A scaled up version of Aerodrome No. 5 was adopted, with the addition of an aviator's car (cockpit) and controls for maneuverability. It was named

Aerodrome A. With Manly at the controls, it was twice launched by catapult over the Potomac River. Both launchings failed. The ridicule of the American press that followed deeply hurt Samuel Langley.

A photograph taken at the moment of the first launching suggests to the author that the trailing edge of the fore-wing was excessively limber. The aerodynamical lift had raised the trailing edge higher than the leading edge, the wing being oriented downwards. Aerodrome A had little choice but to yield to the tilted wing and plunge into the water. Presumably, Langley would have corrected this condition with improved guy-wire stiffening, but no statement with regard to this can be found in the literature. On the second launching attempt, the Aerodrome was seriously fouled by the catapult at the moment of launch, ripping away the Peñaud tail and part of the rear wing. The stricken craft hung on its propellors for a brief moment and then settled into the river tail first. Just nine days later, on December 17, 1903, two brothers, Wilbur and Orville Wright, accomplished man's first successful flight in a heavier-than-air craft under power and control. Langley immediately extended to them his congratulations. Today, the very spot where he met his second and final defeat, is bounded by three flying fields: Bolling Air Force Base, Anacostia Naval Air Station and Washington National Airport.[19]

That Langley's Aerodrome A was indeed capable of flight was demonstrated years later by Glenn H. Curtiss. To do so pontoons were added in order that the craft might take off directly from the water. The addition of pontoons now provided a means to tie down the trailing edge of the fore-wing. Indeed, a photograph reveals that this is just what Curtiss did. On May 28 and June 2, 1914, with Curtiss at the controls, Langley's Aerodrome A rose from the surface of Lake Keuka, New York under its own power and each time flew about a hundred and fifty feet. The credit, however, rightfully belongs to the Wright brothers, for they flew a steerable airplane. Langley's steering control was a shiplike rudder placed amid ship and below the craft, a most questionable arrangement. To Langley, though, the Wright brothers were quick to acknowledge their debt and the debt of all of us who fly today.[20] They said:

> The knowledge that the head of the most prominent scientific institution of America believed in the possibility of human flight was one of the influences that led us to undertake the preliminary investigation that preceded our active work.

During his years in Washington Langley received further honors. Langley became Vice-President of the American Philosophical Society and Council member of the National Academy of Sciences. He received honorary degrees from Princeton, Oxford and Cambridge Universities. Dr. Langley also was awarded the Rumford Medal by the American Academy of Arts and Sciences, and both the Janssen Medal of the Institute of France, and the Medal of the Astronomical Society of France.

Langley was traveling with his niece and staying in Aiken, South Carolina when on February 27, 1906, death came to him quietly, the result of a stroke.

In retrospect, Pittsburgh can proudly call Langley one of its own, but so too can the World, for in the truest sense Samuel Pierpont Langley belongs to us all.

[1]Oliver, J. W., Jr. *Samuel Pierpont Langley's Work in Aeronautics.* M. A. Dissertation, unpublished, University of Pittsburgh, 1952, 2.

[2]Vaeth, J. G. *Langley—Man of Science and Flight.* New York: Ronald Press, 1966, 8.

[3]Ibid.

[4]Letter from SPL to William Thaw, Sept. 9, 1887, while with the U. S. Geological Survey, Jemez Pueblo, New Mexico, Allegheny Observatory Archives.

[5]See Oliver, J. W. Jr. *Samuel Pierpont Langley's Work in Aeronautics.* M. A. Dissertation, unpublished, University of Pittsburgh, 1952, 4.

[6]Letter from SPL to A. M. Mayer, Lehigh University, March 12, 1871, Allegheny Observatory Archives.

[7]Holden, E. S. *Sketch of Professor S. P. Langley.* **Popular Science Monthly,** 1885, *27,* 401-409.

[8]Draft of Report to Observatory Committee by SPL, May, 1872, Allegheny Observatory Archives.

[9]Letter from SPL to William Thaw, March 17, 1874, Allegheny Observatory Archives.

[10]Report of Director Allegheny Observatory to Committee of Board of Trustees, Western University of Pa., June 12, 1873. Pittsburgh: Barr & Meyer, Printers, 1873.

[11]Holden, E. S. *Sketch of Professor S. P. Langley.* **Popular Science Monthly,** 1885, *27,* 401-409.

[12]Vaeth, J. G. *Langley—Man of Science and Flight.* New York: Ronald Press, 1966, 32.

[13]Wagman, N. E. *Personalities of the Observatory.* Pitt Magazine, 1941, Winter (1941-1942), 9-13.

[14]Langley, S. P. *The Internal Work of the Wind.* **Smithsonian Contribution to Knowledge,** 1893, *27,* Article 2, 2.

[15]For a full account of these endeavors see Oliver, J. W. Jr. *Samuel Pierpont Langley's Work in Aeronautics,* M. A. Dissertation, unpublished, University of Pittsburgh, 1952.

[16]Ibid.

[17]Entry of date. Allegheny Observatory Year Book for 1887.

[18]A compact summary of the accomplishments of the Whirling Table experiments is presented in the biography of Langley to be found in volume 15 of The Encyclopedia of American Biography.

[19]Vaeth, J. G. *Langley—Man of Science and Flight.* New York: Ronald Press, 1966, 93.

[20]See Oliver, J. W. Jr. *Samuel Pierpont Langley's Work in Aeronautics,* M. A. Dissertation, unpublished, University of Pittsburgh, 1952, 100.

Wallace R. Beardsley

Mr. Beardsley was named astronomer of the Allegheny Observatory and instructor of astronomy at the University of Pittsburgh in 1953 and has been associated with both institutions ever since. He is an internationally recognized astronomer, active in both teaching and research. Presently he is writing a book on Samuel Pierpont Langley.

Charles Martin Hall at age 42. Courtesy Aluminum Company of America.

CHARLES MARTIN HALL

by Arthur W. Lindsley

Charles Martin Hall is one of the towering figures of American science and industry. His discovery of a commercially practical method of producing aluminum solved a problem which had baffled some of the world's leading scientists for more than three quarters of a century. It launched him on a career that led to considerable personal acclaim and fortune, and a lifetime devoted to the technology of the industry he founded. His achievement has been described as "a classic example of American industry at work." It is certainly one of the nation's greatest success stories.

Hall's discovery was extremely significant for industrial progress. When Hall found the key to his process on February 23, 1886, aluminum was available for about eight dollars a pound. Today, aluminum supplied at a fraction of the price in 1886 is used in thousands of everyday products. Aluminum is the principal material on which some whole industries rely, creating jobs for hundreds of thousands of workers. Billions of pounds of aluminum are used each year in the United States alone for transportation equipment, packaging, building and construction, electrical applications, consumer durable goods and other uses. And the ubiquitous metal, aluminum, is a worldwide industry.

Pittsburgh is the city where it all began. Hall found here a team of dedicated backers—men of vision, business and technical experience, and ability. He began production on a commercial scale here, using for the first time the process his discovery made possible. The headquarters of his company was established in Pittsburgh and remains here as Aluminum Company of America to this day, even though the necessities of the industry—aluminum-bearing ores, and abundant low-cost electric energy—had to be obtained elsewhere.

Bauxite, the ore of aluminum, is found in many different parts of the world, but predominantly in tropical areas near the Equator. The major companies in the industry have most of their primary smelting facilities in industrialized countries near the markets they serve. There is considerable activity in importing and exporting, however, involving not only bauxite and alumina, but also ingot and semifabricated products.

Electrolysis was the key to Hall's process; but Hall first had to find an electrolyte that would dissolve aluminum oxide. Molten cryolite (sodium aluminum fluoride) was the solvent that permitted the production of pure aluminum.

Hall's discovery is especially important because of the fact that aluminum is one of the most common elements in the earth's crust, and its compounds have been known and used for thousands of years. In its mineral form, it is usually called bauxite.

It is useful to trace some of the events that led to the birth of the aluminum industry in Pittsburgh and its commercial production here. Sir Humphrey Davy, a great English electrochemist, in 1807 decided that alumina, the earth substance, had a metallic base. Davy attempted to isolate the metal, and in 1809 fused iron in contact with alumina (aluminum oxide) in an electric arc, producing an iron-aluminum alloy. Despite Davy's success in isolating potassium, sodium, calcium, barium, boron, magnesium and strontium by electrolytic methods, he remained unsuccessful in isolating aluminum.

In 1825, Hans Christian Oersted, the Danish physicist and chemist, produced the first lump of aluminum. Oersted's method was to heat potassium amalgam with aluminum chloride and then distill the mercury from the resulting amalgam.

Frederick Wohler improved Oersted's chemical method by using metallic potassium in 1845. Nine years later, in 1854, Wohler reported that the resulting aluminum particles were "light, ductile, stable in air, and could be melted with the heat from a laboratory blowpipe."

Henri Sainte-Claire Deville further improved the process by substituting sodium for potassium. He exhibited a solid bar of the bright metal at the Paris Exposition of 1855—next to the crown jewels of France.

Napoleon III was attracted by the metal and its light weight, and conceived the idea of equipping his army with armor made of aluminum. An obstacle was the cost—then $115 per pound. Pursuing his idea still further, Napoleon commissioned Sainte-Claire Deville to find a way to lower the cost of the metal. Deville made considerable progress, but it was not enough to make it practical for use as armor.

Meanwhile, artisans were making use of the treasured metal in ornamental ways. Denmark's King Christian X wore a bright crown of aluminum. Napoleon was so intrigued by the metal that on Royal occasions, he had his banquet table set with forks and spoons of aluminum for his most important guests, allowing less important dignitaries to use the more commonplace silver and gold ones. Napoleon's Minister of State ordered an aluminum baby rattle for the Prince Imperial and Napoleon himself presented an aluminum watch charm to the King of Siam on his visit to Paris. In the United States during the Civil War, our Congress honored General Grant with an aluminum medal.

The first assembly of fabricated aluminum in the United States that can be documented was an engineer's transit in 1876. Another unusual application was as a cap for the Washington Monument. On December 6, 1884, a one hundred-ounce aluminum pyramid was mounted on the top of the Washington Monument after a previous showing in Tiffany's Fifth Avenue window in New York. The metal used had been produced by William Frishmuth of Philadelphia.

Hall's discovery in 1886 abruptly changed the prospect for aluminum. At the then-current price of $8.00 per pound, aluminum was destined to be used primarily for special, or novelty applications and in 1888, the entire U.S. production of aluminum was only 10 tons. By 1900 U.S. production was 2,531 tons. With the Hall Process, the aluminum price was brought down to a level which made thousands of useful applications practical. Only about fifty years later, aluminum had become so widely used that *Life* magazine termed it the "Theme Metal of the Twentieth Century."

Apart from price, aluminum can attribute much of its growth to technical developments which greatly enhanced its wide range of naturally useful characteristics. Charles Martin Hall, throughout his life, continued to greatly influence this process.

Aluminum comes in many alloys and fabricated forms. It is a structural material, it is a conductor of electricity, it is an ideal metal for kitchen utensils and it is a brilliant and colorful packaging material. Aluminum is found in automobiles and airplanes, in cans and cables, in sandwich wraps and skyscrapers, on farms and in pharmaceuticals, on boats and in baseball bats. It is a decorative element of interior design. It is a reflector of light. It is a fuel that helps to propel rockets and missiles and it is an insulating material for homes and industrial equipment. One can say aluminum performs more different functions than any other metal used by man.

The aluminum industry, youngest of the major nonferrous metal industries, has come a long way in a short time. Today, it is first among all nonferrous metals in terms of volume produced. Some 38 different countries produce over 13 million tons of aluminum a year. Yet its development as a commercial product only began in the late nineteenth century.

Charles Martin Hall was born in Thompson, Ohio, December 6, 1863, the son of a Congregational Minister, Heman Bassett Hall and his wife, Sophronia Brooks Hall. Hall was the sixth of eight children. By the time Charles was ready for school, the Halls were living in Dover, Ohio, and Charles began his elementary schooling there. When Charles was ten years old, his family moved to Oberlin, Ohio, the home of Oberlin College. Charles was a good student, and finished his elementary education at such an early age that his parents decided to postpone his entry into high school for a year so that he could study music and the piano for which he had a liking and he proved to be an apt pupil. Throughout his life, Hall's ability to play the piano was a relaxation and source of personal enjoyment to him. To prepare for college, Hall completed the regular three-year course at Oberlin High School and a year at Oberlin Academy, and in 1880 he registered as a freshman at Oberlin College.

As a youth, Charles was intrigued with the study of chemistry. In 1892, he testified:

> I have known about aluminum from the time when I first studied chemistry, probably since 1877 or 1878; I was especially struck with the fact that although the most abundant metal in nature—one of the books on chemistry which I studied stating that every clay bank was a mine of aluminum—and exhibiting many of the qualities of the precious metals, it

yet, owing to the difficulties of its extraction, was made only in small quantity, and at a cost about equal to that of silver; I was acquainted with the then process of its manufacture, namely, by the reduction of its chlorides by metallic sodium (a purely chemical process); also with its various compounds, as well as with the properties of the metal itself, and knew that the oxide of aluminum was by far the cheapest and most easily prepared pure compound of the metal.

Hall also said, "At different times for a number of years, I experimented with different methods or attempts to produce aluminum cheaply. First in 1881 and in 1883 and 1884." His first attempt was to separate aluminum from clay (aluminum silicate) by heating with carbon. Then he tried to improve on the existing process by heating calcium chloride and magnesium chloride with clay. Later, Hall spent a number of weeks trying "mixtures of alumina and carbon with barium salts, with cryolite, and with carbonate of sodium, hoping to get a double reaction by which the final result would be aluminum." From time to time, Hall also worked on other inventions as he had since his childhood.

Hall carried on his experiments at home, first using a room on the third floor of his home as a laboratory. Later, he experimented on the alumina reduction process in a makeshift woodshed laboratory in back of his home. Hall's college chemistry professor, F. F. Jewett, was no doubt a source of inspiration to the young Hall. Jewett was a highly trained scholar with degrees from Yale, a year's study at the University of Goettingen in Germany, a year's experience as an assistant at Harvard and four years as professor of chemistry in the Imperial University of Tokyo, Japan. Hall and his professor developed a strong bond of friendship and mutual interest.

Hall began to work in earnest on the elusive aluminum production process after his graduation from Oberlin College in 1885. As a result of his study and experimentation, Hall theorized that the process he was seeking involved electrolysis, as Sir Humphrey Davy had thought, but that this possibility depended on finding a suitable solvent for alumina (aluminum oxide). After weeks of further work and experimentation, he discovered on February 10 that cryolite, (sodium aluminum fluoride), would dissolve aluminum oxide in its molten state. Success came on February 23, 1886, when, after passing a direct electric current through a molten mixture of cryolite and alumina for several hours in a carbon crucible, Hall found some shining button-sized globules of aluminum at the bottom of the pot when the mixture had cooled.

This discovery made it necessary to secure a patent and to obtain the financial backing necessary for the commercial development of the process. Hall's attorney filed an application with the U.S. Patent Office, July 9, 1886.[1]

Within a few months, the patent office reported that another application with a similar claim had been filed by a Frenchman, Paul L. T. Heroult. Although neither man had ever heard of the other, they had strangely parallel lives. Both had been born in the same year (1863), developed identical processes at the same early age of 22 and later died in the same year (1914). Heroult's patent "interference" helped to delay granting patents to Hall, but

Original specimens of pure aluminum produced by Hall in 1886. Courtesy Aluminum Company of America.

Hall was able to prove beyond question that he had reduced his invention to practice on February 23, 1886, while Heroult had to rely on his filing date in France, April 23, 1886. Five U.S. patents were issued to Hall on April 2, 1889.

In 1911 the two inventors met face-to-face. The occasion was a dramatic one, for Hall was being awarded one of Chemistry's highest honors—the Perkin Medal. Heroult was present for the dinner and ceremony of presentation in New York and was introduced and given an opportunity to speak. His remarks were most gracious as he reminisced about the growth of the industry, and in conclusion he said:

> My friend Hall and myself have been fighting for fifteen years, most of the shots going wild on account of the long range over the Atlantic Ocean. Since we met, however, we conceived a better opinion of each other, and I take great pleasure tonight in extending to my friend Hall my sincere congratulations on the award to him of the Perkin Medal.

While patent decisions were pending, Hall began looking for backers who would enable him to put his discovery to productive use. He took some preliminary steps with people in Boston and later in Cleveland, but neither arrangement proved satisfactory. While in Cleveland, he met a young man named Romaine Cole who had worked briefly in Pittsburgh and knew a number of people there. One of Cole's acquaintances was Captain Alfred E. Hunt, distinguished citizen of Pittsburgh, military leader and MIT-trained metallurgist.[2] Captain Hunt was a partner with George Hubbard Clapp in owning and operating The Pittsburgh Testing Laboratory. Cole had worked for Captain Hunt and knew personally of his interest in aluminum, for Hunt had asked him to investigate the possibility of obtaining aluminum by using the intense heat of the open hearth furnace. These efforts were, of course, unsuccessful.

With this information, Hall decided to place his process before Hunt, and sent Cole to Pittsburgh to pave the way. Quick to grasp the importance of Hall's discovery, Hunt immediately contacted some of his friends and assembled "seed capital" of $20,000 to launch a pilot plant operation. Besides Hunt and Clapp, the original investors in the venture were Howard Lush, head of Carbon Steel Company, Millard Hunsiker, general sales manager of Carbon Steel, Robert Scott, superintendent of the Carnegie Steel Company's mills and W. S. Sample, chief chemist of Hunt and Clapp's Pittsburgh Testing Laboratory. At meetings in late July and August 1888, a company took shape and began to function. The name of the new company was The Pittsburgh Reduction Company.

An intriguing, but presumably apocryphal story is told about the early decision to reject the European-style spelling, "aluminium," in favor of the present American style "aluminum." This story attributes the change to a printer's error. The second "i" is supposed to have been inadvertently dropped in producing some company stationery. When the printer went bankrupt before the correction could be made, the financially hard-pressed aluminum company decided to adopt the change rather than pay an additional $300 for new stationery. Unfortunately, the facts do not support this legend.

Paul L. T. Heroult, c. 1910.

A more believable story is associated with the change from The Pittsburgh Reduction Company to Aluminum Company of America in 1907. The story is that the struggling young Pittsburgh Reduction Company was constantly being confused with some sort of garbage disposal outfit. A legendary "last straw" came when one of the company officials was called late one night and was roundly denounced for not removing a dead horse from a near-by alley!

For Hall and the others in the new company, autumn of 1888 was an extremely busy season, filled with preparations for production. The Smallman Street location—between Thirty-Second and Thirty-Third Streets—was chosen for the plant site. Here, a building (24' x 16' x 70') had to be constructed, equipment needs had to be planned and installation accomplished. This end of the business was Hall's primary responsibility.

On September 1, 1888, a young man arrived in Pittsburgh who was destined to play a key role in the business. Arthur Vining Davis, a graduate of Amherst College, had come to Pittsburgh to work for Captain Hunt. Davis was the son of a Boston minister, Rev. Perley Davis, whose family had been friends of the Hunt family for many years. Davis and Hall become close friends and, when the experimental plant was ready to begin production in late November 1888, Davis shared with Hall the experience of pouring the first commercial ingot of aluminum ever to be produced.

Both Davis and Hunt became officers and directors of the Aluminum Company of America and were major shareholders. Their period of service differed greatly, however; as Davis outlived Hall by nearly 48 years, dying in 1962. For much of his later years, Davis was chairman of the board, and was long the guiding genius of the Aluminum Company of America.

Romaine Cole, the young man who directed Hall to Captain Hunt, did not choose to retain a position in the management of the company and by mid-December, because of illness, terminated his employment. For his valued services, however, Hall had promised him a share in the return from the patents, and that promise was kept.

Producing and marketing a new metal meant many new problems for Hall and his associates. At first, as expected, there were technical problems involved in scaling up from a laboratory operation to a pilot plant, and the first few weeks production was somewhat erratic. Hall soon had the problems under control, and aluminum began piling up in the office at a rate of thirty to fifty pounds per day. At first, it was the practice to store the aluminum in the office safe, but this soon became impractical. As conditions changed, the problem of how to market the newly produced aluminum took on the greatest urgency.

There were two main aspects to that early marketing problem. First, aluminum had to be made increasingly convenient and desirable to use. Second, it was necessary that the public be made aware of the many products that could be produced from this metal. Hall applied his genius to both these technical challenges.

Hall's inventive zest continued to motivate him throughout an unusually productive life. From his company's very beginning, he worked long hours to increase the efficiency of his process. Letters from Hall throughout his career give evidence of his constant concern with technological innovation and improvement. One of the inventor's notebooks gives data and suggestions for experimentation on twenty projects he had in progress between February 14, 1888 and November 15, 1889. During his lifetime, Hall was granted 21 U. S. patents. His genius (and that of his associates) brought aluminum from a laboratory curiosity to common usage in just a few years. From his Alma Mater, Oberlin College, Hall received the honorary degree, L.L.D., in 1910. The award had special significance because Orville and Wilbur Wright received the same honor at the same time in an almost prophetic act foretelling the importance of aluminum to aeronautics. Hall maintained an active role in the company through its rapid technical development until his death in 1914. He had never married, so he had no direct heirs. During his life time he had provided for his sisters and he divided the bulk of his estate among designated educational and religious institutions in the United States and abroad. Oberlin College was a principal beneficiary.

When the U.S. Patent Office celebrated the 150th Anniversary of the American patent system in 1940, it called on 75 industrialists, scientists and statesmen to select the greatest American inventors. On the list—along with Whitney and the cotton gin, Fulton and his steamboat, McCormick and his reaper and the Wright brothers and their airplane—stood Charles Martin Hall and his economical method for producing aluminum.

In the Bicentennial year of 1976, Charles Martin Hall was elected to the National Inventors Hall of Fame located in the U. S. Patent Office, Washington, D.C. Hall had achieved his ambitions beyond the fondest hopes of most men. He had "laid up a great fortune" and become a true benefactor of mankind.

Selected References

Carr, Charles C.
> *Alcoa, An American Enterprise,* Rinehart & Company, Inc., New York 1952

Edwards, J. D.
> Frary, F. C.; and Jeffries, Z., *The Aluminum Industry* McGraw-Hill Book Company, Inc., New York 1930

Edwards, Junius D.
> *The Immortal Woodshed,* Dodd, Mead & Company, New York 1955

Van Horn, Kent R., ed.
> *Aluminum,* vol. 2, American Society for Metals, Metals Park, Ohio 1967

ALUMINUM COMPANY OF AMERICA—Charles Martin Hall correspondence and other papers.

[1] Incidentally, Hall's attorney was Homer Johnson, father of Philip Johnson, the noted architect.

[2] Captain Alfred M. Hunt was the father of Roy A. Hunt and grandfather of Alfred M., Torrence M., Roy A., Jr. and Richard M. Hunt.

Arthur W. Lindsley

Mr. Lindsley has been senior editor in the public relations department of the Aluminum Company of America since 1976, and has been with the company since 1948. He is a graduate of Greenville College, holds a degree from the University of Pittsburgh and a Ph.D. in government from New York University. Mr. Lindsley is a member of the International Public Relations Association, the American Political Science Association and the American Academy of Political and Social Science.

Willa Cather, 1902. Courtesy of Mrs. Philip L. Southwick of Pittsburgh.

WILLA CATHER

by Dr. Kathleen Byrne

Although Willa Cather had worked with the University of Nebraska
Literary Magazine and had done free-lance writing for the *Lincoln Courier*, the
Nebraska State Journal, and the *Lincoln Evening News*, her first book was
published during the ten years she lived in Pittsburgh. The book, a collection
of poems, *April Twilights*, was published in 1903 by Richard G. Badger,
Boston, and sold for one dollar. Willa Cather was not pleased with this volume
and gathered and destroyed as many copies as possible. Several years ago, a
copy was found and it was priced at $125.00. There is now a volume, by Willa
Cather, edited with an introduction by Bernice Slote who is one of the
foremost Cather scholars in the world. Ms. Slote has done much writing on
Willa Cather, as has Mildred Bennett, founder of the Willa Cather Pioneer
Memorial and Educational Foundation. To date many volumes have been
published about Willa Cather and her writings including E. K. Brown and
Leon Edel's Biography. The list is too long to enumerate, and the main
interest here is Cather's Pittsburgh years. I mention the numerous writings
and these few in particular, for inevitably much of the material concerning
these Pittsburgh years has been mentioned in some of these publications.[1]

In 1896, Willa Cather, twenty-two and one year out of college, arrived in
Pittsburgh on a Baltimore and Ohio train, looking so happy along the way that
the railway conductor asked whether she was, "getting back home." No doubt
Willa was excited by what she was seeing in Pennsylvania and by thoughts of
Pittsburgh. The hills and streams seemed to gladden her eyes, nevertheless in
her first letter to Mariel Gere, a friend in Lincoln, Nebraska, she described
Pittsburgh as the city of dreadful dirt—but in the same letter she describes the
beauty of the neighborhood in which the Axtells were living.

It was through Mariel Gere's father, Charles Gere, editor of the Nebraska
State Journal that Willa Cather heard of James W. Axtell, who was starting a
family magazine. Axtell was a partner in the firm of Axtell, Orr and Company.
They had recently purchased the two year old *Ladies Journal* and intended to
change its name to the *Home Monthly*. They wanted their magazine to be a
rival of the nationally popular *Ladies Home Journal*. What Axtell and Orr
heard from Charles Gere about Willa Cather's qualifications must have
impressed them, for they agreed to pay her $100 a month to act as a kind of
managing editor.

James Axtell met Willa Cather at the Baltimore and Ohio Railroad Station
when she arrived in Pittsburgh and she spent her first week as the Axtell's

guest at 6338 Marchand Street. The family consisted of Mr. and Mrs. Axtell, a son Philip and a daughter, Lida. When Willa Cather arrived, the daughter had gone to Waynesburg to be tutored in Greek by an Aunt, for Lida was to enter Vassar in the fall. However, Willa Cather suspected that this explanation was a substitute for the real reason that Lida was not at home at that time; it was to protect her from any negative influence of this free-spirited woman from Nebraska!

In working with the *Home Monthly* Willa Cather was forced to yield some of her aesthetic values. She tried hard to produce the magazine Axtell and Orr wanted, the one outlined in an editorial of its first issue, August, 1896.

"Only talent of high order will be employed, although a little time will be required for the organizing of such a corps of contributors as is desired. Nothing need be said further than that these pages will be kept clean and pure in tone, and that all plans for *The Home Monthly* center in the aim to entertain, to educate, to elevate." Willa Cather worked long hours, largely unsupervised in the *Home Monthly* offices at 203 Shady Avenue in East Liberty. Axtell had left the project entirely up to her and had gone on a trip West. Willa Cather needed all the experience she had had at the University of Nebraska with the literary magazine and in free-lance writing for the *Lincoln Courier,* the *Nebraska State Journal,* and the *Lincoln Evening News* in order to complete the first number of the *Home Monthly.* She wrote half the first issue herself. It was necessary since other material was not at hand. Besides she had to read and edit all manuscripts that came in, write filler and make up the pages. Working with an inexperienced foreman in the composing room required long hours. And with her secretary, (who sometimes scolded her for doing too much work), Willa Cather handled the flow of ordinary business letters and letters to would-be contributors. For her own independence and confidence, she was determined to succeed. It was her first fulltime job.

According to the City Directory of 1897, Willa Cather's first regular residence in Pittsburgh was at the boarding house of Mrs. Harriet J. Meskimem at 309 Highland Avenue, just a pleasant walk or ride of six blocks from the *Home Monthly* office on Shady Avenue. Mrs. Meskimem moved the following year to 304 Craig Street in Oakland and Willa Cather went with her. The Craig Street house at the corner of Winthrop Street was closer to the downtown offices of the *Pittsburgh Leader* for which Willa Cather was, by that time, working. It was also near the Carnegie Institute, Pittsburgh's cultural center. Despite these advantages, Willa Cather chose to move back to East Liberty in 1899 to the home of Eliza Davis at 341 Sheridan Avenue. The next year she moved a short distance into the boarding house of Mrs. Marie Eyth at 6012 Harvard Street where she remained until she moved into the home of her friend, Isabelle McClung, in the spring of 1901.

All four of these houses where Cather had lived have been destroyed. The Craig Street site is now part of the Pittsburgh Chapter of the Western Pennsylvania Blind Association. When it was demolished, one first-floor mantelpiece and a peerglass of extraordinary size from a second-floor bedroom, (two of the house's many features in the Charles Eastlake gothic or late medieval design) were given to the Pittsburgh History & Landmarks Foundation.

During these first years in Pittsburgh, Willa Cather spent a great deal of time with the George Seibel family. With them she found comfort for her loneliness, knowledge for her eager mind, and stimuli for her imagination. The Seibels lived in a second-floor apartment of a small brick house at 114 Seventeenth Street. George Seibel had sought out the new editor of the *Home Monthly,* Willa Cather, because he was eager to sell her a feature article.

George Seibel's first impression of Willa Cather was that she looked about eighteen; she was plump and dimpled, with dreamy eyes and an eager mind. Her hair was pulled back in Gibson-girl style, tied with a knot in the back. An instant friendship sprang up. Soon Willa Cather was having dinner once or twice a week with George Seibel and his wife, the former Helen Hiller whom he had married in 1894, (incidentally, through the author's interest in Willa Cather and an introduction from the late Anna Jane Phillips Shuman, the author had the privilege of a real friendship with Helen Seibel for a number of years before her death at the age of 97). George Seibel described those evening meals as "simple suppers." It was before the day of calories or vitamins. Noodle soup, plebeian but nourishing, potato salad, larded with delicious slices of cucumber, cookies of crisp and crackling texture. Helen Seibel found Willa Cather a "very nice young woman," blessed with "strikingly brilliant eyes, a sense of humor, one never heard to say a nasty thing about anyone. Willa Cather was not a gossip." They talked about journalism, poetry, fiction, theater, local art exhibitions, opera and other forms of music. All three in their early twenties, Willa Cather and the Seibels enjoyed discovering their common enthusiasms and they learned much from each other. Often following their dinners together, Willa Cather read in French with her host and hostess and other such guests as Isabelle McClung.

Each Christmas Eve Willa Cather helped to trim the Seibel's Christmas tree. In 1897 she brought her friend Dorothy Canfield with her. Dorothy Canfield's father, Chancellor of the University of Nebraska during Willa Cather's undergraduate days there, had become President of Ohio State University in 1895, and Dorothy had stopped in Pittsburgh for a short visit on the way from Columbus to the family home in Arlington, Vermont. Almost six years Willa Cather's junior, Dorothy Canfield looked upon Willa Cather as a successful woman, one able to pay her own room and board, to buy her own clothes, to provide her own amusements, and to send money she had earned home.

Partly to mark the special occasion and partly to save the young women a long streetcar ride back to Willa Cather's boardinghouse, the Seibels found room for them to stay overnight. George Seibel wondered in his *New Colophon* article whether Dorothy Canfield remembered that he had "allowed her to stay up an hour later and drink an extra cup of coffee." She did remember and in a newspaper feature printed in 1947, she wrote, "It was (although I didn't tell anybody this) the first time I had drunk coffee like a grownup—a great event." That evening too, Hasenpfeffer, the Seibel's cat, delighted the guests by repeatedly tinkling a bell on the lower branch of the Christmas tree and Willa Cather clapped her hands in glee. In the Seibel apartment Dorothy Canfield Fisher felt that she had caught the full essence of Christmas, even more so than in her later life when she celebrated Christmas with her own husband and children. This feeling caused her to describe the city of her Christmas with Willa Cather and the Seibels in 1897, not as "dirty, dark, noisy, grimy," but as "bright-colored and enlivening."

In two letters written by Helen Seibel she agrees that the Engelhardt home described in Willa Cather's short story "Double Birthday" is a just representation of the Seibel home. The Engelhardts of "Double Birthday"

> Lived, certainly, in a queer part of the city, on one of the dingy streets that turn uphill off noisy Carson Street, in a two-story brick house, a workingman's house . . . Albert and his uncle occupied only the upper floor of their house . . . The house opened directly upon the street, and to reach Albert's apartment one went down a narrow paved alley at the side of the building and mounted an outside flight of wooden stairs at the back. They had only four rooms—two bedrooms, a snug sitting room in which they dined, and a small kitchen. The court was bricked, and had an old-fashioned cistern and hydrant, and three ailanthus trees.

The house on Seventeenth Street still stands, in good condition from a recent renovation. The steep steps, which Willa Cather and Albert Engelhardt used, are in their original position, running across the back of the house to an alley at the right side. The yard has been cleared. Instead of the three ailanthus trees, there is only one and it looks over into the yard from next door.

The distance of the Seibels' home from Willa Cather's boardinghouses, from the first on Highland Avenue to the last on Harvard Street, created something of a problem. In "Double Birthday" the home of Judge Hammersley creates the same kind of problem for Albert Englehardt on a late November evening. "He took the streetcar across the Twenty-second Street Bridge by the blazing steel mills. As he waited on Soho Hill to catch a Fifth Avenue car the heavy, frosty air suddenly began to descend in snowflakes . . . He was hesitating about a taxi when his car came bound for the East End. He got off at the foot of one of the streets running up Squirrel Hill, and slowly mounted. Everything was white with the softly-falling snow." Willa Cather did not have Albert's additional problem of climbing the Squirrel Hill streets until she moved to Murrayhill Avenue in 1901. But then, such problems did not phase this vigorous young woman.

A special attraction for Willa Cather at the Seibel residence was Erna. The Seibel's only child born to them on February 24, 1897. Her father says that Erna may have been only a day and a half old when Willa Cather first met her. We must leave the Seibels, however reluctantly, and discover something of Willa Cather's days with the *Leader,* of her teaching days in Pittsburgh, some of her students, and of other friends she made during these Pittsburgh years.

Willa Cather had known Ethelbert Nevin's songs from childhood, but the exact date she met Nevin in person is not certain. It must have been after September, 1897 when the composer returned from two years in Italy and

France because of the illness of his mother. The Nevins lived in Edgeworth, and sometime during the fall of 1897, Mrs. John Slack, a neighbor and close friend of the Nevins, may have introduced Willa Cather to Ethelbert Nevin. Margaret Hall Slack might well have qualified as a professional pianist. She went to New York twice yearly to study under Eugene Heffly. Willa Cather enjoyed many musical evenings at the Slack residence; she recreated something of the musical atmosphere of the place in her short story, "Uncle Valentine." If Margaret Slack was not the one who introduced Willa Cather to Nevin, perhaps one of the Nevin men did. They were the owners of the *Pittsburgh Leader* who had hired Willa Cather the same fall Ethelbert Nevin returned from Europe. Many of the male members of the Nevin family were at sometime involved in the management of the paper before 1904, when Alexander Moore bought it from Theodore and Joseph Nevin.

The meeting with Nevin had taken place before January 10, 1898, when Willa Cather wrote Mariel Gere that she had attended a dinner in Nevin's honor. She described Nevin as the "prince and king of them all." She had seen Nevin before their first meeting at his homecoming concert at Oakland's Carnegie Music Hall. She recreated some of the scene for her *Lincoln Courier* readers on February 5, 1898, perhaps a month after the concert:

> Then there stepped, or rather sprang, upon the stage a youth scarcely five feet three in height with the slender, sloping shoulders and shapely hips of a girl, and that was Nevin! Barely two-and-thirty in fact, with the face of a boy of twenty . . . The roses kept going over the footlights until they were stacked half as high as the piano and the applause did not cease.

This description besides reflecting the audience's enthusiasm for a native son and his music, has an almost verbatim parallel in Willa Cather's "A Death in the Desert." Willa Cather did become acquainted with the Nevins and was invited to their home, Queen Ann's Lodge, for delightful musical evenings. Willa Cather was almost as shocked as the rest of the world when Nevin died suddenly on February 17, 1901 from a stroke of apoplexy. He was only 38 years old. That afternoon, Willa Cather telegraphed Anne Nevin, "By my own sorrow, I can understand yours a little. I think there is no more music left on earth."

Another friend of these years was Lizzie Hudson Collier, leading lady for the Avenue Theater Stock Company during its theatrical season, 1896-1897. Later she moved to the New Grand Opera Stock Company where she played leading roles until 1901. In the spring of 1899 Willa Cather took a night off to go to the theatre. After the performance she hurried backstage. There, according to most Cather biographers, her friend introduced her to another caller, Isabelle McClung. The two women were immediately attracted to one another. Each enjoyed not only the theater, but also music and literature. Isabelle McClung had earned for herself the reputation for Bohemianism of which James Axtell had suspected Willa Cather. Miss McClung knew a great deal about the arts and wanted to know a great deal more. She was twenty-two and spent much of her time with artists. According to Elizabeth Moorhead Vermorcken, she appeared to have an "infallible instinct for all the arts." Isabelle McClung was

Carnegie Music Hall, 1900. Carnegie Library of Pittsburgh.

the daughter of an important Pittsburgh judge; as a jurist, Judge McClung is particularly remembered for having presided at the trial of Alexander Berkman, the anarchist who shot and wounded Henry Clay Frick on July 23, 1892. Following the jury's decision, Judge McClung sentenced Berkman to prison for the maximum of 22 years—he served fourteen.

Isabelle McClung who enjoyed the intellectual stimulation of Willa Cather, came to realize the difficulties of Cather's life when she became a school teacher and an apprentice writer, living in a boardinghouse. She also enjoyed the intellectual stimulation of Willa Cather. Approximately two years after their meeting, Isabelle McClung decided to invite Willa Cather to share the McClung household in Pittsburgh's fashionable Squirrel Hill, and before long, she had persuaded her parents and Willa Cather to adopt the idea. Isabelle McClung and Willa Cather enjoyed a warm friendship as long as Isabelle McClung lived. At the McClung home, a small sewing room on the third floor was converted into a private study for Willa Cather. From this room there was a view over the roofs of many homes, the tops of trees, and banks of flowers and green shrubbery, such as the honeysuckle which still surrounds the residence.

Willa Cather spent from 1897 to 1901 working with the *Leader* and after deciding that such employment left no time for her creative writing, and with the fortunate move to the McClung residence giving her greater freedom to write, she began her Pittsburgh public school teaching at Central High School in March, 1901 as a replacement for a Latin teacher, Belle Weidman. Cather may have received help in getting the job through George Seibel's influence. He was then writing for the Pittsburgh Gazette, (owned by George T. Oliver who had been president of the Central Board of Education from 1880 to 1883). Cather finished the spring term and when Burkey Hunter Patterson, English teacher, resigned in 1901, Willa Cather transferred to the English Department. Norman Foerster, one of Cather's pupils who has himself achieved fame as teacher, editor, and critic has described Central High:

> The Central High School Building was a dismal, grimy structure on a bluff looking down on the Union Station. The darkness of fog and smoke in fall and winter, the dirt of the squalid streets that led up to it, must have made Willa Cather feel that the great plains and skies of Nebraska were very far away—as they were.

Within these grimy walls Willa Cather's classroom-homeroom was where she taught not only Norman Foerster but also Donald Miller, later principal at Peabody High School, and John O'Connor, the future associate director of the Fine Arts Department of Carnegie Institute.

Thanks to her former students' testimony in personal conversations, telephone interviews, and letters, one can make a synthesis of Willa Cather's activities as a high school teacher. Whenever she strolled into her classroom at Central or at Allegheny High School, where she began teaching in 1903, her students saw a determined young woman. For some of them, such as Jean G. Weaver, it was Willa Cather's youth that was impressive. Willa Cather was "one of the very few young teachers in a faculty of gray-haired veterans who seemed like veritable Methuselahs to a thirteen year old." Though these witnesses differ in such specifics as the color of her eyes, all agree on her daily costume. More often than not, she wore what she had worn to the newspaper office, a white shirtwaist with stiffly starched collar, sometimes of the Buster Brown model, with a long red tie or a black Windsor tie, and a dark skirt which some believed exposed too much of her ankle. Her shoes usually had rubber heels.

Her manner too affected the students, just as it had the adults she had already met in Pittsburgh and whom she would later meet all over the world. Her approach to students, according to Frances Kelly, who studied with her at Central, "Was usually forthright, impressively so. She called the boys by their last names (which was new to us); her voice was low, pleasant, almost rolling— but commanded attention. She certainly wanted to have something good in our response to her and sometimes she got results. Everyone seemed to know she was really interested in him or her." Professor Foerster agrees.

John O'Connor, Jr. cherished for most of his life a yellowed story about the "tragic melting down of a favorite lead soldier" which Willa Cather had marked "Good." At the time of her death, O'Connor commented on the fondness of her pupils for her. They had been inspired by the breezy, Western way she had with people. Most of her students had been startled the first day they had walked into class; they had found Willa Cather sitting on top of her desk!

Phyllis Martin Hutchinson mentions that she profited from Willa Cather's methods of teaching composition. "She knew that the only way to learn to write was to write, and she set us to writing themes, one every class day." In the novel *Démeuble* Willa Cather refers to "That drudge, the theme-writing high school student," and thus described us perfectly.

Both Mabel Watts Lovelace, Class of 1904, (who now sometimes meets with the Cather group) and Phyllis Hutchinson, Class of 1905, praised Willa Cather for her beautiful, even teeth, teeth often glimpsed, says Mrs. Lovelace, since Willa Cather had a habit of ending a conversation with a smile. "In Miss Cather's class we never thought about grades; we just enjoyed learning about literature." Mrs. Hutchinson on the other hand, did keep an eye on the grading system. "Seldom did she grade beyond 85 . . . Mostly we got seventies and occasionally achieved an 80 on our themes which were all carefully corrected and returned to us."

Willa Cather was, of course, not so effective with all her students. For instance, it might have chagrined her that she did not convert to literature the nephew of her former employer, Newell H. Orr, who attended one of her English classes at Central; young Newell was the nephew of Thomas E. Orr, one of the publishers of the *Home Monthly.* His letter of 1962 praises her as an able English teacher and as a strict disciplinarian, though "a very pleasant person." He confesses that he has read none of Willa Cather's novels, being "not so much of a book reader."

In September, 1903, Willa Cather left Central for a new teaching position in the English Department at Allegheny High School. Her annual salary increased from $650 (probably as much as she had made at the *Leader*) to $750. By 1906, when she resigned, she was earning $1,300.

Willa Cather's students at Allegheny High School have not been hesitant to express their opinions. Two of the songs sung at the Class Night ceremonies held at the Gayety Theatre on June 23, 1905, the first by the graduating class and the second by a chorus, twit Willa Cather.

Among the seniors who received their diplomas that evening were Walter P. Smart, later judge of the Court of Common Pleas, and Raymond Frodey, who became a gynecological surgeon at Mercy Hospital. Both had been Willa Cather's students.

Margaret Case, another student, in an interview about Willa Cather's teaching at Central offered a two-edged analysis. As a high school adolescent, Miss Case had "unbounded admiration" for her English teacher. And she felt Willa Cather admired her, for once in a while Willa Cather read one of Miss Case's themes in class. In 1962, as a retired English teacher (Peabody High School) and librarian, Miss Case felt that Willa Cather had demanded too much of her pupils. Phyllis Hutchinson also offers an estimate with the same single negative note. "A perfectionist, Willa Cather had little patience with the stupid or careless student." Some of the same criticism was heard at Allegheny High School. Grace Miller, who did not begin teaching there until 1913, seven years after Miss Cather left, recalled critical and bitter feelings still existing among the faculty members because of Miss Cather's devotion to the brilliant student and her intolerance of those who had not learned quickly.

Pittsburgh and its people became part of Willa Cather's emotions, intellect and psychology. Never again was Willa Cather to live as the extrovert she had been in Pittsburgh. Once her genius began to be recognized, Willa Cather deliberately withdrew from public scrutiny.

Another source of much information on Cather's Pittsburgh years is Dr. Richard Snyder of the University of Pittsburgh. Dr. Snyder and I have been working on Cather's Pittsburgh years and hope before too long to have this material ready for publication. [3]This article is just a brief view of Cather's Pittsburgh years and will end with this brief glimpse of Cather's Pittsburgh years by quoting from JoAnna Lathrop's introduction to her checklist of Willa Cather's published writing. (JoAnna Lathrop is a past Director of the Willa Cather Pioneer Memorial in Red Cloud). Her statement sums up the stature of Willa Cather.

> It is not the least unusual feature of Willa Cather's extraordinary career that today, almost three decades after her death, after numerous and widespread observances of the centenary of her birth, after a score of biographical and critical volumes and countless articles, reviews, dissertations, and theses devoted to her work, there is still no definitive Cather bibliography and what is more no immediate prospect of one. Why should this be so? One reason that might be advanced is the duration of her literary career, which spanned nearly fifty years; another is the heterogeneous character and scope of that career—Willa Cather was a newspaperwoman (columnist, drama and music critic, book reviewer, reporter) a feature writer for magazines, an editor, poet, short-story writer,

essayist, and novelist. Moreover, particularly during her first two decades as a professional writer, her work more often than not was unsigned or appeared under a bewildering variety of pseudonyms. Finally, and quite apart from these problems, the author herself created difficulties for the bibliographer. In Bernice Slote's words, "We have not known the extent of Willa Cather's accomplishments, partly because she did not talk about them. An experienced writer does not boast of routine accomplishment, or even remember it all. And for her, as time went by, it became unimportant to talk of past successes when greater ones were at hand.

---

[1] See references.

---

[2] George Seibel

---

[3] *Chrysalis,* Western Pennsylvania Historical Society, March 1980.

REFERENCES

Bennett, Mildred R.
  The World of Willa Cather. Lincoln: University of Nebraska Press, 1961.

Bennett, Mildred R.
  "Willa Cather in Pittsburgh." *Prairie Schooner.* XXXIII (Spring, 1959), 64-76

Brown, E. K. and Edel, Leon.
  Willa Cather: *A Critical Biography.* New York: Alfred A. Knopt, 1953.

Cather, Willa.
  Pioneer Memorial. Letters of Willa Cather.

Curtin, William M.
  The World and the Parish, 2V. Lincoln: University of Nebraska Press, 1970.

Faulkner, Virginia, ed.
  Willa Cather's Collected Short Fiction. Introduction by Mildred Bennett. Lincoln: University of Nebraska Press, 1970.

Howard, John Tasker.
  Ethelbert Nevin. New York: Thomas Y. Crowell Company, 1935.

Hutchinson, Phyllis Martin.
  "Reminiscences of Willa Cather as a Teacher." *Bulletin of the New York Public Library.* LX (June, 1956), 263-266.

Moorhead, (Vermorcken), Elizabeth.
  These Too Were Here: Louise Homer and Willa Cather. Pittsburgh: University of Pittsburgh Press, 1950.

Nebraska State Historical Society.
  Cather Letters.

Schillinger, Ella.
  "Pittsburgh Recalls Willa Cather." *Book Marks.* I (February and March, 1963), 1-10.

Seibel, Helen.
  Letters.

Seibel, George.
  "Miss Willa Cather from Nebraska." *The New Colophon.* II (September, 1949), 195-208.

Sergeant, Elizabeth Shepley.
  Willa Cather: A Memoir. New York: J. B. Lippincott Company, 1953.

Slote, Bernice, ed.
  Uncle Valentine and Other Stories. Lincoln: University of Nebraska Press, 1973.

Woodress, James
  Willa Cather: Her Life and Art. New York: Western Publishing Company, Inc., 1970.

Kathleen Byrne

Miss Byrne has distinguished herself in a number of ways: her knowledge of the career and work of Willa Cather, her work for the aging, and in the area of mental health, and her teaching at Seton Hill College and Duquesne University. She was named a Distinguished Daughter of Pennsylvania in 1958. Her book **Chrysalis** *, co-authored with Dr. Richard Snyder (about Willa Cather's Pittsburgh years), was published in March 1980.*

Dr. T. Lyle Hazlett in his middle years.

DR. T. LYLE HAZLETT

by Theodore L. Hazlett, Jr.

Doctor T. Lyle Hazlett—a pioneer of industrial medicine, engineer, hardware salesman, doctor, soldier, administrator, educator, writer, farmer, public servant, religious leader and husband and father—was born April 19, 1885, at North Washington, Butler County, Pennsylvania and died March 8, 1967, at Coral Gables, Florida.

His father, William J. Hazlett, arrived in Pittsburgh from Ireland on Friday, August 27, 1880. The ocean trip had begun from Learne, County Antrim, on the S. S. Pennsylvania, State Line, reaching New York on August 25th and then extended by overnight train to Pittsburgh. An unmarried man of thirty-two, a linen weaver and English teacher, he had decided to make his way in the new country as a minister. It is difficult for one to realize the psychological effect of moving from one's birthplace to a foreign land, but interestingly enough you can find on every anniversary date in the diary kept by Reverend Hazlett an entry acknowledging that trip. Graduating from the Western Theological Seminary in 1883, after attending Wooster University, Ohio, Class of '82 in the summer for additional educational credits, he accepted his first pastorate at North Washington in the fall of 1883. His marriage to Margaret Ann Lyle of Allegheny City took place on May 8th, 1884. The Lyle family, also emigrants from northern Ireland, had been in Pittsburgh for some years before and had started a successful hardware business on Water Street, Pittsburgh. It is reported that the two young people met at the Swift Mission of the Second United Presbyterian Church in Allegheny City. This union produced one son, T. Lyle Hazlett, but unfortunately the mother died shortly after his birth. Mary McKay, a niece of Reverend Hazlett who had joined him on his trip across the ocean, came to live with father and son and took care of the young child until the Rev. Hazlett married Jemima Redmond, in 1894.

Not much is known about T. Lyle's youth. It was probably uneventful, and much of his education was undoubtedly received from his father and in the several schools that his father began at his various pastorates. T. Lyle Hazlett attended Grove City College, 1902-1903, and West Virginia Conference Seminary, now known as West Virginia Wesleyan, 1903-1904, concentrating in civil engineering. Leaving the Seminary he took a job as assistant engineer on construction work for the Coal and Coke Railroad in West Virginia. A tunnel he helped build is still in use today. Those were rough days in the mountains, and I remember he told me he had to carry a gun for self-protection! At the end of 1904, T. Lyle Hazlett was prevailed upon by members of his mother's family to come to Pittsburgh as a salesman for the family concern. Hazlett's territory included parts of Ohio, Pennsylvania and West Virginia. During his days at home, in between selling trips, the young man developed a close association with the family doctor, Dr. Black and frequently went on calls with him during the days of the horse and buggy. The work the doctor was doing appealed to him, and in 1908 T. Lyle Hazlett entered the Medical School of the University of Pittsburgh.

Following his graduation in 1912, Dr. Hazlett spent two years—one as an intern and the other as an assistant staff physician—at the South Side Hospital in Pittsburgh. After a few months of private general practice, the spirit of adventure seized him, and he joined the American Red Cross, as one of a group of doctors sent to Russia to assist in the care of the wounded at base hospitals at the beginning of World War I. This assignment lasted from December, 1914 to July, 1916. Most of the time was spent at Kiev and certain small cities in Persia. It was hard and not very glamorous work. The hospitals were extremely primitive and the staffing was inadequate. The injuries were severe and the weather bitter cold. In April, 1916, Dr. Hazlett almost died from typhus. His survival was due in large part to the care given him by an American Red Cross nurse, Clara Barndollar, who came from Western Pennsylvania (Everett, Bedford County). Miss Barndollar had joined the group in 1915, several months after the Doctor. It is interesting to read in the Doctor's diary at this time, in commenting upon the arrival of the new nurses. His statement implied none of the group was very good looking! His ideas on this subject must have changed, since by the time he was to leave Russia, he was engaged to this lady! Both returned to the United States by way of Japan, she first and then he, several months later; so both experienced a round-the-world trip. While abroad, Dr. Hazlett was commissioned a Lt. Colonel in the Russian army.

In April, 1917, America was at war. The Doctor was a part of the Pennsylvania National Guard, and he organized a group of men from Pittsburgh to form a Field Hospital Unit. It became known as Field Hospital No. 112 of the 103 Sanitary Train, Twenty-eighth Division. In July the group was at Mt. Gretna, Pennsylvania for training and then in September moved to Camp Hancock, Georgia. While stationed there, he married Miss Barndollar at Savannah, Georgia on November 21, 1917. On May 18, 1918, Doctor Hazlett sailed for England and in June was in France at the front where he served as Commanding Officer of Field Hospital 112 until March 6, 1919. At that time Dr. Hazlett was promoted to Lt. Colonel, Medical Corps. Until his return to the United States and discharge from service at Camp Dix, New Jersey in June, 1919, Dr. Hazlett served as Director of Field Hospitals of 103 Sanitary Train. During his army service, he participated in the battles of Aisne-Marne; Champagne-Marne; Meuse-Argonne; Vise-Aise, Defensive Sector. Field Hospital 112 was the first American Hospital to be located at Chateau Thierry. I vividly remember the war stories told to my brother and me when we were young as a Sunday evening ritual. Father described the time a bomb was dropped next to the tent but fortunately turned out to be a dud. He described the way certain men of the unit were able to pilfer chickens and other food. . . and the very warm relationship the Doctor had with those serving with him.

Soon after his return, Doctor Hazlett served as Medical Director of the Pennsylvania State Sanitorium for Tuberculosis at Mt. Alto where he stayed until 1920. While occupying this post, Dr. Hazlett became aware of the large number of patients coming from industry, and his work on behalf of workers in industry began at this time.

On December 1, 1920, he was offered the post of Medical Director of Westinghouse Electric Corporation which he accepted and served in that capacity with the able support of his secretary, Miss Mary O'Rourke, until his retirement, May 1, 1950. He became the first Medical Director of a large corporation in the United States. With the assistance of enlightened management and his own vision, Dr. T. Lyle Hazlett brought many changes to industry which improved the health and safety of the employees. One of the first industrial hygiene laboratories was set up at the East Pittsburgh works and the fruitful joining of medicine and engineering techniques took place under the leadership of Dr. Edgar Barnes. I am not qualified to assess the value of his work, the qualities of the ideas developed and their application to modern society. I am able to report that in 1942, Doctor Hazlett received the Westinghouse Silver "W" Order of Merit and in 1948, the coveted Knudsen Award of the American Association of Industrial Physicians. In 1941, he was elected President of the Industrial Medical Association.

The history of the development of industrial medicine has been divided into several periods. Prior to 1916, the emphasis was placed on the surgical and curative aspects. From 1916 to 1930, it was the period of preventive medicine. This direction developed overnight with the enactment of the Pennsylvania Workmen's Compensation Law. Most of the large, well-established industries introduced pre-employment physical examinations as part of their medical programs, and many began to establish hospitals, create medical departments and hire "industrial physicians." There was increased emphasis on the education of the industrial worker in first-aid, the installation of restrooms and showers. The growing concern with tuberculosis led to the creation by the Westinghouse Corporation of a T. B. Dispensary. Even dental services for employees were established. It was between the years 1930 to 1941, that medical engineering became prominent in industrial medicine. It arose because of the depression with increased accident compensation claims pressed by employees and contested by employers; the appearance of new occupational disease hazards as a result of new processes; and the adoption of new and more efficient methods of compiling industrial accident statistics. This period was also the time of the development of a formal educational program for the industrial physician. A Department of Industrial Nursing was created within the University of Pittsburgh School of Nursing. With the coming of World War II in 1941, industrial medicine came of age. It became important to save every man-hour lost to illness and accident. Attention was directed to the areas of nutrition, syphilis, alcoholism, mental health and industrial

Dr. Hazlett receiving the Knudsen Award, 1948.

dermatosis. It was the period of growth for the Pittsburgh Diagnostic Clinic founded in 1932, by Dr. R. R. Snowden (who has publicly acknowledged the contribution of Dr. Hazlett, there being a better understanding of the usefulness of periodic physical examinations). The professional life of Dr. Hazlett cuts across all of these periods.

The Doctor's interest in education was broad. He was not only concerned about the education of industrial physicians and nurses but also of the industrial workers. He attempted to show them the importance of industrial hygiene and its impact upon industrial efficiency. Dr. Hazlett promoted the introduction of first-aid courses, mine rescue courses, home-nursing courses, lectures on nutrition and personal health, discussions of industrial health and hygiene in company house organs and distribution of literature on industrial medical subjects. In 1936, a new plateau was reached when the Department of Industrial Hygiene of the School of Medicine at the University of Pittsburgh was created. Doctor Hazlett was made Professor of Industrial Hygiene and head of this department, a position he held until his retirement in 1950. An advisory committee for the Department had been organized of which Dr. Edward Weidlein (then head of Mellon Institute) was Chairman and T. Lyle Hazlett was Secretary. This group was instrumental in developing projects in the fields of fever therapy, nuclear physics and numerous other innovative programs. In 1944, a graduate fellowship course was established, leading to a graduate degree of Doctor of Industrial Medicine. Dr. D. John Lauer, now Medical Director of International Telephone and Telegraph, was one of its first recipients. Dr. Hazlett was also one of the group that organized in 1941, the Industrial Hygiene Foundation, now known as the Industrial Health Foundation (presently directed by Dr. David Braun). This organization is a nationally recognized, non-profit research group supported by industry in the field of industrial health.

A list of Dr. Hazlett's publications at the conclusion of this chapter gives you some insight into his concerns and contributions.

Into his busy life, the Doctor added a new interest; he became a part-time farmer! In 1941 he bought a farm on Bulltown Road, near Murrysville, Westmoreland County, Pennsylvania, and worked it for ten years. During the War years from his farm he was able to provide the Westinghouse cafeteria at East Pittsburgh with fresh vegetables. I know because many mornings I had to rise early to help pick the corn for the day's consumption. The farm was sold when Dr. Hazlett and his wife began to spend more time in the South. For a number of years Dr. Hazlett also served as Chairman of the Occupational Disease Board, an agency created to assist in determining the validity of silicosis claims of workers. Dr. Hazlett was also an active church goer and served for many years as elder of the Third Presbyterian Church in Pittsburgh.

Dr. Hazlett's retirement years were spent in Coral Gables, Florida. These were happy times for him. He lived near a nine-hole golf course, and played frequently. The friends he made through the country club and church filled his time with pleasure. Bridge was a favorite game, and for several years he studied creative writing at the University of Miami. He and Mrs. Hazlett traveled to the Near East, South America and in the Caribbean. When he died, he left a widow now living in Pittsburgh and two sons, Robert D. and Theodore L.; a step-brother, William, and two step-sisters, Annie and Mary.

Doctor Hazlett led a full and constructive life by any standards. Shortly before his death when I last saw him, he was completely at ease and his mind was still strong, but he was beginning to live more in the past. His death came quickly, a heart attack at night, (a heart probably weakened by typhus in Persia many years before). Dr. Hazlett was a man of vision and compassion with a fine sense of humor, religious and with a deep concern for his fellow man. I would like to relate two personal stories. I never heard my father swear but once. It was when I came across an item in grandfather's diary which related that he had been visited by the elders of the church he was then serving, and they asked him to resign. When I showed this to Dad, it must have brought to his mind the incident because he angrily let loose a torrent of four-letter words, and I stood there with my mouth open. The last statement I can remember Dad making was, "I brought them all back alive. I brought them all back alive." He of course was referring to the Field Hospital Unit in

World War I. This he considered one of his greatest achievements. Yes, he did bring them all back alive, but because of his efforts many, many more were brought back alive and are alive in our industrial society, and it in turn is a more humane society because of the life of this honorable man, my father, Dr. T. Lyle Hazlett.

TUBERCULOSIS PREVENTION WORK IN A LARGE PLANT
Journal—Outdoor Life, 1925
PRACTICAL RESULTS OF PHYSICAL EXAMINATIONS IN INDUSTRY
Pennsylvania Labor and Industry, 1928
TUBERCULOSIS IN INDUSTRY
Bulletin of American Association of Industrial Physicians and Surgeons, 1929
VALUE OF GOOD PHYSICAL AND MENTAL HEALTH IN INDUSTRY
Pennsylvania Health, 1930
THE PHYSICIAN ADMINISTRATOR
National Safety Council, Industrial Health Section, 1930
MEDICAL-ENGINEERING CONTROL OF INDUSTRIAL HAZARDS
Industrial Medicine, 1936
FUNDAMENTALS OF INDUSTRIAL HYGIENE
Proceedings of Annual Congress on Medical Education and Licensure, American Medical Association, 1939
THE PRACTICE OF INDUSTRIAL HEALTH
Southern Medical Journal, 1941
PLACEMENT OF THE WORKER
Industrial Medicine, 1941
INSTRUCTION IN INDUSTRIAL MEDICINE FOR MEDICAL STUDENTS
Industrial Medicine, 1942
SAFEGUARDING WORKER HEALTH
Factory Management and Maintenance, 1942
WHAT ARE WE EXAMINING FOR?
Industrial Medicine, 1942
INDUSTRIAL MEDICAL PROBLEMS IN WAR PRODUCTION
Industrial Medicine, 1944
TUBERCULOSIS AND INDUSTRY
Industrial Medicine, 1944
EXECUTIVES' HEALTH IN INDUSTRY
Hygeia, 1946
VALUE OF INDUSTRIAL HYGIENE
American Journal of Public Health, 1947

Editor

INTRODUCTION TO INDUSTRIAL MEDICINE, 1945
Industrial Medical Publishing Company

Co-Author

INDUSTRIAL MEDICINE IN WESTERN PENNSYLVANIA
1980-1950
University Press, Pittsburgh, Pennsylvania, 1959

Theodore L. Hazlett, Jr.

Theodore Hazlett, a lawyer, was one of the outstanding figures in the history of public service in Pittsburgh. On graduating from Harvard School of Law in 1944, he became legal secretary for James Drew, chief justice of the state Supreme Court, and soon began a private law practice that lasted until his death in 1979. At the same time, he helped sponsor the Allegheny Conference on Community Development, and in 1946 became its solicitor. In 1948 he became secretary and general counsel of the Urban Redevelopment Authority of Pittsburgh. In 1965 he became president and a trustee of the A. W. Mellon Educational and Charitable Trust. In addition, he served on the Pennsylvania State Planning Board, the Commonwealth of Pennsylvania Council on the Arts, and the Western Pennsylvania Conservancy. One of his service-related legal posts was as solicitor for the Pittsburgh Regional Planning Association and the Southwestern Pennsylvania Regional Planning Association.

John Kane, c. 1930. Photograph by David Craig, Museum of Art, Carnegie Institute of Pittsburgh.

JOHN KANE

by Leon Arkus

There are those who believe that Pittsburgh was created in the image of John Kane's paintings. I'm inclined to agree.

He also painted in Philadelphia, in Harrisburg, on the Juniata River; but it was Pittsburgh he loved. Pittsburgh was the subject of the major part of his oeuvre. And it was here that he created his greatest paintings. Now let us talk about Kane, the man, and without slides for a spell.* The reason for this is that virtually all of Kane's paintings that are known were done in the last six years of his life.

I quote: "You will find no more magnificent paradox than this: that an immigrant day-laborer, who had no time to paint, no money to paint, no earthly provocation or encouragement to paint, should emerge, at the age of 67, as the most significant painter America produced during the past quarter-century." Frank Crowninshield wrote that in his foreword to SKY HOOKS, the autobiography of John Kane as recorded by Marie McSwigan during the last years of Kane's life. Told with candor, humor, and much warmth, it is the story of a man of little education who developed a profound wisdom and perception in life and in art. Poverty and incessant toil were his lot, and he accepted his lot without any illusions. In his last years when he achieved recognition, he rejoiced in it, but he knew his worth and it changed him little; rather it provided the impetus and freedom of assurance to further his art. Of his life Kane wrote, "It is in the main a simple story but like my paintings it contains many details."

Kane was born of Irish parentage in West Calder, Scotland, on August 19, 1860. When he was ten years old, his father died, leaving a widow and seven children. Kane quit school to work in the coal mines while he was in "the third reader." His mother remarried; and in 1879 he joined his stepfather and older brother, Patrick, who had preceded the family to America and were working in Braddock, Pennsylvania.

His first job was gandy-dancing, or stamping down rocks between railroad ties. This he did for the Baltimore and Ohio Railroad at McKeesport. After another stint working at the National Tube Company, Kane left McKeesport for Connellsville to try his fortune in the coke region of western Pennsylvania. He helped dig foundations for an addition to the Edgar Thompson Steel Works and for the Westinghouse plant at East Pittsburgh. He subsequently worked seven days a week at the Bessemer blast furnaces.

Shuttling from job to job in the ever-insecure labor market, sometimes destitute, always poor, John Kane was one of the millions of unskilled and semi-skilled laborers who built America's industrial might. He took great pride in his work, in his physical strength, and in his adopted country. He said, "As a boy in Scotland I had always thought that 'a man's a man,' as our poet Burns tells. If he was good at his work he was a good man."

Between 1884 and 1886 Kane mined coal in Alabama, Tennessee, and Kentucky. His body, tempered by strenuous labor, was spare and muscular. He stood six feet tall and weighed under 180 pounds. He loved to box, a sport he favored even after he lost a leg. (More of this later). It was at Glenmary, Tennessee, that he had his first moment of glory. A professional boxer arrived at the local saloon asking whether anyone might be willing to fight four or five rounds in a practice bout. Kane accepted the challenge. There were no knockdowns, and, when it was over, it was called a draw. Kane commented, "He was five or six years younger than I, and I was pretty powerful. I knew I could do away with him if I wanted to." His opponent? Gentleman Jim Corbett, the man destined to defeat the great John L. Sullivan for the heavyweight championship of the world!

Wanting to be close to his family, Kane returned to Braddock in 1887 and once again mined coal in the Connellsville area. In 1890 he started to work as a street paver in Pittsburgh and McKeesport. In later years Kane would point to streets in his paintings that "*I* paved." He began to sketch things that interested him—mills, industrial plants, highways, and surrounding landscapes. Kane's pencil drawings were poor. It was too difficult for that calloused hand to draw with precision and flare. But sketching became a habit, one he was to keep throughout his life.

At this time—he was 31 years old—John Kane experienced one of the major tragedies of his life. While walking along the railroad tracks of the Baltimore and Ohio, he was struck by an engine running without lights and lost his left leg, cut off five inches below the knee. Not given to self-pity, he learned to wear an artificial leg, and only in his last years were people aware of his disability. Kane became a watchman for the Baltimore and Ohio at thirty-five dollars a month. There he remained for eight years.

In 1897 Kane married Maggie Halloran at St. Mary's of the Point in Pittsburgh. "I was still making only thirty-five dollars a month, but she didn't mind that. Not Maggie Halloran. She was willing to be poor with me." They lived in McKeesport. Following the birth of their first child, Mary, Kane left his job at the B & O and started painting steel railroad cars at the Pressed Steel Car Company in McKees Rocks. It was there, incidentally, that his second daughter, Margaret, was born.

During his lunch hours, when he would draw on the side of a railroad car and "fill in the colors," (to use his phrase) Kane realized his first opportunity to create paintings in oil. After lunch, the picture would disappear beneath the monotonous, standard railroad car paint. Kane always mixed his own colors, rarely using prepared paint in tubes. He once decided to try ready-made colors and applied to A & B Smith's for some "sunshine paint!" The reply probably deterred him forever.

Kane transferred to the Standard Steel Car Company at Butler, Pennsylvania, where he worked until the Panic of 1907 shut down that plant. In order to support his family—another child was on the way—he took up enlarging and coloring photographs. And at last John Kane had the son he longed for, John, Jr. The child lived only one day.

John Kane could face poverty, loss of limb, and the erratic, strenuous life of an itinerant laborer, but the death of a son he had prayed to have was the greatest blow of his life. He took to drinking heavily, and soon his wife, in despair, left him. Except for brief intervals, during the following twenty-five years, the Kanes were to lead separate lives. He would rejoin his family for several months, then disappear for years.

The great depression of 1907 was the most bitter time of Kane's life. For seven weeks he slept on the floor of the Salvation Army building in Pittsburgh. There was no work to be had, and he grieved for his son. "But discouraged and all as I was, I never lost the idea that I wanted to paint beautiful pictures." He did odd jobs and also worked at painting two amusement parks. Next he secured work as a house painter in Charleston, West Virginia, where he tried to enter an art school but couldn't afford the tuition since he was earning only two dollars a day. He had attempted to enroll at the Carnegie Institute of Technology when its art school was first opened but the cost of materials and tuition was too high. Another opportunity for formal art instruction came just before this country's entry into World War I, when a teacher in the Cleveland School of Art made arrangements for him to attend night classes. By this time, however, Kane was working such long and irregular hours that he had to turn down the offer. All we can say is, how fortunate for art!

In order to augment his earnings Kane became a carpenter's apprentice in Youngstown, Ohio. He moved to Akron in 1910 and worked there in the construction of the Firestone, Goodyear, and Goodrich and General Tire Company plants. In his own words, "I preferred to paint. But if there was no painting to be done, I could fall back on my full-fledged carpenter's card to show. I was never sorry I learned this work. Like outdoor painting, it helped me with my art. It has been said that I am able to apply a technical knowledge to my industrial scenes, my paintings of steel mills, furnaces, pipe factories and of buildings of all sorts. If I paint a building you may be sure it sits square on solid foundations and is built according to the laws of construction which take into consideration the laws of nature and of gravity."

Kane's "pictorial" paintings date from his stay in Akron. Beaverboard odds and ends that were discarded by the construction crew became an economical surface for the paintings he worked on at night and after church on Sundays. None of the oils of this period has been discovered, and it is difficult, if not impossible, to date Kane's works prior to 1928.

Throughout SKY HOOKS, Kane refers to "beauty." For him, beauty was not detached from everyday life; he found it in the written word, in the poetry of Robert Burns, the Bible, the Gettysburg Address. It was in the melodies he played on his tin flute. He sought it in people's faces, in the natural world of forests, hills and rivers, and in the accomplishments of man. "You don't have to go far to find beauty. It is all over, everywhere, even in the street on which you work. All you need is observation. You must look for beauty and you will find it."

Kane submitted paintings to the 1925 and 1926 Pittsburgh Internationals, but his works were rejected. However, in 1927 the Jury of Admissions accepted *Scene in the Scottish Highlands.* Andrew Dasburg not only insisted on its inclusion but purchased the painting for fifty dollars to show his good faith.

The sudden emergence of the sixty-seven-year-old untaught laborer as an artist worthy of admission to an International was heralded in the press. After all, there were 400 entries and most of the major painters of the decade were represented. He was visited by dealers. Newspaper writers and photographers descended upon him, and his story was exploited nationally.

Kane had been painting a house in Ingram when the letter advising him of his acceptance arrived. In his own words, "When you walk the way of life all your days with the poor, as I have, one honor the more, one rebuff the less, is nothing. I was content. I was proud and glad to have this recognition at last. But beyond that it was of little importance. I have had too many hardships in a long life. I have lived too long the life of the poor to attach undue importance to the honors of the art world or to any honors that come from man and not from God."

Shortly after the exhibition opened, Mrs. Kane, who had completely lost contact with her husband for ten years and was living with her younger daughter in West Virginia, saw his picture in a New York newspaper. Neither had known whether the other was still alive. She returned to Pittsburgh, and, you will be happy to know, they remained together during the last seven years of his life.

Kane was included in all the Carnegie Internationals from 1927 until the year of his death. He joined the Associated Artists of Pittsburgh in 1928 and exhibited regularly with that group, winning second prize in 1928, the Carnegie Institute Award in 1929 for the best three or more works, and first prize in 1933 for *Liberty Bridge, Pittsburgh.*

Sudden success, as it usually does, brought on detractors—academic painters who scoffed at his technical deficiencies and Pittsburgh artists who were startled by the acclaim given to a mere "Sunday painter." But not Henry McBride, the great art critic of the *New York Sun*, always a champion of Kane. In 1930 he wrote, "John Kane of Pittsburgh is a house painter who paints only in his hours of ease. His uninstructed but genuinely poetic pictures found their way into the Pittsburgh International, where they were singled out for praise by the New York critics. Pittsburgh was somewhat surprised at this, but has become resigned to having a 'man of feeling' in its midst."

Kane's works were now borrowed by museums; The Toledo Museum of Art, The Museum of Modern Art, the Addison Gallery of American Art, the

Larimer Avenue Bridge, 1932. Museum of Art, Carnegie Institute of Pittsburgh.

Whitney Museum of American Art (for its first and second Biennials in 1932 and 1934), and the Pennsylvania Academy of the Fine Arts. In 1931 his first New York one-man exhibition took place at the Contemporary Arts Galleries, where twenty paintings were shown. A year later Manfred Schwartz exhibited Kane's works in his Gallery 144. Edward Duff Balken, John Dewey, Leon Kroll, Mrs. John D. Rockefeller, Jr., and G. David Thompson were among the first to buy his paintings. The Phillips Memorial Gallery in Washington acquired *Across the Strip* in 1930, thus becoming the first museum to own a Kane.

John Kane died on August 10, 1934 of tuberculosis, a condition no one seemed aware of until his last days. He was buried in Calvary Cemetery in Pittsburgh in a plot of single graves adjacent to the area reserved for the St. Vincent de Paul Society for the Poor.

One of the pallbearers at Kane's funeral was John O'Connor, Jr. (former associate director of the Museum of Art), who on numerous occasions had befriended the artist and who in 1936 assembled forty-six oils for the John Kane Memorial Exhibition at Carnegie Institute. O'Connor wrote: "There were three realities for John Kane—God, nature, and himself. In his very limited and humble way he rejoiced, as few men have, in the world that God created; and he felt called, for the greater honor and glory of God, to transmit to his fellow men his impression of the small but glorious world his eyes encompassed."

I believe no artist before or after Kane equaled him in portraying the industrial scene. Steel mills are organic, monumental structures; railroad tracks have a purposeful yet graceful sweep through his paintings; and houses cluster together as though they had sprung forth from seeds planted in close, orderly rows. Smoke pours from the stacks of factories and river boats, providing a dynamic contrast to the serene green hills. The reflections of bridges in the rivers, as in *Homestead*, provide a contrapuntal pattern.

The Redon-like fantasy of the setting sun in *Sunset, Coleman Hollow* was a reality he literally saw, not a product of his mind's eye. Greyed clouds have a heavy shadow, and Kane painted them that way even though they made Frank Crowninshield feel that "If Kane's clouds were ever to crash to earth, they would produce a sound as of collapsing skyscrapers."

Self-Portrait is unquestionably one of the most moving works of its genre. Kane was sixty-nine years old when he painted himself, stripped to the waist, before a mirror. His body was aging but proudly strong, keenly observed. You sense the layers of muscles and tendons beneath the skin. The veins in his hands and arms are pronounced, and the erect head strains the muscles of his throat. His lips are compressed, his hair carefully combed. The arched ornamental bars at the top of the painting center our attention on his eyes, which belie the realism of the torso and return us to the sensitive artist before the mirror. The formal arrangement of the hands counterbalances the architectural forms above, producing in all a composition of incredible sophistication.

Touching Up, c. 1931-32. Museum of Art, Carnegie Institute of Pittsburgh. Gift of Thomas Mellon Evans.

In *Pieta,* a modern dress version of the 15th century School of Avignon painting, Kane portrays himself as the donor and adds a background of St. Paul's Cathedral in Pittsburgh.

A third likeness appears in *Touching Up.* It is a brilliantly composed work, which is very reminiscent of Vuillard in its faithful recreation of his "studio," with its patterned wallpaper and closely hung paintings across the upper section. So strong is the concentration of the artist on his painting that the infinite detailing recedes into the background.

Unfortunately, one of the tendencies in contemporary criticism is a frantic effort to lump artists into categories and movements. This may provide the critic and historian with a certain amount of intellectual security, but it will not help them or the viewer to evaluate the genius of John Kane, who remains a lone, unclassified figure. Kane transcended his technical deficiencies by breathing into his works a rare personal poetry. To judge Kane by academic standards is to rebuke Giotto for his lack of perspective, or, more significantly perhaps, to decry the mystique of art itself.

---

*At various intervals, this talk was accompanied by slides of Kane's paintings.

Leon Anthony Arkus
Mr. Arkus, recently retired director of the Carnegie Institute Museum of Art, is one of the best-known personalities in the art world of Pittsburgh. He came to Pittsburgh in 1954 from New York, joining the staff of the Museum of Art, Carnegie Institute, as assistant director. In 1962 he was promoted to associate director, and was elected director in 1968. Under his administration the museum grew, and most notably with the opening of the Sarah Scaife Gallery, in whose planning he was closely associated. Some of the museum's most notable shows have been organized by Mr. Arkus. He has been active in a number of other institutions as well, and has been a governor of the Pittsburgh Plan for Art since its beginning in 1958. He has written numerous articles and a book, **John Kane, Painter.** *He retired as director of the Museum of Art in 1980.*

John Gabbert Bowman, c. 1938. University of Pittsburgh Archives.

JOHN GABBERT BOWMAN

by Agnes Lynch Starrett

To begin with, I stress the word *Plan*. Dr. John Bowman always insisted that his work was not a "dream," as many characterized it. It was his *Plan*, he said, with a purpose to fill space needs at the University. He presented realistic cost figures to the Board of Trustees for providing sound, attractive building space: places to gather good teachers, and libraries and laboratories equipped to give the youth of Western Pennsylvania the kind of learning which could provide good doctors, dentists, nurses, pharmacists, lawyers, teachers, engineers, politicians, business personnel, citizens and homemakers. Students were to have the best opportunities possible in this community for becoming skilled men and women, for awakening their responsibility to satisfy for themselves and their neighbors the practical everyday needs and the more sensitive deeper needs of the heart and spirit. Dr. Bowman said, "To be useful is good; to be useful and happy is best of all."

Dr. Bowman brought to Pittsburghers fresh interpretation of their own best efforts which had made Pittsburgh an industrial capital, one of the world's great manufacturing marketplaces, a center for science and invention. He revived their faith in the importance of having a strong university in the important city they had built at the junction of three rivers. And his combination—almost a contrast—of strong practical common sense, expressed in language which sounded like poetry, penetrated to the heart of every problem, and said to those he depended upon for help, "It can be done. Together we can do it." In 1921 there had come to Pittsburgh a new kind of schoolmaster to be Chancellor of the University of Pittsburgh.

It is not my purpose here to canonize John Bowman. His temper was often too short and he was oversensitive to criticism. He was shy and impatient with himself for being shy and for his quick loss of temper. But above any faults, he had great strengths. He had honesty, energy and vision together with great determination to complete his "plan". His natural charm won many to listen and to help.

Dr. Bowman's writings and his reports to trustees, to parents, and to the community show his realistic facing of costs and the practical mundane matters of building a university worthy of the city. They also characterize him as an artist, a perfectionist—one who would accept nothing but the best for the University and its students. He often had to remind himself, he said, that "Bankers and successful corporation heads might not trust a poet." And so he always carried in his breast pocket a three-by-five card with facts and figures about student enrollments and space needs, and other practical matters to buttress his urging of support from a prospective donor.

In appearance John Bowman was a lean, spare man, straight as an arrow, always impeccably dressed in darker tones which brought into prominence his fair skin and very blue eyes. He met visitors to his office courteously at the door, greeted them with a warm handshake and a smile, and invited them to sit opposite him at his desk. Those who had asked to come were invited to speak first. To those whom he had invited he spoke first. Thoughtful silences between responses were much in order—time for thought on both sides of the desk. There never was a bell or buzzer to summon his secretary. He walked to the door and said, "Mrs. Stegeman, will you come in a moment?" He explained the absence of a bell thus: "I should not want anyone to call me with a bell, and I do not wish to call anyone that way." Those who knew him well recognized certain danger signals. His habit of tugging at a forelock when he was disturbed or displeased was a sure sign that the interview had better terminate so he could get on with his day's work.

The Chancellor was at his best when talking around a table to a small group, rather than before a mass gathering. In smaller groups he could reach each person directly, speak in lower tones more natural to him, and at his moments of deepest feeling, light up like a burning bush! On those more intimate occasions, his charm, sincerity, and enthusiasm carried his meaning direct to each individual listener. Each left feeling that he and the Chancellor spoke a common language of clear purpose. And the Chancellor was wise enough to know that flashes of understanding fade and need rekindling again and again.

John Gabbert Bowman, grandson of early pioneers and teachers, was born in Davenport, Iowa, on May 18, 1877. One grandfather came to Iowa from Virginia in 1835; the other from Pittsburgh to Iowa in the 1850's. Pittsburgh was a kind of coming home for the Chancellor. After three years in Davenport High School and a year's teaching in a one-room prairie school John Bowman entered the State University of Iowa from which he received a Bachelor of Arts degree in 1899 and thereafter, for about two and one-half years, he worked on newspapers in Davenport, Waterloo and Chicago. In 1901, he returned to Iowa University to teach English Composition, a subject he said he preferred because "It carried the student along by a real pleasure in creating." John Bowman and Percival Hunt became fast friends during their teaching years at Iowa, and Dr. Bowman often admitted publicly that he learned much about writing from his young colleague whom, soon after his own coming to Pittsburgh as Chancellor, he called to head the Department of English. P. Hunt, as the great teacher called himself, taught and inspired good teachers and writers in Iowa and in Pittsburgh who spread his superb teaching techniques far and wide.

When John Bowman received a Master's degree in 1904, he enrolled as a student in Columbia University, and became an instructor in Columbia's English Department before the year was out. While he was teaching at Columbia, he was also employed by the Carnegie Foundation for the Advancement of Teaching to classify American colleges. From 1907 to 1911, as secretary of the Carnegie Foundation, he visited many colleges and universities in North America, viewing at first hand the field of American higher education. In 1911 he returned to the State University of Iowa as its president.

Four years later, as a result of his work in reorganizing Iowa Medical College, Dr. Bowman became the *first* director of the American College of Surgeons. Its purpose was to put surgery on a more ethical and scientific basis, to eliminate fee splitting, to insist on proper diagnoses, and to advocate that hospital trustees accept responsibility for the competence of their hospital staff. In five years, between 1915 and 1920, Dr. Bowman developed the American College of Surgeons into an organization with a membership of four thousand of the best surgeons in North and South America, and had an endowment of $1,500,000. Bowman won the lasting friendship and respect of such physicians as Drs. Charles and Will Mayo.

After he came to Pittsburgh Dr. Bowman produced with professional technique photographs of interesting people and animals, cultivated for his own pleasure the arts of pottery and ceramics, and became a collector of fine printing.

John Bowman never would accept any printing second-rate in character or design. Anyone who received a diploma in Chancellor Bowman's era has real parchment, imprinted with beautiful authentic Roman type. He sent directly to Italy for letters cut as on old Roman tombstones and other Roman memorials. A diploma, he said, should be worthy to be treasured as a prized family heirloom! Every University printed notice, invitation or brochure represented real quality (paper, type, composition and content)—the quality of true and valued learning.

Among these varied hobbies and interests, Dr. Bowman raised pedigreed Jersey cows at his farm home near Schellsburg, Pennsylvania, adjacent to the farm of his friend, Leon Falk, Jr., a trustee of the University who also raised prize cattle. Their farm neighbors came to appreciate the resulting improvement in Bedford County stock.

In 1920, at age forty-three, while he was director of the College of Surgeons, John Bowman came to deliver a speech to the Pittsburgh Chamber of Commerce before an audience of fifteen hundred men, which unknown to him included trustees of the University. That speech challenged Pittsburghers to revive the spirit which had built an industrial capital on the edge of the nation's first western frontier, and as worthy heirs of Pittsburgh's courageous and creative beginnings to carry the city to ever greater victories in science and in art. Those who heard that speech, or read it, were fired to fresh purpose, and for some it sparked what later came to be called "the Pittsburgh Renaissance." The immediate reaction of the trustees present was to invite Dr. Bowman to become Chancellor of the University of Pittsburgh. Dr. Will Mayo told them, "If you get John Bowman to Pittsburgh, you will have a great university."

Late in 1920 Dr. Bowman accepted the post and assumed the office of chancellor in January 1921. He brought with him to their home on Dithridge

Street his wife, Florence Ridgeway Berry of St. Louis, and their two children, John R., (who became a chemical engineer and teacher), and Florence, a painter, who married Theodore Bowman, a gifted architect, calligrapher and artist.

Dr. Bowman was aware, as were the trustees who elected him, that every great city throughout history grew in cultural strength with a university at its center which encouraged citizens and those who gathered there to learn from great teachers; to preserve and understand their best human heritage; and to add for every new generation new ideas and fresh interpretations of older ones. No need to remind Pittsburghers, so well and widely travelled and so well acquainted with Pittsburgh's Nationality Classrooms, or the reverence for learning that is the well-spring of each national group which has made its home in Pittsburgh.

The beautifully illustrated brochures Dr. Bowman created, written with charm and skill, were distributed and read widely. These highlight and record his first fifteen years at the University, years wherein a man and his friends accomplished more for education in Pittsburgh than it is often given citizens to realize in so brief a span. They are preserved in the University of Pittsburgh's Library archives, as are the leaflets called "Good Teaching." To these, Professors Lee Paul Sieg, Percival Hunt, John Oliver, and other teachers contributed short articles when they met once a month, in formal dress, to discuss the art of great teaching to which their lives and best talents were dedicated. A notable publication was produced by the Fine Arts Department as a memorial of honor and remembrance to Chancellor John G. Bowman. Its content lists in John Bowman's honor some of the choice and rare possessions of the Department.

The Fine Arts Department was one addition to the College of Liberal Arts of which Dr. Bowman was especially proud. Miss Helen Clay Frick, his good friend, built on the campus a beautiful building to house the offices, classrooms, art exhibits (travelling or permanent), and a great library of books, art journals, teaching slides and prints, and other teaching aids. Dr. Frederick Mortimer Clapp administered the department in its earliest years. Dr. Walter Read Hovey, Dr. Clapp's successor, travelled over three continents to purchase books and other materials which made the library equal, at the time, in quality to any fine arts library in the United States. Miss Virginia Lewis, Dr. Hovey's student and teaching colleague, lectured on good printing and bookmaking and was in charge of displays and exhibits. Mr. Thomas Jarrett prepared hundreds of photographs and slides as teaching aids. Professor Andrey Avinoff, Director of the Carnegie Institute Museum, from his rich storehouse of knowledge and with his inimitable Old World courtesy and charm, taught and lectured on art symbols as universal affirmation of noble living to spellbound audiences of young people and adults. Those were halcyon days for graduate students and teachers of history, English, philosophy and the sciences whose Master's degree requirements were permitted to include fine arts electives. The several young assistants, concentrating directly on study in the Fine Arts Department, today staff art museums in many distinguished museums, galleries, and art faculties of colleges in this country and abroad.

Another teaching department featuring the 1920's was the University's pioneer college radio station. On March 31, 1924, through a happy arrangement between the University and Radio Station KDKA, the so-called "University Studio of Westinghouse Station KDKA" opened on the campus in old State Hall. Under the management of Miss Mary Philput, the studio broadcast over half the earth, short talks by University teachers, administrators, trustees, leading Pittsburgh citizens, and neighboring cultural and educational institutions on a variety of subjects as broad in scope as the University curriculum. Professor Glen King (who in a self-equipped, closet-sized laboratory in Thaw Hall isolated Vitamin C) lectured on nutrition in the radio series. He and his colleagues in science teaching received grants from local and national foundations in recognition of their contributions to research in science and to the teaching of science. Professor John Oliver, historian, talked on the need for American historians to know foreign affairs. Drs. Edward Weidlein and William A. Hamor and their colleagues of Mellon Institute (outgrowth of the University's School of Chemistry) lectured on "science for industry." On the third Friday of each month audiences eagerly awaited Frederick Mayer's reviews of current novels. Dr. Florence Teagarden, psychologist, presented a series on children, parents and home environment, and their relation to education for adulthood. The talks were published in individual brochures and distributed free on request. I am told that requests still come in , although the studio's publication supplies are long since exhausted. Distribution of more than sixty talks circulated from 1924 to 1930 when, for reasons of economy, the studio was closed. In those six years the University sent education over the air far beyond its walls to a world-wide audience.

During Dr. Bowman's thirty-five years as Chancellor he accomplished much. Gifts from 17,000 men and women and 97,000 school children, gifts from thirty corporations made possible, by 1937, the dedication of the Chancellor's "Tower of Learning" for which ground had been broken in 1929. The tower was a solid reality in stone, visible as it is today above hilltops and across the rivers. Inside, with a careful selection of beautiful and lasting materials, the best work of the most skilled artists and craftsmen, at home and abroad, was executed in corridors and classrooms, in wrought iron, wood, woven and embroidered fabrics, and carved stone. Pittsburgh men and women with Old World skills and artists and craftsmen from abroad were afforded a chance to apply their talents. The architect, Charles Z. Klauder, took three years to work out the details of the high building and the great Commons Room to make them fit suitably into Dr. Bowman's plan. Mr. Klauder's chief architect--assistant, Albert Klimcheck, became University architect in residence. He adapted all plans for special classrooms submitted by the best artists from abroad to the space allotted them in the building. Mrs. Ruth Crawford Mitchell—because her knowledge, energy, and enthusiasm offered her expertise to work with the various nationality committees and the faculty and

Bowman with students, c. 1940: A fireside chat. University of Pittsburgh Archives.

helped the Chancellor carry out this part of the "great plan": classrooms to keep alive for citizens and for teachers and students the Old World cultural traditions of Pittsburgh's people. There were many who helped. Their contributions are well recorded and the letters to and from Joseph K. Lilly which concerned the gift to the University of the Foster Memorial Collection are preserved there. These books and manuscripts about our native born composer Stephen Collins Foster comprise one of the City's great treasures.

Gifts from the family of H. J. Heinz, Sr. made possible the beautiful Gothic chapel whose spire throws into the air a message similar to the one sent proudly upward by the high building—a university company of scholars seeking the eternal verities in a world of everyday demands. Christian teaching in literature, song and charitable love by courageous men and women is the chapel's theme in twenty-three beautiful stained glass windows designed and executed by Mr. Charles J. Connick. Among the faculty, Professor John Weber (Engineering) and Professor George Hatfield (History) were special help as advisors to Mr. Connick on the theme for the series.

On the hills above the Cathedral of Learning and on property surrounding it, stands the Medical Center, with hospitals and clinics and a library, all gathered for the betterment of public health, care of the sick, and the education of medical personnel—a project for which Dr. Bowman worked with philanthropic foundations and Pittsburgh medical leaders. Dr. Bowman would not wish me to omit the names of the Deans, Drs. Raleigh R. Huggins and William McElroy in Medicine; Charles F. Lewis, whose Buhl Foundation gifts to learning were everywhere on the campus (notably science and history and the University Press); Andrew and R. B. Mellon, who gave without restriction the nineteen-acre plot upon which stand three of the University's beautiful buildings. He would want included gifts of lasting meaning from the Falks, Maurice, Leon Sr. and Leon Jr.: the Falk Clinic, the Falk hilltop observation school for elementary and junior high school education, and eventually the great Falk Medical Library. He would include Drs. Steele Gow and C. V. Starrett, young men whose imagination and skills helped push forward communication and understanding concerning the "great Plan." Dean of College Stanton C. Crawford, who consistently stood by with encouragement and professional advice during the troubled times of the 1930's (long past now and acknowledged as a "tempest in a teapot"). And most surely Dr. and Mrs. George Hubbard Clapp whose gifts, great and small, touch every facet of University life. Names and pictures of prominent donors and helpers are preserved in the cornerstone of the Cathedral of Learning, set in 1937 at the University's celebration of its one hundred and fiftieth birthday. Mrs. Maxine Bruhns, director of the Nationality Rooms and Educational Exchange Programs, has published a beautiful book on the Nationality Classrooms in the Cathedral of Learning. They are inspiration for students and teachers who use them and for the many, many visitors from all over the world who come to view them. They memorialize the ancestry of Pittsburghers whose talents and works have united to make our City and our Nation. Their very names resound with hope and love and the strength that is in a unity of purpose: Chinese, Czechoslovak, English, French, German, Greek, Hungarian, Irish, Italian, Lithuanian, Norwegian, Polish, Rumanian, Russian, Scottish, Swedish, Syrian-Lebanese, Yugoslav, Early American. And there are more rooms to come which are nearing completion.

All of us who lived and worked during the Bowman years felt that we were part of a great adventure, almost beyond the telling of it. The University, for one hundred ninety years, has been fortunate with administrative heads and Chancellors who, with time, come and go. Dr. Bowman and the men and women he gathered here have followed and preceded strong Chancellors and great teachers. Each Chancellor, from Robert Bruce to Wesley Posvar, has brought what the community and the University needed in his own time. There have always been great teachers—long and affectionately remembered by alumni for sharing the good life of learning with their students. Dr. Bowman consistently asked for teaching which had the power to awaken the student to his best life purpose and to the strength which comes from good companionship along the way—so that the student geared with the whole armor of learning can make his own discoveries and face alone life's frustrations and victories.

He said:

> I want the student to know what life can mean for him. After that, he can

decide what to do. I want him to believe that he is a good fellow and that he will get along; and that he is not the only good fellow and the only one who will get along. I want him to hold his head up, to play fair, to control his temper, and to like people. I want him to think for himself; to see beauty and meaning in common things and in human character; and to know that he is part of a great design of which grass and neighbors and stars are also parts.

If the University could cause even one man or woman to be an intellect strong enough to hold the fire of youth steadily toward a useful end, the result would justify all that all of us here could do about it throughout our lives. One Shakespeare or one Bacon telling about life here would give Pittsburgh more than the city could measure in a hundred years.

And now, may the University and Pittsburgh remember this great citizen of Pittsburgh and of the wide world of learning who showed us what a great university here could mean. And may the generations which come after him go on building this University for Pittsburgh with faith and courage like those of John Gabbert Bowman.

Agnes Lynch Starrett
Mrs. Starrett, born in 1889, is director emeritus of the University of Pittsburgh Press. Her entire career has been associated with the University of Pittsburgh: there she received her B.A. in 1920 and her M.A. in 1925, and taught in its Department of English from 1922 to 1964 (she is also a professor emeritus). She remains a freelance writer, editor, and book designer, and is the author of three books. In 1954 she was named a Distinguished Daughter of Pennsylvania.

This book was typeset in Century Schoolbook with Craw Modern Bold chapter headings, by Mangis & Associates, Pittsburgh. It was printed on 60 lb. Warren Olde Style by William G. Johnston Company, Pittsburgh. Cover and book design by Thomas S. Stevenson, Jr., Pittsburgh History & Landmarks Foundation. Photo of Agnes Lynch Starrett by Harry Hull.